IOWA
INSIDE OUT

written and illustrated by
Herb Hake

IOWA STATE UNIVERSITY PRESS

IOWA INSIDE OUT

IOWA INSIDE

LARCHWOOD
QUARTZITE OUTCROP
Rock River
SIBLEY
×OCHEYEDAN MOUND
DUST STORMS
ARNOLDS PARK
ESTHERVILLE
SITE OF METEORITE FALL 1879
Waldorf "SURVIVOR OF 'BATTLE OF THE HOTELS' 1899"
FOREST CITY
CLEAR LAKE
BRITT
WOODEN SHOE FACTORY
SPENCER
CLAY COUNTY FAIR
GARDNER CABIN
SPIRIT LAKE MASSACRE
PILOT KNOB TOWER
HOB CONV
ORANGE CITY
PHEASANTS
GROTTO OF THE REDEMPTION
WEST BEND
BEEF
Iowa River
REMSEN
IOWA'S FIRST PLANETARIUM
Floyd River
CAPTAIN FENTON'S BARN
OLD ENGLISH COLONY
CHEROKEE
STATE TREE: OAK
BIRTH-PLACE of CARDIFF GIANT
Big Sioux River
GRAVE OF SERGEANT FLOYD 1804
STORM LAKE "SAVE THE LAKE"
PALMER
KALSOW PRAIRIE ×
GYPSUM MINES
SIOUX CITY
FORT DODGE
WATERFOWL MIGRATION STOP
Little Sioux River
ADAMS RANCH
ODEBOLT
Raccoon River
LOHRVILLE
WORLD PONY SHOWDEO
SHELDALL
STORY CITY
STATE BIRD: GOLDFINCH
Soldier River
BIRTHPLACE of MAMIE EISENHOWER
BOONE
AMES
NEVA
Missouri River
LEWIS & CLARK EXPEDITION 1804
LINCOLN LAND
BELL LOG CABIN
DENISON
CORN
KATE SHELLEY DEPOT
MOINGONA
BOY HO BIL
Boyer River
STATE FLOWER: WILD ROSE
Rock Island R.R.
HISTORIC OLD FARMHOUSE
I.S.U. CAMPUS
FIRST
JESSE JAMES TRAIN ROBBERY 1873
TERRACE HILL
Des Moines River
GRENVILLE DODGE HOUSE
LEWIS & CLARK MEMORIAL
SHEEP
ADAIR ×
DES MOINES
COVERED BRIDGES
WINTERSET
RELIC of ORIGIN DELICIOUS APPL
Silver Creek
West Nishnabotna River
COUNCIL BLUFFS
LEWIS "JOHN BROWN HOUSE"
HENRY A. WALLACE BIRTHPLACE
ORIENT
EAST PERU
BIRTHPLACE JOHN L. LEWIS
SILVER CITY
OLD STAGE COACH INN
East Nishnabotna River
Nodaway River
MONUMENT to MORMON DEAD
LORIMOR
LUCAS
REV. JOHN TODD HOUSE ... STATION ON UNDERGROUND RAILROAD
TABOR
SIDNEY RODEO
SHENANDOAH
CORNING
DINING HOUSE OF ICARIAN COMMUNITY — NOW PRIVATE FARM HOME
Grand River
GARDEN GROV FIRST SETT ON MORMON 1846
SIDNEY
BIRTHPLACE HENRY FIELD
LAMONI
HOME of JOSEPH SMITH III SON of THE PROPHET

OUT

Written and Illustrated by HERBERT V.

HAKE

Published by the

IOWA STATE

UNIVERSITY

PRESS

Ames, Iowa

Map labels:
BOYHOOD HOME OF HAMLIN GARLAND
DVORAK HOME & CLOCK MUSEUM
SPILLVILLE
FT. ATKINSON
FESTINA
DECORAH
NORWEGIAN OUTDOOR MUSEUM
LANSING
MOUNT HOSMER
Upper Iowa River
PIKE'S PEAK
McGREGOR
EFFIGY MOUNDS
MARQUETTE
"SMALLEST CHURCH"
Turkey River
PIONEER ROCK CHURCH
GUTTENBERG
OLD SHOT TOWER
BACKBONE STATE PARK
FIRST IN IOWA
STRAWBERRY POINT
"LEXINGTON OF THE NORTH" 1890
MINOR BASILICA
DYERSVILLE
DUBUQUE
OUTDOOR STATIONS OF THE CROSS
TRAPPIST ABBEY NEW MELLERAY
SAINT DONATUS
CATTLE CONGRESS
WATERLOO
CEMETERY CEDAR FALLS
INDEPENDENCE
Cedar River
Maquoketa River
GRANT WOOD ART COLONY
ANDREW
HOME OF ANSEL BRIGGS
"TAMA JIM" WILSON BIRTHPLACE
TRAER
GRANT WOOD STUDIO
STONE CITY
CEDAR RAPIDS
Wapsipinicon River
LUMBER PORT
CLINTON
MESQUAKIE INDIANS
TAMA
KING CHAPEL
MT. VERNON
OATMEAL FACTORY
WORKSHOP OF BILLY ROBINSON, PIONEER AVIATOR
GRINNELL
AMANA COLONY
WOOLEN MILL
IOWA CITY OLD STONE CAPITOL
PLUM GROVE-HOME OF ROBERT LUCAS
WEST BRANCH
BIRTHPLACE HERBERT HOOVER & PRESIDENTIAL LIBRARY
BUFFALO BILL'S BOYHOOD TOWN
LE CLAIRE
Skunk River
SITE OF "COPPERHEAD WAR"
SOUTH ENGLISH
DAVENPORT
MUSCATINE
LE CLAIRE HOUSE, FIRST R.R. DEPOT IN IOWA
JOHN F. BOEPPLE CUT FOOT ON CLAM AND STARTED BUTTON INDUSTRY 1890
LANDMARKS
OSKALOOSA
HOME OF FREDERICK KNIGHT LOGAN
FAIRFIELD
GRAVE OF WAPELLO
AGENCY
FIRST STATE FAIR 1854
FIRST IOWA LANDING BY WHITE MEN 1673
OAKVILLE
HARLAN-LINCOLN HOME
OTTUMWA
VAN BUREN CO. COURTHOUSE 1842
KEOSAUQUA
MT. PLEASANT
OLD JUG FACTORY
SALEM
LEWELLING HOUSE
LOWELL
HOME OF JAMES W. GRIMES
BURLINGTON
BENTONSPORT
CANNONBALLS FELL HERE
CROTON
LONE CHIMNEY MONUMENT
FORT MADISON
FIRST SCHOOL IN IOWA
The MASON HOUSE OLD STEAMBOAT HOTEL
BATTLE OF ATHENS, MO. 1861
GALLAND
KEOKUK GRAVE
KEOKUK
HERB HAKE

HERBERT V. HAKE was the producer of "Landmarks in Iowa History," a film series appearing on several Iowa television stations. In addition, he produced the midwestern history film series, "History with Herb Hake," for the National Educational Television Network. He was Director of Radio and Television at the University of Northern Iowa, Cedar Falls, for many years. He died in 1980. A graduate of Central Wesleyan College, Warrenton, Missouri, Mr. Hake received his M.A. from the University of Iowa.

Before moving into the field of radio and television education, Mr. Hake served as an instructor of speech and drama at the University of Missouri and the University of Iowa. He conducted "The Technician's Question Box," a monthly column in *Lagniappe,* for 24 years. Besides this book, he is the author of *Here's How: A Basic Stagecraft Book.*

In 1955, Mr. Hake received the First Place award for his Iowa History series in the American Exhibition of Educational Radio-Television Programs, sponsored by the Institute for Radio-Television at Ohio State University.

© 1968 Iowa State University Press, Ames, Iowa 50010

Composed by Iowa State University Press
Printed in the United States of America

First edition, 1968
Second printing, 1968
Third printing, 1969
Iowa Heritage Collection edition, 1987

Library of Congress Cataloging-in-Publication Data

Hake, Herbert V.
    Iowa inside out.

    (Iowa heritage collection)
    Bibliography: p.
    Includes index.
    1. Iowa—History. I. Title.
F621.5.H3 1987   977.7   86-27317
ISBN 0-8138-0844-8

To my wife MONABELLE
whose faith and forbearance never faltered

FOREWORD

For the past twenty years, I have produced a weekly radio or television program on Iowa history as part of my work of broadcaster for the University of Northern Iowa. In preparation for the program, I have traveled widely throughout the state in search of data.

Old books, magazines, and newspaper files have been fruitful sources of information. But my camera, recorder, and notebook too have gone with me into many unusual corners of Iowa. I have crawled through caves and mine tunnels, climbed ladders in church steeples and ruined towers, probed the dungeons of old jails, explored hiding places of the Underground Railroad, struggled for footholds on rocky bluffs, fasted with Trappists in a monastery, wrestled with river currents in a rowboat, and searched for firsthand material in a hundred other exciting ways.

The translation of this research into print has been attempted by beginning at the *inside* of Iowa history and proceeding, level by level, to the *outside*. In brief, I have tried to tell the story of the state from the inside out.

The places and personalities of the present are all around us, chronicled in detail by our current news media. The places and personalities of the past have been largely forgotten. It is because I believe they merit at least a concise chronicle that this book has been written.

Hundreds of people have helped me to assemble the material which is contained in this book. Wherever I have traveled in Iowa, librarians, newspaper editors, local historians, and long-time residents have shared their knowledge with me. I am grateful to all of them for answering my questions and for guiding me to sources of reliable information.

I appreciate, also, the interest of many radio and television listeners who have urged me to condense my program material into book form. This encouragement has been highly gratifying.

The invitation to submit a manuscript was first extended to me by Raymond P. Fassel, the assistant director of the Iowa State University Press. I express my thanks to him and to Merritt E. Bailey, the director of Book Publishing at the Press, for furnishing the incentive to do the actual writing.

Richard E. Gage, consultant in history for the State Department of Public Instruction, paid me the compliment of giving the first draft his critical appraisal. I esteem this service as both a personal and a professional favor.

My secretary, Mrs. Marilyn Oleson, patiently typed and retyped the manuscript during time that was not committed to her regular work schedule at the university. I am indebted to her for the diligence of many hours that would otherwise have been given to her family.

Finally, I wish to acknowledge the detailed and perceptive assistance which I received from Mrs. Joy Banyas. As the editor assigned to the book, Mrs. Banyas had the responsibility of shaping the material into a format acceptable to the Press. Her cheerful attention to this assignment and her skill and tact in communicating with the author are gratefully remembered.

Herbert V. Hake
Cedar Falls, 1967

CONTENTS

IOWA INSIDE OUT

1. IN THE BEGINNING

IF THE LAND that is Iowa could be turned inside out, it would be just a big mass of rock. There would be no trees, no rivers, no black soil, and no people. It would look as it did millions of years ago when the earth was new.

Nobody knows exactly how old the bedrock of Iowa is. Some scientists have guessed that about three billion years ago a fiery blob of matter broke loose from the sun. This ball of liquid rock went spinning through space and slowly cooled into what we now call the earth.

There were no calendars in those days and no historians to write down what was happening, but men called geologists understand the language of the rocks. As John Ely Briggs wrote in his book *Iowa, Old and New,* "They can read in the mighty book of stone about the process of creation, the eternal struggle of land and sea, the different kinds of climate, and the drama of life."

ROCKS AND WATER

The earth did not remain a shapeless lump of matter for very long. The

RED QUARTZITE is a distinctive type of granular metamorphic rock. This outcropping in Gitchie Manitou State Park is, geologically speaking, the oldest rock in Iowa.

crust hardened, but there were liquid stone and gas inside the ball and they erupted in volcanoes. The shell of the earth bulged and cracked. The air and the ocean flowed into the openings. Earthquakes caused the rocky crust to buckle and change in shape. Great valleys were filled with water, and all of what is now Iowa was a part of the sea.

During the millions of years in which all of this was taking place, the shells of small sea creatures fell to the bottom of the Iowa ocean. Layers of shell were packed down to form what we now call limestone. (This is the kind of stone that was used for the Old Stone Capitol in Iowa City.) The sea pounded the rocks and gouged tiny particles of sand from them. The sand piled up and, in millions of years, hardened into sandstone. In Iowa, the shelf of sandstone formed in this manner slants in a southwesterly direction from the northeastern corner of the state. It is exposed in a tall bluff along the Mississippi River in Clayton County. Where the slanting shelf of St. Peter sandstone crosses the southwestern corner of the state, it is more than half a mile below the surface.

The oldest rock that can still be seen in Iowa is the outcropping of red quartzite in northwest Iowa. It is found in Gitchie Manitou State Park beside Jasper Pool. But, as we look at the red quartzite in northwest Iowa and the cliff of sandstone in northeast Iowa, we must remember that all of this rock was once under the sea.

LEAD AND COAL

Earthquakes and other upheavals of Nature raised Iowa's land above the ocean, but there was no grass to cover the rock. Wind and rain carved deep ruts in the layers of stone. Streams carried algae and other forms of simple plant and animal life into cracks of the rock and they were changed into minerals. Some of these minerals were dissolved and, under pressure, became lead (which was to make Julien Dubuque a rich man millions of years later).

THE TOP of the "backbone" in Backbone State Park is covered with millions of stone molds of primitive sea creatures.

But the sea had not given up. As the rock mass strained and twisted, the ocean flowed back into the part of the world which now includes Iowa. This time it brought strange creatures with it. Animal life had developed beyond the soft sponges and jellyfish which had floated in the warm water a million years earlier. Quoting Briggs again, "The time had come when living things came out of the water and found a home on land. The ferns were among the first of the plants to venture ashore, and then came the rushes. . . . Slimy snails moved sluggishly along the stems of leafless weeds, while thousand-legged worms scooted in and out of the mold."

Fish had grown into species of considerable size, and some of them had acquired the ability to live briefly on land, where they preyed on the worms and snails that were trying to get a start in the world. Some of these "fish out of water" had to return to the sea. Others didn't get back in time. Their remains sank into the mud and slime and fertilized the land which was finally exposed when the sea retreated.

Then the weather of Iowa became tropical. Giant ferns and great trees grew in the swamps and marshes. Summer lasted for thousands of years. The plants and trees died and fell into the water. When the sea came again, it placed more layers of stone over the dead vegetation. The pressure of this rock caused the fallen trees and ferns to turn into coal.

THE DINOSAURS

When the land won its battle with the sea again, monsters roamed the earth. These were land animals much larger than the simple amphibians which had lived in the sea in earlier times. Their story is written in the remains found in the ooze which later turned into stone. We are told about them by the geologists. Some of the monsters were giant lizards that walked on their hind legs. Scientists have named them *dinosaurs,* a word which means "terrible reptiles." The Brontosaurus was a 60-foot dinosaur that weighed 25 tons. With all this weight to throw around, the Brontosaurus had a brain that weighed only two and one-half ounces! It is not surprising, therefore, that it didn't have enough sense to take care of itself. In eighty million years, the Brontosaurus, the Tyrannosaurus, the Triceratops, and all their relatives were gone. It took brains to survive in those days.

The sea came again to wash over the remains of the dinosaurs and the flood carried silt and sand and shale into the low places where they were buried. When the sea left Iowa for the last time, a great deal of sediment remained behind, and trees and vegetables grew in abundance. That was about sixty million years ago.

THE ICE AGE

The climate changed at the close of the long tropical era, and it went to the opposite extreme. Winters lasted the year 'round. The snow and ice piled up into huge glaciers which were more than a mile in thickness at some points. The first of these great ice sheets was called the *Nebraskan*. Of course, there was no state of Nebraska at that time. The glacier got its name later, because it covered the country all the way down to what is now Nebraska. As it grew, it spread over all of Iowa. When the spell of cold weather ended, the glacier melted and left drifts of topsoil formed by the water of the melting ice.

In one part of northeast Iowa, the ice of the Nebraskan glacier was not thick enough to change the surface of the land a great deal. This part of Iowa—sometimes called "Little Switzerland"—has been described as "the country the glaciers forgot." The Nebraskan ice sheet covered it, but its weight was so slight that it did little damage. The later glaciers didn't touch it at all.

The area around Backbone State Park in northeast Iowa is believed to have been a kind of "Noah's Ark of North America," because the continental ice sheets made it an island in a great white sea. Here, the northern plants and some of the hardier animals continued to exist. After the white sea had melted away, they spread abroad and reclaimed the rest of the country. The Backbone in the Park, with its millions of stone molds of primitive sea creatures called "lampshells," looks much as it did

when it was a ridge at the bottom of the sea.

As primeval time is measured, only a short summer followed the first ice sheet. The weather turned cold again, the second glacier (the *Kansan*) was formed in Canada, and it began moving south at a speed of about an inch per week. It crushed the soft rocks beneath it into a fine powder. The harder stone was not crushed, but a lot of it was moved a long way from home. Hills were leveled, river beds were filled, new valleys were plowed in the earth, and there was a great scraping and gouging of the landscape in general. The glacier finally melted, but the rock-powder, sand, gravel, sticky clay, and dead vegetation remained where the ice sheet had carried them. Time and the chemistry of Nature were to change this deposit into the black soil of Iowa.

Two more glaciers, the *Illinoisan* and the *Wisconsin*, followed. The last one was stubborn about melting. When most of Iowa had been cleared of ice, cold weather settled down once more, and a new tongue of the Wisconsin ice sheet licked the land as far south as Des Moines. Since this late impulse began where Mankato, Minnesota, is now located, the final thrust was called the *Mankato Drift*.

The rolling hills left by the various drifts of the glaciers are called *moraines*, and many of them can still be seen by the traveler who crosses the state. Large granite boulders as well as rich loam were left by the ice sheets as they bulldozed their way across Iowa. The farmer who plows his land today is still reminded of the Ice Age by rocks from Canada which at times break his plowshare.

It is doubtful that man appeared on Iowa soil until the last glacier was gone, some 20,000 years ago. But, when he came, he found a country which had experienced three billion years of turmoil and change. Whatever he did to the land was insignificant by comparison with the work done by the forces of Nature in the millions of years before he arrived. His activity had *human* interest, however, and this accounts for the fact that we give more attention to it than we give to the story of the earth in earlier times.

2. THE FIRST PEOPLE

MAN DID NOT venture into Iowa until the last of the great ice sheets was gone. It was too cold and slippery. But there were men in other parts of the world. Scientists tell us that man has been living on this old earth for at least a million years. The first men lived in what is called the Paleolithic Age. "Paleo" means old, and "lithic" means stone. It is not surprising that the two words together mean the Old Stone Age. The Stone Age takes its name from the fact that men made their weapons and tools out of stone. They hunted with homemade spears tipped with flint or some other hard rock. Paleolithic man had not learned that food could be raised by planting seeds. He lived on a diet of meat and fish.

STONE AGE MAN IN AMERICA

The first men made their homes in what is now called the Old World —Africa, Europe, and Asia. As time went on, some of the hunters followed their food supply across the land between northeastern Siberia and Alaska. Before Bering Strait separated the two continents, there was a wide bridge of land between Asia and North America. Moreover, the ice which covered Canada and the north-central part of the United States didn't come near this corner of the world, so the plants, animals, and men had a free passage.

Marshall McKusick in his *Men of Ancient Iowa* asks: "When were North and South America first settled by Indians?" His answer: "Generally, a date somewhere around 20,000 B.C. appears to be a reasonable estimate for the first migrations of Indians into the American continent."

Now, this was about the time that the last of the great ice sheets was melting in Iowa. Since there was still a lot of ice in the north-central part of the country, the people who had come to America probably wandered down to the southern part of the United States to escape the cold.

Fortunately, man had stopped going around on all fours and had mastered the trick of balancing himself on his legs. As he gained confidence in walking erect, he learned to run, and this proved to be a great help in chasing animals. His brain was more highly developed than the brain of the animal he hunted, so he thought of ways to outsmart his prey. There are places where piles of bones have been found at the bottom of high cliffs. Archeologists believe that men of the Stone Age stampeded animals off these bluffs and got them to break their own necks. This saved a lot of time—and running.

A layer of bison bones has been found under fifteen feet of soil in Cherokee County along the west bank of the Little Sioux River. W. D. Frankforter of the Sanford Museum in Cherokee identified the bison as belonging to a species long extinct in North America.

THE INDIANS AND THE BEGINNINGS OF AGRICULTURE

In 1925, flint spearpoints were found in a pile of animal bones at Folsom, New Mexico. The fossilized remains were those of bison which were different from any modern bison. The fact that manmade weapons were found among these ancient bones proved that there had been human hunters in America in the long ago. How long ago? The carbon tests, which tell the age of old bones, showed that the bison had lived 15,000 to 20,000 years ago. The hunter of the Folsom bison was therefore called the "Folsom Man." He was the first Indian of whom we have a scientific record. The word "Indian," of course, was the name Columbus gave the Americans when he thought he had found a short cut to India. The name stuck, even though the natives had nothing to do with India.

But Columbus is far ahead of our story. Before any white men crossed the ocean, there were thousands of years in which the hunting parties spread over the continent. Nobody was in any special hurry. The time was spent in camping, exploring, and raising families.

About 8000 B.C. Indians living in

the middle of America discovered a wild plant which had kernels that were good to eat. By some accident some of these kernels fell to the ground, were covered with dirt, and grew new plants. This must have happened in a camp where the hunters had decided to stay for a while. Usually the hunting parties trailed the herds of deer and buffalo from one part of the country to another. Perhaps there was such a good supply of game in this valley that the hunters decided it would be foolish to move elsewhere. In any case, they stayed long enough to see the strange plants grow and produce a new crop of corn. This was a red letter day on the Stone Age calendar. Now food could be raised by planting seeds.

The story of corn must have spread from one hunting party to another. As far as the men were concerned, it made little difference in their habits of life. They still brought in the meat. The women had nothing to do except cook the meat, carry the baggage, and take care of the children. The men therefore decided that their wives and daughters had plenty of spare time for planting and harvesting the corn, as well as pounding it into meal and making mush out of it. The effect of all this was that food became more varied than it had been in earlier times. It also brought the Paleolithic Age to an end. The age which began with the development of agriculture was to be known as the Neolithic or New Stone Age.

During the Old Stone Age, the keeping of food had been impossible. Meat had to be fresh when it was eaten. If there was more than the group could eat, the leftovers were thrown away. Nobody had an icebox. But corn could be kept for a long time if it were stored in some kind of a container. Some unknown genius invented pottery for this purpose. But pottery didn't stand up very well when the group decided to travel. Bags made out of animal skins or baskets woven out of reeds were used to carry the corn from place to place. Settlements are usually marked by the remains of earthenware pots, and it is evident that these pots were used for cooking as well as storage.

INDIANS COME TO IOWA

No one knows exactly when man first came to Iowa. Spearpoints have been found in some parts of the state which indicate that there were hunters in Iowa as early as 10,000 B.C. But the hunters who used them were probably nomads who didn't stay in any one place very long. The earliest pottery-bearing sites in Iowa date from about 1000 B.C.

How did the first people come to Iowa? The early hunters probably walked. It is believed that the later Indians came in canoes. The many streams of America gave somebody the idea of using his stone axe to gouge a crude boat out of a log. He must have seen logs floating down the river, and reasoned that he might as well let the water take him where he wanted to go. If he wanted to go downstream, the river could carry him a lot faster than he could walk. Going upstream was a different proposition, but he could manage it by forcing his dugout to go against the current with a pole or a paddle.

Then, somebody decided that a much lighter boat could be made by sewing pieces of birch bark together with strips of animal skin, mounting the birch bark on a wooden frame, and covering the cracks with pitch to make them watertight. Such a canoe was light enough to be carried (instead of dragged) from one stream to another, and it could go much faster than the boats made of logs. Our earliest Americans traveled either on foot or by boats. They had no horses. The horse was brought into America by the Spaniards many years later.

The pottery-bearing sites in Iowa are found along the larger streams. This fact supports the belief that our first farmers came to the Iowa country in canoes or dugouts. They framed their shelters with poles and covered them with bark, reeds, or animal skins. We call these early farmers Woodland Indians to distinguish them from the Archaic, or non-farming, Indians who roamed the plains and prairies in more primitive times.

It was the Woodland people who built the mounds in Iowa. Indeed, the name of Mound Builders is often applied to them. The mounds were built for burial of the dead. Sometimes the bodies were buried immediately after death with the knees drawn up against the chest. At other times, the bodies were exposed until the flesh was gone. Then, the bones were gathered for a "bundle burial." Pottery containing food for the departed spirit was often placed in the mound.

Effigy Mounds

Archeologists who have studied the contents of Indian mounds have found evidence of a religion which made use of stone altars and rich grave offerings. One cult has been called Hopewell after an enormous burial mound site in Ohio. Another cult, which developed somewhat later, is named Effigy Mound after the animal- and birdlike shape of the mounds built along the bluffs of the Mississippi River in northeast Iowa.

Effigy mounds were made to resemble birds and animals. The word "effigy" means a likeness. Nobody knows exactly why the mound builders took the time and trouble to pile up dirt in the shapes of animals and birds. Perhaps it had something to do with their religion. Or it may have been done to frighten away the bears and buzzards that plundered the village. Whatever the reason, the building of an effigy mound was a tremendous job. The dirt had to be carried in baskets and shaped with pointed sticks and crude tools, and some of it had to be carried for a long distance.

Different colors of earth have been discovered in the mounds. If the right color could not be found near the mound site, a group of basket carriers might be sent a long way from home to find it and bring it back.

There are conical and linear mounds on the Mississippi bluffs too, but they are found elsewhere in the state as well. The conical mounds have a circular ground plan, and they are so named because of the shallow cone of earth which gives them their basic profile. Some of the conical mounds may have been used as elevations for stone altars. In areas of low terrain, they may have served as islands on which lodges were built in times of high water.

The linear mound was often built by filling the gap between two conical mounds and thus forming a short line of fortification. The mound provided an effective shield in case of enemy attack. The linear mounds may have been designed primarily as ramparts, but burials have been found in them. Whether these burials were made by the builders of the mounds, or by later people who found them suited to this purpose, is not known.

The effigy mounds, like some of the conical and linear mounds, were used for burials, but only people of special importance were buried in them. In the bear mound, for example, there was a burial pit in the part of the mound representing the head. There was another in the region of the heart, and still another in the hindquarters. The head man or the chief might have been buried in the head or heart region, but what dignitary would have been buried in the hindquarters? Maybe it was a "rear admiral."

The effigy mounds in northeast Iowa were proclaimed a National Monument by President Harry Truman in 1949. The Monument area is divided into two parts by the Yellow River. The Fire Point Mound Group north of the Yellow River has conical and linear mounds as well as effigy mounds. The larger of the two bear effigies in this group is the largest bear effigy remaining in Iowa. This effigy, the Great Bear Mound, is 70 feet across the shoulders and front legs, 137 feet long, and 5 feet high.

South of the Yellow River, the Marching Bear Mound Group contains a line of 10 bear effigies, 3 bird effigies, and 2 linear mounds. Almost a mile northeast of the Marching Bear Group are 3 mounds—a bear effigy, a bird effigy, and a long combination of conical and linear mounds measuring 450 feet from end to end.

Most of the mounds in the Monument are covered with a heavy forest growth, but a trail has been cleared for visitors to the Fire Point Mound Group. This trail makes a loop which passes the Little Bear Mound, a long row of conical mounds, and a linear mound. There is a side trail leading to the Great Bear Mound. The Visitor Center is near the highway at the foot of the bluff, and dioramas prepared by

CONICAL MOUND is shown in cross section (lower right) in a diorama at the Villa Louis Historical Museum, Prairie du Chien, Wisconsin.

the United States Department of the Interior tell the story of the Mound Builders.

The tour of the mounds is self-guided. There are markers along the trail which identify the various mounds, and the two-mile round trip from the Visitor Center and back takes about an hour of steady walking. There is a 350-foot rise within the first half-mile of the trail, and tourists of today are usually puffing by the time they reach the top of the bluff. The Mound Builders must have been sound in both wind and limb.

Fate of the Mound Builders

What happened to the Woodland Indians whom we have called the Mound Builders? No one knows for sure. They may have been destroyed by newcomers from the south who arrived in Iowa about 1200 A.D. These Upper Mississippian newcomers were

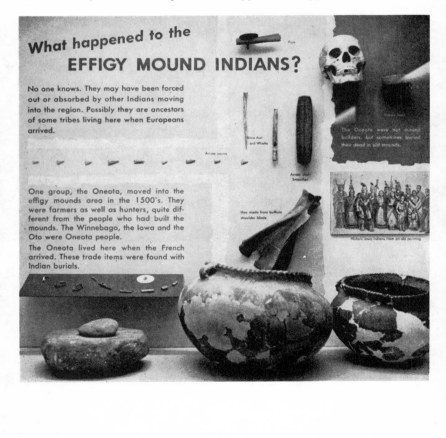

What happened to the
EFFIGY MOUND INDIANS?

No one knows. They may have been forced out or absorbed by other Indians moving into the region. Possibly they are ancestors of some tribes living here when Europeans arrived.

One group, the Oneota, moved into the effigy mounds area in the 1500's. They were farmers as well as hunters, quite different from the people who had built the mounds. The Winnebago, the Iowa and the Oto were Oneota people.

The Oneota lived here when the French arrived. These trade items were found with Indian burials.

The Oneota were not mound builders, but sometimes buried their dead in old mounds.

Historic Iowa Indians, from an old painting

warlike, because the remains of their villages show that they built moats and stockades around their settlements. The three main groups of Mississippians were: the Oneota group which lived in northern and northeastern Iowa; the Mill Creek group, centered near Cherokee; and the Glenwood group, along the bluffs of the Missouri River in the southwest corner of the state.

Dr. Reynold Ruppe, professor of archeology at the University of Iowa, has called attention to the fact that the Oneota people were cannibals. There doesn't seem to have been any good reason for this, because Iowa, then as now, provided plenty of food. One theory is that the Oneota thought

POTTERY and other relics found in mounds at Effigy Mounds National Monument are displayed in the Visitor Center at the monument.

they could take on the strength of their victims by eating them. The mounds left by the Woodland Indians prove that they were people of enormous strength and energy, so it is possible that the Oneota ate the Mound Builders.

When Jacques Cartier sailed into the St. Lawrence River in 1534, the Indians in the eastern part of the continent started moving westward. This began a chain reaction. The Oneota gave ground in eastern Iowa and moved into the area occupied by the Mill Creek and Glenwood cultures. These weaker groups had no choice but to cross the Missouri River and find hunting grounds elsewhere.

In the years to come, the tide of white settlement would dispossess the Indians of all their lands. Only the earthen mounds, an occasional spearpoint, and patches of flint rubble would be left as reminders of the Stone Age.

★ ★

3.
A NEW BREED

THE FIRST MEN who came to America were only looking for food. As long as they could hunt in peace and keep their families from starving, they were content. If one bison would provide enough food for the hunting party, only one was killed. They saw no sense in killing more than they needed. Thus, the supply of wild game always remained greater than the demand.

Sometimes the Indians had to walk or paddle their canoes a long way to find their supply of food. The herds of wild animals were constantly moving from place to place in search of grazing land. Sometimes other Indians found the good hunting grounds first. Then there would be fighting, and the stronger group would drive the other group away. But the conti-

nent was big enough to provide food for all who were willing to work for it.

Then a new breed of men came to America. This breed had no interest in hunting or farming. It was interested only in gold. The invaders had white skins and they came from Europe. Their kings had expensive tastes and they needed gold to pay for their luxuries.

Columbus had figured out that the earth was round. He believed that he could sail west and bring gold from India without going all the way around Africa. He didn't bring back the loads of gold he had expected, but he *did* discover the West Indies, and nobody had ever done *that* before.

DIVIDING THE WORLD

The King of Spain was sure that Columbus had found a new continent which undoubtedly had gold on it somewhere, and he didn't want anybody else to get it. In 1493, he persuaded the Pope to draw a line on the map from the North Pole to the South Pole. Everything east of this line, which was not already claimed, was to belong to Portugal. Everything west

of it was to belong to Spain. As things turned out, Portugal got nothing but a lot of water. Spain got all of North and South America.

If the King of England knew about the Pope's line, he paid no attention to it. It was out in the Atlantic Ocean somewhere, and nobody could be expected to see a line "drawn" on the water. The King of England sent John Cabot across the Atlantic to see what he could find. In 1497 Cabot landed on Labrador and promptly claimed the entire continent for England. The Indians of Iowa didn't know that their hunting grounds had been claimed by both the King of Spain and the King of England. Even if they had known, they wouldn't have believed it. How could human beings own land? It belonged to the Great Spirit. Man could use it, but it could not be taken just because somebody held a flag over it. The Indians were to learn that the white man had other ideas about this whole business of ownership.

THE FRENCH DISCOVER IOWA

For a long time Spain and England didn't do anything about the lands they had claimed in North America. They certainly weren't interested in raising crops on it. Now and then Spanish pirates plundered Mexico, but if any Spaniard ever set foot in Iowa while he was looking for gold, he never wrote home about it.

After the first excitement of finding a new world had died down, the Spanish and the English decided that America didn't amount to much. There weren't enough rich Indians to rob of their gold, and they weren't interested in digging for it. (Work was against their principles.) It was not until the French arrived in America that the Spanish and the English began establishing colonies.

In 1534 Jacques Cartier discovered the St. Lawrence River. The French soon had a line of settlements extending along the full length of this river, and the whole country was given the name of New France. French traders, explorers, and missionaries made friends with the Indians. France thus became the first of all the nations of Europe to recognize the importance of the Mississippi Valley. Spain had ignored it.

Marquette and Joliet's Journey

On June 17, 1673, the land which is now Iowa was discovered by white men. This was no accident. A Jesuit priest named Jacques Marquette had been working among the Indians at a mission on Lake Superior. He had learned their language, and he had heard much talk about a great river toward the west. Later, when he established the mission of St. Ignace on Lake Huron, he wrote a letter to his Father Superior in Quebec. In his letter he told of his wish to look for this river and to bring Christianity to the Indians living in its valley.

The Father Superior asked Count Frontenac, the governor of New France, if he had ever heard anything about such a river. The governor hadn't, but he promised to send somebody to look into it. Maybe this river was a passage leading across the continent to India. Wouldn't that be a joke on the Spanish? After they had been stopped in their tracks by an unexpected continent, the French might be the first to find a secret waterway to the other side of the world.

Count Frontenac picked an experienced trader and woodsman named Louis Joliet to look for the river. He told Joliet to find out all he could from Father Marquette. He might even take the priest with him if it seemed like a good idea.

Joliet reached St. Ignace in the winter, and he and Father Marquette spent the time until spring planning their trip. Since Marquette could speak the Indian language, there was never any question about his partnership in the project. Five "voyageurs," or oarsmen, were hired to paddle the two canoes which were outfitted for the journey. It was agreed that Marquette would ride in one canoe and Joliet in the other. If anything happened to one canoe, there would still be a leader in the other canoe to take charge.

On May 17, 1673, the little company left the mission to look for the Great River. Marquette was sure that it would be found by going due west. All of the Indians who had told him about it had pointed in that direction. The explorers drove their canoes through the Straits of Mackinac, then, along the northern edge of Lake Michigan and into Green Bay. At a village of Menomonee Indians, they stopped for a short visit. When Marquette told the Indians why his people were traveling westward, the Menomonees tried to talk him into going back to St. Ignace.

The Indians had heard many tales about the Great River. Did the Frenchmen know that a monster lived in it? This demon of the deep could swallow their canoes and all its passengers in one gulp. Its roaring could be heard for miles, and the water around it boiled like a huge cauldron. Marquette thanked the Menomonees for their concern but assured them that, having come this far, they would take a chance on escaping.

The voyageurs paddled their canoes out of Green Bay into the Lower Fox River, then across Lake Winnebago, and into the Upper Fox River. They rested for a few days in a village of the Mascoutin Indians. The Mascoutins told Father Marquette that the Upper Fox River would not take them much further west. However, they knew of a place where the Frenchmen could carry their canoes and supplies across a short strip of land to the Wisconsin River. Marquette and Joliet hired two Indian guides to show them this place. The Indians accompanied the white men to the portage, or carrying place, and returned to their village. They had heard about the monster too, and they didn't want to meet it.

Now Marquette and Joliet and their five oarsmen were alone in the wilderness. The last known village had been left behind. They launched their canoes on the Wisconsin River and floated with the current into country that no white man had ever seen. On June 17, 1673, just one month after they had left St. Ignace, the travelers reached the mouth of the Wisconsin. They had found the broad, surging stream of the Mississippi. Across the wide river to the west was a row of high bluffs which Marquette called "mountains." He and his companions were the first white men to see Iowa.

They were not the first white men to see the Mississippi, however. The Spanish explorer, Fernando de

Soto, had discovered the great inland waterway much further south, in 1541, while he was looking for gold. But Marquette and Joliet were the first white men who really explored it.

We have a full account of their observations in Marquette's Journal, which is still preserved in *The Jesuit Relations*. (This is not a book about the relatives of the Jesuits. It is a story of the experiences of the Jesuit missionaries as related in their journals.) Father Marquette named the mighty stream the "Riviere de la Conception," in honor of the Virgin Mary, but the Indian name "Misisibi" is the one we have adopted.

As the Frenchmen let their canoes follow the swift current southward, they noticed the beautiful landscape on both sides of the river. No monster appeared, but Marquette wrote that one large fish—possibly a sturgeon—"struck our canoe with such violence that I thought it was a large tree, about to break our canoe in pieces." In all this part of the journey, they saw no human beings except themselves—"only deer, cattle, cranes and swans." The "cattle" were probably buffalo.

For eight days, the voyageurs steered their way southward, stopping at night on small islands in the river. On June 25, they noticed "some tracks of men" near the mouth of a stream entering the Great River from the west. We know this smaller stream now as the Iowa River. It enters the Mississippi near the town of Oakville. Of course, there was no town at the mouth of the Iowa in 1673. There were only "some tracks of men."

Marquette and Joliet agreed that they should look for the men who had made these tracks. Leaving their canoes and guns in the care of the oarsmen, the two leaders began following what Marquette described as "a narrow and somewhat beaten path." After walking several miles, they reached an Indian village at the place where Toolesboro is now located.

There was no one in sight. Deciding that it was time to reveal themselves, they stopped and shouted. "On hearing the shout," Marquette wrote in his Journal, "the savages quickly issued from their cabins. Having probably recognized us as Frenchmen, especially when they saw a black gown, they sent four old men to come and

INDIAN VILLAGES like this one, reproduced as a diorama at Villa Louis Historical Museum, Prairie du Chien, Wisconsin, were familiar sights to Marquette and Joliet. The wickiup (right center) served as a snug and weatherproof dwelling.

speak to us. Two of these bore tobacco pipes, finely ornamented with feathers. They walked slowly toward us and raised their pipes toward the sun, without saying a word."

Marquette asked them who they were. The Indians were overjoyed to hear a stranger speaking to them in their own language. They told Marquette they were Illinois Indians and, as a token of peace, they offered the white men their pipes to smoke. Then they invited them into their village. Marquette told the Indians that the Frenchmen were on a journey to learn the direction and length of the Great River, and that they came as friends of the people living beside it.

After gifts had been exchanged, the visitors were given a great feast. A master of ceremonies fed the strangers with a wooden spoon. The first course was an appetizer of Indian cornmeal mush seasoned with bear fat. Next, the Indians picked the bones out of some fried fish and thrust the pieces of fish into the mouths of Marquette and Joliet with their fingers. The third course was roast dog—the first time white men were given the pleasure of eating a "hot dog" in Iowa. The final course was buffalo meat, which the visitors liked most of all. That night Marquette and Joliet slept in the lodge of the chief.

The next day the chief and six hundred braves walked with their two guests along the path to the Mississippi. The voyageurs, who thought that Marquette and Joliet had been

killed, were at the point of hurrying back home.

With the shouts of their new friends bidding them farewell, the Frenchmen resumed their journey. They traveled past the Missouri and Ohio rivers as far as the mouth of the Arkansas River. Here, friendly Indians told them that the Spanish were in possession of the lower part of the Mississippi, and it was decided to turn back.

They had learned what they wanted to know. The Great River ran from north to south. Count Frontenac would be disappointed be-

REFLECTIONS SHIMMER as Iowa River joins the Mississippi—seen in the far background against the shoreline of Illinois. History records Marquette and Joliet followed the bank of the Iowa on the side now fringed by trees.

cause it did not run from east to west. It provided no passage to India, but it was to become a great highway for the fur traders and the settlers who followed them.

Marquette and Joliet returned to Lake Michigan by way of the Illinois and Chicago rivers. They never saw Iowa again, but the Mississippi would be their lasting monument in Iowa history.

4. THE FRENCH MOVE IN

THE TWO WHITE MEN who led the first expedition into the Upper Mississippi were good friends, but they had little in common beyond their interest in finding the Great River. Marquette was a frail missionary; Joliet was a rugged woodsman. The missionary zeal of the priest had sustained him on the long journey. There had been little time for him to bring the story of Christ to the Indians while he and Joliet were making their trip into the wilderness.

After a short rest at St. Ignace, Father Marquette returned to an Indian village on the Illinois River and worked there as long as his failing strength would permit. When he became ill, his Indian friends knew that the end was near. They started to take him back to his mission on Lake Huron, but he died on the way. The year was 1675, only two years after his discovery of the Great River.

Joliet, meanwhile, had gone to Quebec to report to Governor Frontenac. The governor was excited about the prospect of getting a lot of new country for France, but he was disappointed because Marquette and Joliet had not followed the Mississippi all the way to its mouth. Maybe it took a turn somewhere and still flowed into the Pacific Ocean. There was one way to find out. He would send the most fearless of his explorers all the way down the Great River. The man he picked was Robert Chevalier de la Salle.

LA SALLE EXPLORES THE MISSISSIPPI

La Salle did not have an easy trip. He started out in fine style aboard a big sailing vessel named "The Griffon." By September of 1679 he had reached Green Bay and the ship was sent back with a full cargo of furs. Nobody knows what happened to it on the return voyage. It was never seen again.

Of course, La Salle didn't know that his ship was going to be lost. With a missionary named Louis Hennepin and a few others, La Salle pushed on. By New Year's Day of 1680, the little company had reached the foot of Lake Michigan. Since "The Griffon" had not come back, La Salle knew that he would need more supplies before he could complete his trip to the mouth of the Mississippi. He set off in the spring of 1680 to paddle back to Montreal. La Salle left Father Hennepin and two other members of his company to see if Marquette and Joliet had missed anything. They were to go down the Illinois River and up the Mississippi, and report to him when he got back.

Marquette and Joliet had enjoyed their trip down the Father of Waters in 1673, but Father Hennepin soon found that going up the Mississippi wasn't as pleasant as going down. The Indians weren't as friendly, either. One afternooon, as the priest and his two companions were cooking their dinner, a fleet of fifty canoes came down the Mississippi. The canoes were filled with Sioux Indians. They paid no attention to the black gown or the peace pipe of Father Hennepin, and carried the three Frenchmen back to their camp as prisoners. All summer, the captives were in constant fear that they would be murdered. They were finally rescued by a French explorer named Daniel DuLuth.

La Salle came back from Montreal with new supplies and men and, in 1682, he went down the Illinois River to the Mississippi, then down the Great River all the way to the Gulf of Mexico. As Marquette and Joliet had observed nine years earlier, the direction of the massive waterway was toward the south along its entire course. But, if La Salle couldn't get to the Pacific Ocean by following the Mississippi, he could at least claim the whole valley for France, and he did.

Spain had some colonies along the Gulf, but La Salle built a fort at the mouth of the Mississippi to prevent the Spaniards from using the river. Then he unfurled the flag of France and claimed all the country drained by the Mississippi in the name of King Louis XIV. Just to be sure that the rest of the world would know who owned this vast territory, he named it Louisiana. (Of course, the Spaniards kept calling it New Spain, but by this time France was stronger than Spain, so the Spaniards didn't make an issue of it.)

The Indians in Iowa weren't paying any attention to the names that were being given to their country. And, by the way, the Illinois Indians who had entertained Marquette and Joliet in 1673 had just been "spending their vacation" in Iowa. By the time Marquette came down the Illinois River to do his last missionary work, they were back home, and were glad to see their old friend again.

THE IOWAYS AND THE SIOUX

Dr. Marshall McKusick has pointed out, in his *Men of Ancient Iowa* that, "at the time of French exploration, the resident Indians of the state were called Ioways." Charles R. Keyes, writing about prehistoric man in Iowa, held the theory that the Ioways were related to the Oneota Indians, who had destroyed the Mound Builders.

There is a legend that the Indians who later called themselves Ioways entered Iowa by crossing the Mississippi from Illinois. Looking at these new hunting grounds from a high bluff along the river, they saw a land richly endowed with timber and sparkling streams. The prairie was carpeted with many colors of wild flowers, and wild game flashed in and out of the natural cover. Delighted with what they saw, one of the Indians shouted: "Ayooez" (pronounced "Ah-you-ways"). Translated into English, this meant "Beautiful Land." The expression was adopted by the Indians as their name.

Now, of course, it is possible that somebody made up this whole story long after the Ioways had moved in, but it *could* have happened like that. One thing is certain: By the time the French were exploring the Mississippi, the Ioways were living along the Des Moines River. Eventually, their name would be given to the entire state.

The Dakota, or Sioux, Indians moved into Iowa from the north, where they had been carrying on a running battle with the Chippewas for years. When Father Hennepin and his two companions ventured into their territory in 1680, the Sioux promptly pounced on them as intruders, and DuLuth had a hard time getting them released. For a while after that, the French stayed out of Sioux country.

A NEW BUSINESS

In 1685, Nicolas Perrot was given control of the fur trade. He built a trading post on the Wisconsin side of the Mississippi at a place which is now called Prairie du Chien. Indians discovered that they could bring beaver and otter skins to the trading post and get guns, powder, hatchets, cloth, and whiskey for them. The fur trade made

TRADING POSTS enabled Indians to exchange furs for products of the white man's world. Note the heavy interior shutters in the diorama at the Villa Louis Historical Museum, Prairie du Chien, Wsiconsin.

a great difference in the life of the Indians. Now, instead of using animal skins only for clothing and shelter, they could use them as money to buy white man's goods.

The search for furs took the Indians far from their homes, and the French traders followed them to pick up the pelts. A map published in 1703 shows one of these trails leading from Prairie du Chien all the way across Iowa to the Big Sioux River. Even the Sioux were willing to do business with the French instead of kidnapping them.

TROUBLE WITH THE SAUKS AND FOXES

But all of this was too good to last. The Fox Indians, who lived in Wisconsin, resented the French traffic across their lands. They didn't like the French very much anyhow. It was the French who called them Foxes because they were so sly. They preferred to be known as Mesquakie, or "red-earth people."

The Foxes lived along the Wisconsin River. They made it so difficult for Frenchmen to use the old canoe route to the Mississippi that the French government ordered the traders to leave their posts. For 50 years, the fur trade on the Mississippi was closed, and it was not opened again until the Fox Indians and their neighbors were chased out of Wisconsin.

These neighbors were the Sauks, or "yellow-earth people," and they didn't like Frenchmen either. At one time they had lived in upper Michigan. Then they moved into the neighborhood of Green Bay. In 1733, a French officer was killed by the Sauks while he was inspecting their village. The Sauks knew the French wouldn't be very happy about that, so they moved in with their neighbors for greater protection. The Foxes didn't think they could fight the whole French army, even with the help of the Sauks. The combined tribes therefore decided to "get lost" by crossing the Mississippi into Iowa.

A French Army is Mobilized

The French government at Quebec couldn't let the Sauks kill a French officer and get away with it. The governor of New France ordered Captain Nicolas des Noyelles to lead an expedition against the murderers. The captain was told that he might pardon the Sauks if they agreed to break up their alliance with the Foxes. If they refused, he was to destroy *both* the Sauks and the Foxes.

Eighty-four Frenchmen and 200 Iroquois, Huron, and Pottawattamie Indians made up Des Noyelles' "army." This mixed lot of white soldiers and Indian braves started from Montreal in the late summer of 1734. At Detroit, more Indians joined the group, because they all hated the Sauks and Foxes. The motley militia left Detroit in January of 1735.

It was not easy to march hundreds of miles in the dead of winter. The snow was deep, and the "army" couldn't go very fast on snowshoes. Food was hard to find. The party had grown so large that supplies ran out, and there were times when the soldiers had to eat horse and dog meat.

The eastern Indians didn't know the Iowa country and they often missed the trail. But, on April 19, 1735, the French and Indian army finally caught up with the Sauks and Foxes at the junction of the Raccoon and Des Moines rivers. Here, at the site of the present state capital, the first battle between white men and Indians was fought on Iowa soil. It was just 40 years to the day before the battles of Lexington and Concord.

The fight settled nothing. As so often happens in war, nobody won. After the smoke had cleared away, Captain Des Noyelles sent word to the Sauks that the governor of New France would pardon them if they would leave the Foxes. The Sauks gave their solemn promise that they would do this. Des Noyelles led his soldiers away and never came back.

The Sauks, of course, didn't leave the Foxes. They became strong allies and settled along the Mississippi River, where they were to give the Americans a lot of trouble in the years to come. They became firm friends of the British, who were beginning to crowd the hated French.

FRANCE LOSES ITS GRIP

The French and Indian War broke out in 1754. It was fought between the French and the English, and the French were helped by eastern Indians who didn't like the way the English were taking over the country.

The French and the Indians fought their British enemies for seven years, but the French finally had to give up. At the close of the war, France lost all of Canada as well as the part of Louisiana east of the Mississippi.

The French didn't want to lose everything in America, so they made a secret deal with Spain. If Spain would agree to return the part of Louisiana west of the Mississippi by 1800, the French would go through the motions of giving it to the Spanish. By that time, France hoped to be strong enough to fight England again —and Spain, too, if the Spanish forgot their agreement. Iowa thus became Spanish territory. The American colonies were to win their independence a few years later, but Spain and France would continue to own Iowa until President Jefferson bought it for the United States in 1803.

5. THE SPANISH LAND GRANTS

SPAIN and France didn't agree on many things, but on one thing they were in complete agreement: they both hated England. When England defeated France in the French and Indian War, France had to give up all of Canada and the part of the Louisiana Territory east of the Mississippi.

The Louisiana Territory west of the Mississippi was ceded to Spain in the hope that the Spanish would stop England at the Great River. France and Spain were encouraged when the Revolutionary War broke out. It established a new nation in the western hemisphere. This took a sizable chunk of land out of the British dominions.

However, England still had Canada and many Indian allies along the eastern side of the Mississippi. Spain could not build military posts every few miles on its border, but it could give land to French trappers and traders. This would put friends of the Spanish where they might be needed. The Spanish governor in St. Louis knew that the French were his friends. He had been given proof of it before the Revolutionary War ended. In 1780, a Frenchman named Jean Marie Cardinal had been driven away from his lead mines on the northern Mississippi by a British force which had come down from Canada. Cardinal and some of his friends had escaped and had hurried down the river to warn the people of St. Louis. So the Spanish governor knew he could depend on the French.

FIRST SETTLER IN IOWA: JULIEN DUBUQUE

The first white man who made a permanent home in Iowa was a French-Canadian named Julien Dubuque. He had come to Prairie du Chien from Canada to try his luck in the fur trade. In the course of his proposed to Kettle Chief that the Indians turn over the operation of the mines to him. "Ugh-Ugh," the Chief replied, and this meant "No," just as it does today.

Dubuque tried to explain the advantages of his way of doing things. The Indians were not getting much money for their impure lead. Dubuque proposed the building of a smelter, which would extract the pure lead from the ore. He would then take this lead to St. Louis, where he would get a better price for it than the Indians were getting. Kettle Chief still said "No."

But Dubuque was a resourceful man. He had expected resistance to his proposal, and, before he began his conference with Kettle Chief he had sent some of his friends a short distance upstream on Catfish Creek. While nobody was looking, these friends had poured oil on the slow-moving water. Dubuque kept his eye on the creek and when he saw the oil coming downstream he picked a burning brand from the campfire. As soon as Kettle Chief turned him down the second time, Dubuque announced that if he could not have his way he would set Catfish Creek on fire. Kettle Chief made no reply until Dubuque threw the burning brand into the patch of oil and the water burst into flames.

Then Dubuque repeated his question: Would the Indians allow him to operate the mines? This time, Kettle Chief had a different answer.

STONE TOWER marks the grave of Julien Dubuque, first white settler in Iowa. It is on a high bluff south of the city of Dubuque overlooking the junction of Catfish Creek with the Mississippi River.

traffic in pelts, he learned that the Fox Indians had found rich deposits of lead in the bluffs near Catfish Creek, which flows into the Mississippi. This was not too far from Prairie du Chien, so Dubuque decided to visit the lead mines on the west side of the great river. He liked what he saw, and he made a proposal to Kettle Chief. (That really was his name: "Kettle Chief" not "Chief Kettle.") Dubuque

He said, "Ugh-Huh," which meant "Yes," just as it does today.

To make the whole thing legal, Dubuque persuaded the Fox to give him written permission to work the lead mines, and a contract was signed at Prairie du Chien on September 22, 1788. He immediately moved into the camp of Kettle Chief, built himself a cabin and constructed a furnace to smelt the lead for the St. Louis market. The women of the Fox village continued to do the actual mining, but Dubuque and a crew of French-Canadians from Prairie du Chien worked the smelter and molded the lead into neat bars—or "pigs," as they were called. He kept working at the fur trade on the side.

Twice a year he loaded his lead and furs on a flotilla of boats and went down the Mississippi to St. Louis. The Fox chiefs and braves, whose wives had been working the mines, went with him for a vacation. The arrival of Dubuque and his party in St. Louis was always a special event, and banquets were given in honor of the rich trader from the north. The lead and furs were sold, and supplies were purchased to make life on Catfish Creek as comfortable as possible.

The Mines of Spain

Naturally, the Spanish governor was pleased to have a powerful ally on the Upper Mississippi. When Julien Dubuque decided to strengthen his hold on the land he occupied, he called his operations The Mines of Spain. Then he asked the Governor-General, Baron de Carondelet, to give him a Spanish land grant covering the area around Catfish Creek. Carondelet gladly gave him official title to a tract of land extending 21 miles along the river and 9 miles inland.

With his claim to the mining country thus doubly secured, Dubuque should have piled up a tidy fortune because he lived in Iowa for 22 years and, in that time, he mined and sold a great deal of lead. However, Julien Dubuque was not a good business man. Before he died in 1810, he had exchanged half his land in Iowa for goods he had bought on credit from a St. Louis merchant named Auguste Chouteau. The rest of his holdings were to go to Chouteau at the time of his death.

It was a poor bargain for the St. Louis merchant. When Dubuque died, the Fox Indians gave him a funeral befitting a chief and buried him on top of the bluff overlooking Catfish Creek. But they denied the claims of Chouteau to the lead mines. They said their arrangement had been made with Dubuque only, and his rights could not be passed on to anybody else. Chouteau took his case to court but, by that time, the United States had bought the territory west of the Mississippi, and the Supreme Court ruled that Spanish grants were not legally binding upon the new government. So Chouteau and his heirs got nothing.

Today, there is an imposing memorial on the bluff above Catfish Creek which marks the grave of the first white settler in Iowa. On the riverfront of the city named in his honor stands the old Shot Tower, which is another monument to what John Rider Wallis has called "The Lure of Lead." It was not built until 1856, which was almost a half-century after the death of Julien Dubuque, but it is a symbol of an industry which was begun by the French-Canadian trader in 1788.

BASIL GIARD

Julien Dubuque was not the only Iowa settler who received a land grant from the Spanish. There were at least two others. One of them was a Frenchman named Basil Giard, who had become acquainted with Julien Dubuque while both were living in Prairie du Chien. In 1795, when Giard applied for a grant of land on the Iowa side of the river, he told the Spanish governor that he had lived there for fifteen years. This would have put him in Iowa in 1780, eight years before Dubuque began operating the Mines of Spain. (It is unlikely that Giard ever lived on the Iowa land. He might have gone across the river to hunt or fish on Saturday afternoons, but he had a business to run in Prairie du Chien, and his home was on the Wisconsin side of the Mississippi. The tract that he got from the governor in what is now Clayton County covered 5,760 acres, and this made Giard an important landholder, whether he lived in Iowa or not. The hired men who worked the land and cut the timber probably had their homes in Prairie du Chien, too.)

TESSON'S APPLE ORCHARD

The third man who received a Spanish land grant was also a Frenchman. His name was Louis Honore Tesson. Tesson was given a tract, "a league square," which included the present town of Montrose. The grant signed by the Spanish governor in 1799 gave Tesson permission "to establish himself at the head of the rapids of the River Des Moines and, his establishment once formed, notice of it to be given to the Governor-General, in order to obtain for him a commission of a space sufficient to give value to such establishment, and at the same time to render it useful to the commerce of the peltries of this country, to watch the Indians and to keep them in the fidelity which they owe to His Majesty."

In that very long sentence, the part about "His Majesty" referred to the King of Spain. The Spanish governor in St. Louis wanted to prevent English traders from coming into the northern Mississippi Valley and buying up all the furs. He figured that a man like Tesson could keep the Indians from doing business with the British—if he treated them well and showed them how to be Christians in

30

the Spanish manner. This worked out pretty well for a while. Tesson went down to St. Louis and brought back supplies, such as calico, blankets, guns, powder, traps, and knives, to trade for the Indian furs. But he had to get credit for the goods he bought, and, like Julien Dubuque, his bills piled up.

In an effort to make more money, Tesson went to St. Charles, Missouri, and brought home some apple tree seedlings. The orchard he planted was the first in Iowa, but it didn't bear fruit soon enough to do him much good. By 1803, he was so deeply in debt that the Tesson farm was sold at auction in St. Louis for $150.

Tesson lived on the farm for at least two years after it was sold, because Lieutenant Zebulon Pike found him there when he went up the Mississippi in 1805. Tesson tried to get a job with Pike as an interpreter, since Pike didn't know the Indian language, but the United States government didn't have as much money then as it has now. Pike couldn't afford to hire him. Since Tesson couldn't make a living in Iowa, he had to look for work somewhere else. Nobody knows where he went.

What happened to the apple orchard? The trees finally bore fruit, and the apples were picked by the In-

LEWIS AND CLARK MONUMENT on the heights above Council Bluffs gestures, like outstretched arms, toward the Nebraska side of the wide Missouri. Although the historic meeting with the Missouri and Otoe Indians actually took place on the west bank of the river, the Iowa city took its name from the meeting site—Council Bluffs.

dians. They didn't know that the apples had to turn red before they were ripe, so the Indians ate them while they were still green. Even the stumps of the old trees are gone now. At least, they are out of sight. In 1912, a great dam was built across the Mississippi at Keokuk. When the flood gates were closed in 1913, the river was backed up to form a huge lake which covered the ground where Louis Honore Tesson had planted his apple trees. There is a stone marker at Montrose which reminds the traveler of the old orchard, but it is on high ground, far from the place where Indians once picked green apples.

Napoleon Bonaparte forced Spain to give the Louisiana Territory back to France in 1800, but, as we shall see in our next chapter, the United States got it in 1803.

★ ★

6. A GOOD BUY

THE UNITED STATES OF AMERICA began to feel growing pains almost as soon as it was born. Settlers moved into the land west of the Alleghenies in search of new opportunities to make a living. Since there were no interstate highways and no railroads, the rivers were the main avenues of travel. They also carried the products which the settlers wanted to buy and sell.

The boundary separating the United States and the Louisiana Territory was an imaginary line in the middle of the Mississippi River. The river provided plenty of room for American commerce, but there was a bottleneck at the mouth of the stream. New Orleans belonged to Spain, and the Spanish commander could shut off the traffic whenever he felt like it.

France took the Louisiana Territory away from Spain in 1800, but President Jefferson didn't hear about it until 1802. During the Revolutionary War, France had been a big help to the colonies in winning their independence, but the former ally was now under the powerful leadership of Napoleon. Jefferson didn't feel very comfortable about having Napoleon in control of the Mississippi.

"SHOPPING" IN PARIS

There was no immediate cause for alarm, because Napoleon had his hands full in Europe. He was making plans to conquer England. Since wars take money, Jefferson thought it might be a good time to do a little spending in France. He asked Congress for two million dollars. Then, he told James Monroe and the American minister, Robert Livingston, to get an appointment with Napoleon and try to buy New Orleans and West Florida from him. If Napoleon didn't want to sell this much, they were to spend *all* of the two million dollars, if necessary, for New Orleans alone.

The appointment was made, but the deal didn't work out quite the way it was planned. When he heard the offer, Napoleon shook his head. He didn't want to sell just New Orleans and Florida. His financial needs were urgent, and he startled the Americans by making a counterproposal. Would they be interested in buying *all* the land still owned by France in North America?

Well! This was a bigger bite than Monroe and Livingston were prepared to swallow. They couldn't call the President by transatlantic telephone, because it hadn't been invented yet. They would have to use their own judgment.

Napoleon was waiting for an offer, and he acted as though he wasn't going to wait very long. Monroe and Livingston began to dicker. After a while, Napoleon agreed to accept fifteen million dollars for all of the Louisiana Territory from the Mississippi to the Rocky Mountains. Monroe had enough for a down payment. The deal was closed April 30, 1803.

President Jefferson was a little shaken when he found out what his ministers had done, but he soon realized that the whole thing had worked out better than he had expected. There were complaints in Congress, of course. For one thing, the purchase was called unconstitutional. (Some Congressmen pointed out that fifteen million would make a pile of silver dollars three miles high, and this was going too far with government spending.) But the people supported the President and so, finally, did Congress. The balance due was borrowed, and by the time the interest had been paid, the total outlay amounted to something like 27 million dollars.

The Louisiana Purchase added over 900,000 square miles of territory to the United States at a cost of less than five cents an acre. All of six states and parts of seven others were to be carved out of this immense area. It was the biggest real estate bargain in history. Perhaps Napoleon had the idea that he was just letting go of the land temporarily. Maybe he planned to take it all back after completing his conquests in Europe, but it didn't work out that way. The sale in 1803 was final.

LOOKING OVER THE LAND

Now that the Louisiana Purchase had doubled the size of the United States, President Jefferson was eager to take inventory of it. Nobody knew exactly what the nation had bought. There was a settlement called St. Louis near the junction of the Mississippi and Missouri rivers, and the President decided that this would be a good place to start. Two expeditions were to be sent from St. Louis. One of them was to go up the Missouri River, and the other the Mississippi.

First, however, the ownership of the territory had to be straightened out. Even though France had reclaimed Louisiana in 1800, St. Louis was still in the hands of the Spanish. The French prefect in New Orleans commissioned Captain Amos Stoddard, an American artillery officer, to receive the territory of Upper Louisiana in the name of France. This was done on March 9, 1804. The next day, Captain Stoddard transferred the territory to himself as a representative of the United States. By this act, on March 10, 1804, Iowa became a part of the United States for the first time in its history.

THE LEWIS AND CLARK EXPEDITION

As soon as the American flag was raised over St. Louis, the explorers began to get ready for their journeys into the wilderness. President Jefferson had chosen Captain Meriwether Lewis of the infantry and Lieutenant William Clark of the artillery to lead the expedition up the Missouri River. For some reason, the War Department refused to promote Clark to the rank of captain, as Jefferson had requested. This didn't make any difference to Lewis. He called his friend "Captain" anyhow, and he insisted that the forty men in the company follow his example. Since the leadership was shared equally by the two men, the great adventure became known as the Lewis and Clark expedition.

Congress appropriated only $2,500 for the trip. (After borrowing all that money to *buy* the land, Congress thought it was time to watch expenses.) One large keel boat and two smaller boats called "pirogues" were outfitted with supplies, and the journey was begun on May 14, 1804. It took over two months to pole and haul the boats against the strong current of the Missouri as far as the southwest corner of Iowa.

Stops Along the Iowa Border

On August 3, a council with the Missouri and Otoe Indians was held on the Nebraska side of the river. It was opposite a bluff on the Iowa side which later became known as the Council Bluff, and, still later, gave the city of Council Bluffs its name. The Indians were friendly, gifts were exchanged, and everyone had a good time—all except Sergeant Charles

Floyd. He had not been feeling well for some time. On August 19, he took a sudden turn for the worse, and he died the following day. It is believed that he had a ruptured appendix and in those days this was fatal.

The sergeant died when the expedition had reached the place where Sioux City is located today. He was buried at the top of a bluff on the Iowa side of the river, and his grave was marked by a cedar post bearing his name. Now, a one-hundred-foot sandstone shaft called the Floyd Monument crowns the bluff. It honors the memory of the first soldier of the United States to be buried in Iowa, as well as the only member of the Lewis and Clark expedition who died on the long journey.

FLOYD MONUMENT towers above Sioux City, marking the grave of Sergeant Charles Floyd. A member of the Lewis and Clark expedition, Floyd died, probably of a ruptured appendix, and was buried in Iowa.

Results of the Expedition

The trip to the headwaters of the Missouri took the explorers to the Rocky Mountains, which marked the western boundary of the Louisiana Purchase. Since they had come this far, the leaders decided they might as well go all the way to the Pacific Ocean. Robert Gray's earlier discovery of the Columbia River had given the United States a claim to the Oregon country. Lewis and Clark strengthened this American claim by their visit.

On September 23, 1806, the expedition returned to St. Louis. Lewis and Clark had been gone for more than two years, and nobody had expected to see them again. They brought back the first reliable information about the unknown and mysterious Northwest. The journals of the two leaders were eagerly studied by scholars and politicians, and the reports on the natural wealth of the region started the trappers, the traders, and the settlers moving westward.

ZEBULON PIKE ON THE MISSISSIPPI

While Lewis and Clark were learning about the Missouri River country, another military officer was exploring the Mississippi. He was Zebulon Pike, a lieutenant in the infantry. Lewis and Clark had been sent up the Missouri by the President of the United States. Pike was under orders from the Army. He was told to select points along the river where forts might be built. He was also told to look for British traders who were trespassing on United States territory. These traders, acting as agents of the British government, were stirring up the Indians against the Americans. Lieutenant Pike didn't have as large a company as Lewis and Clark. One keel boat held the entire party of twenty men, plus provisions for a four-month trip. The Pike expedition left St. Louis on August 9, 1805. The Lieutenant thought he could go all the way to the source of the Mississippi and get back to St. Louis before the river froze over.

Travel upstream was slow, and the rapids along Iowa's eastern border made progress especially difficult. However, Pike found two excellent places for forts. One was on the high ground where Burlington is now located. The other was on one of the "mountains" which Father Marquette had noted when he left the mouth of the Wisconsin River in 1673. This bluff in Clayton County is now called "Pike's Peak." Since Pike discovered it before he found the more famous peak in Colorado, Iowa claims the honor of having Pike's Peak No. 1. Although the young lieutenant strongly recommended the building of forts at Burlington and on the heights above McGregor, the Army paid no attention to him.

Nobody else paid much attention to Lieutenant Pike either. Julien Dubuque was still living on Catfish Creek, but he was suspicious of Americans, and he refused to give Pike any precise information about his mines.

Pike Meets Black Hawk

On the Illinois side of the river, the British flag was flying over a camp of the Sauk Indians. Pike tried to get Black Hawk to haul it down. He explained that the American flag should be displayed, now that the country belonged to the United States. Black Hawk was willing to fly both the British and the American flags, but he wouldn't settle for one—unless it was the British. He made no secret of his loyalty to the redcoats, and no amount of argument would change it. Lieutenant Pike was the first, but not the last, American officer who had trouble with Black Hawk.

The Pike expedition had to spend the winter in the frozen wilds of Minnesota. Even there, Pike did not discover the true source of the Mississippi. This discovery was not made until 1832, when Henry Schoolcraft found the headwaters in Lake Itasca. Lieutenant Pike returned to St. Louis on April 30, 1806. The trip hadn't been much fun for him, and the Army didn't think it had been worth the time or the trouble either. It would be several more years before the full value of the Mississippi would be recognized by the United States.

★ ★

7. WAR ON THE MISSISSIPPI

Captain Amos Stoddard was the first American governor of Upper Louisiana. He was the man who accepted the territory for France on one day and turned it over to the United States on the next. But being governor was just a temporary job for him. By the late summer of 1804, William Henry Harrison, governor of the Indiana Territory, was on his way to St. Louis to take over the duties of governor of the Louisiana District in addition to his other chores.

The Louisiana Purchase in 1803 had disposed of the French danger in America, but there were still British agents who were encouraging the Indians to revolt against the United States. President Jefferson wanted to get the Sauks and Foxes to sign a treaty with the new government. He didn't want to push them off their land without paying them for it, but he had to get them moved to a place

where they couldn't cause any trouble. Governor Harrison had been trying to get the job done for years, but the Indians didn't trust the Americans.

A TRAP, A TREAT, AND A TREATY

Shortly before Harrison arrived in St. Louis, two settlers in the back country had been killed by a party of Sauk warriors. There was nothing unusual about this. A settler who built his home on Indian land in those days took the same chance that a hunter takes when he pitches his camp in the jungle today. However, this incident turned out to be something special. Word of the killing was brought to the Sauk village, and, since the Indians didn't want to invite trouble with the United States, a chief went down to St. Louis to apologize.

Here was a golden opportunity. The military commander in St. Louis

LONE CHIMNEY MONUMENT overlooks the riverfront at Fort Madison. For many years the chimney was considered to be merely a symbol of Iowa's first fort. It was believed that the actual fort site had been covered by the river.

knew that Governor Harrison was due almost any day. "Go back to your village," said the Army man. "This is a serious matter, and you must round up all the chiefs of the Sauk and Fox nations. Bring them here, and the Great White Father will tell them what must be done."

The big chiefs got the word and shook their heads. After all, only two settlers had been killed, and they had no business being on Indian land in the first place. The Americans had been trespassing, and it shouldn't require a full-dress delegation to prove it. A few Sauk and Fox chiefs appeared in St. Louis on the appointed day, but they were not the top chiefs. The matter wasn't considered important enough for the head men to settle.

The Indians were given whiskey and smooth talk and, when they were thoroughly befuddled, they were told to touch the end of a goose quill while an American officer made marks beside their names on a piece of paper. It all seemed like "good clean fun," but, after the hangover, the chiefs discovered that they had signed away fifteen million acres of land.

Governor Harrison told the bewildered Indians that they might stay on their land until the government had sold it to settlers. He also said that everything would be delightful for them, because the Great White Father was going to provide a blacksmith who would repair their guns and traps. He would also set up a trading post where they could bring their furs and lead and exchange them for supplies and trinkets. And, besides all that, the Indians would be paid a thousand dollars in annuities as long as they behaved themselves. But they must understand that all of their former property east of the Mississippi now belonged to the United States.

Well, of course, this wasn't exactly good news to take back to the villages of the Sauks and Foxes. The wonder is that the United States didn't have an Indian war on its hands as soon as word of the swindle got around. But most of the Sauks and the Foxes knew that they had to get along with their new neighbors, whether they liked them or not, so nothing was done about it.

A POOR PLACE FOR KEEPING PEACE: FORT MADISON

Lewis and Clark had returned from their long journey on the Missouri River, and, since they had shown real talent in dealing with Indians, they were given special assignments as soon as they got back to St. Louis. Meriwether Lewis was appointed governor of the territory, and William Clark was made the superintendent of Indian affairs. Together, they decided to keep Governor Harrison's promise of a trading post on the Upper Mississippi. And, while they were about it, they thought a fort would be a good idea, too. The trading post was to be stocked with enough goods to persuade the Indians to do business with the Americans instead of the British. The fort was to keep the peace.

Colonel Thomas Hunt was placed in command of the project, but, a few days before the convoy was ready to leave St. Louis, the colonel died, and the whole job was turned over to Lieutenant Alpha Kingsley. The lieutenant had never been in command of such an expedition, and he had never built a fort, but he promised to do his best. As it turned out, his best wasn't good enough.

In September of 1808, Kingsley and his soldiers reached the Des Moines River. The Secretary of War in Washington had given orders that a post was to be built at the mouth of this river. But there were rapids boiling in the Mississippi all the way from the mouth of the Des Moines to a point eleven miles upstream. Kingsley thought the location might be flooded in times of high water, so he pushed his way to the head of the rapids, where Governor Lewis had bought some land from the Indians.

The lieutenant didn't like the looks of this place either. He didn't think there would be enough white oak timber to build a stockade. Zebulon Pike had recommended the location for a trading post, with a fort on *high* ground at the place where Burlington is today. The War Department had given no heed to this recommendation, and Kingsley probably didn't even know about it. He proceeded up the river to a point about ten miles north of the rapids. This, he decided, was the place! Kingsley wrote the Secretary of War that the location commanded an extensive view of the river, and that it had an excellent spring of drinking water. He even called it Fort Bellevue because the scenery was so beautiful.

As a location for a fort, it was about the worst place he could have picked. Donald Jackson, in an article for *The Palimpsest* of January, 1958, declared that, "the location could never be defended. Behind it ran a ridge where the Indians could take cover while firing down at the garrison, and along the west was a ravine where war parties could infiltrate without being seen."

Kingsley had passed up the places which had been bought by the government, so he got as many Indians together as he could find and talked them into selling him the land for $300. Black Hawk was delighted. The location would make things easy for him when he got ready to attack.

Black Hawk Begins His Campaign

Black Hawk didn't wait very long. During the winter of 1808-9, most of the fort was completed. The trading post was built outside the stockade, so the Indians wouldn't be able to do their shopping inside the fort. Black Hawk hadn't counted on this, but he thought he was cunning enough to get inside the stockade anyhow. In the spring of 1809, he and his braves came across the river to trade their furs and lead for traps, blankets, and whiskey. After they had finished their business, they sent word inside the fort that they would like to dance for the white soldiers.

Lieutenant Kingsley had kept his men locked inside the stockade in case there might be trouble. Now, he got his soldiers to face the closed gate and aim their muskets at it. A cannon was wheeled to a spot where its load of grapeshot couldn't possibly miss. Then the lieutenant ordered the gate opened. The great door of the stockade swung open. The Indians took one look at the receiving line and decided they didn't feel like dancing after all.

But this was only the beginning. Black Hawk came back again and again. He didn't try to get his warriors inside the fort on these return trips, but he kept the soldiers jumping by shooting down at them from his position on the ridge. To make things even more exciting, he shot fire arrows at the wooden barracks, and the soldiers had to work fast to keep the buildings from burning down. This kind of sniping went on for some time, and nobody in Washington did much about it. Now and then, supplies and reinforcements were sent up the river from St. Louis, but this didn't help matters a great deal. In the hope that the President would do something for his namesake, Lieutenant Kingsley changed Fort Bellevue to Fort Madison when Madison was elected President. (But two other forts in different parts of the country did the same thing, and the only result of this renaming was that mail for the soldiers in the three Fort Madisons got all mixed up.)

The War of 1812

Then fighting broke out between England and the United States. The friends the British had made among the Indians now openly supported England. Of course, not all of the Sauks, Foxes, and Ioways fought on the side of the British in the War of

1812. Most of them remained neutral, even though many were tempted to take back their land while they had the chance. However, Black Hawk and his warriors and a band of tough Winnebagoes were on the side of the British all the way.

During 1812 and 1813, Iowa's Fort Madison was attacked so many times that the soldiers lost count. They could do nothing but lock themselves inside the stockade and hope the Indians would go away. If a soldier ventured outside the walls, he was shot and scalped by the Indians, and no one even dared to go after his body. Lieutenant Thomas Hamilton, who was now in command, decided that the garrison could not defend itself against Black Hawk.

ACTUAL FOUNDATIONS of old Fort Madison were discovered in the summer of 1965 by a crew working under State Archeologist Marshall McKusick. Remains were uncovered on both sides of the Lone Chimney Monument. The stone paving in the foreground was in front of the officers' barracks.

The Fort Is Abandoned

On the night of September 3, 1813, a trench was dug from the fort to the river. The men had to work very quietly, because the Indians were hiding within easy gunshot of the stockade. Their work completed, the soldiers crawled on their hands and knees to waiting boats, and the last man to leave the fort set fire to it. By the time the Indians discovered that their prize was in flames, Lieutenant Hamilton and his entire command were safely out of reach on the dark Mississippi.

The war was over for Fort Madison, and the Indians called the charred ruins "Po-to-wo-noc," or "Place of Fire." One chimney of the officers' barracks remained standing on the river bank for many years, and steamboat captains called it "The Lone Chimney." In time to come, a city would take the name of the old fort, and a stone monument would mark the general area which Lieutenant Kingsley had chosen for its beautiful view.

Historians assumed that the remains of the fort had been hidden by the waters of the Mississippi when the river was backed up by the Keokuk Dam. But, in the summer of 1965, foundations of blockhouses and barracks were uncovered on both sides of the monument. The long-buried ruins exactly matched a ground plan which had been sent to the War Department in 1810.

Fort Madison was not a success as a military bastion, but it taught the War Department a few lessons which would be remembered in building later forts. It also gave Black Hawk a reputation which wouldn't do him much good in his future dealings with Americans. His faith in the British had been misplaced, and he would live to regret it.

★ ★

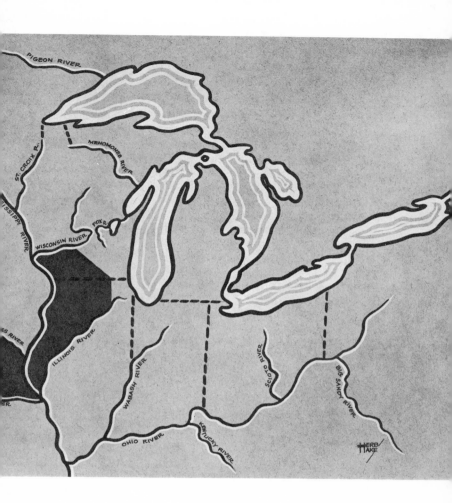

8. RED AND WHITE

IN 1812, when Black Hawk was taking pot shots at the sitting ducks in Fort Madison, the land that is now Iowa was a part of the Territory of Missouri. It had been in the Louisiana Territory only nine years earlier, when the vast region between the Mississippi and the Rocky Mountains had been purchased from France.

As soon as American title to the Louisiana Territory was established in 1804, Congress divided it into the Territory of Orleans and the District of Louisiana. Iowa was in the District

SHADED PORTION of the map indicates the land signed away by the Sauk and Fox Indians in 1804 while they were too "tipsy" to realize what they were doing.

of Louisiana, which was the northern part of the new property. Then, in 1805, the District of Louisiana was renamed the Territory of Louisiana. Seven years later, the Iowa country became a part of the Territory of Missouri. All of this was done to achieve greater convenience in local government.

Iowa remained in the Territory of Missouri until 1821, when Missouri became a state. For the next thirteen years, Iowa was an orphan, without government of any kind. Congress probably reasoned that the Indians living in Iowa wouldn't pay any attention to a government even if they had it.

RUNNING A LINE: THE SULLIVAN BOUNDARY

You will remember that Governor Harrison had "persuaded" the Sauk and Fox Indians to part with fifteen million acres of land. Most of this land was east of the Mississippi River in what is now Illinois and Wisconsin. But there was also a sizable piece west of the Mississippi and north of the Missouri River. In 1808, the United States obtained the rest of the land north of the Missouri by signing a treaty with the Osage Indians.

Settlers who followed Lewis and

Clark up the Missouri River began to establish their homes in this country. The frontier towns of St. Louis and St. Charles were growing in population, and the area which had been cleared of Indian titles was considered ready for statehood.

A man named John C. Sullivan was hired by the government in 1816 to survey the land which the United States had acquired from the Osage Indians. Starting at the junction of the Kansas and Missouri rivers, Sullivan ran a line due north for a distance of one hundred miles. From that point, he ran a line due east to the Des Moines River. Sullivan didn't get this line straight, and his error would cause trouble between Iowa and Missouri in the years to come, but, as yet, nobody knew about it. When Missouri was admitted to statehood, Sullivan's line became the northern boundary of the state, and it was defined as "the parallel of latitude which passes through the rapids of the river Des Moines."

Now, we know that there are no rapids in the Des Moines River. The so-called "rapids of the river Des Moines" were in the *Mississippi* River. They were thought to be caused by the turbulence of the Des Moines River as it entered the larger stream. Sullivan had been told to run his line only as far east as the Des Moines, because the Sauk and Fox had ceded no land north of this river. To make sure he would be understood, he had extended the line to follow "the parallel of latitude" all the way to the Mississippi. Of course, it was a dotted line across the corner of Iowa, and this part of the line didn't count as far as Missouri was concerned. The Des Moines River served as the northern boundary of Missouri on the eastern edge of the state. In theory, the land beyond this northern boundary still belonged to the Indians. (There was a kind of polite understanding among the nations of the world that full ownership of "empty land" could not be established until treaties had been signed with the natives. Political title merely carried with it the option to negotiate. It didn't matter a great deal how signatures to treaties were obtained, so long as the legal formalities were observed. Once the treaty was signed, the transfer of ownership was final.)

THE HALF-BREED TRACT

The Sauk and Fox Indians had signed no treaties with the United States for the cession of any Iowa land. Lieutenant Kingsley had paid $300 for enough land to build Fort Madison, but as things turned out, it was given back to the Indians.

Of course, traders, trappers, and soldiers had been traveling through this wild country for years, and they didn't care whether the United States owned it or not. Some of them got along fine with the Indians and even married Indian women. The children born of these mixed marriages were

SCHOOLDAYS began in Iowa in a little log building at Galland. The present structure is a replica of that first schoolhouse.

called half-breeds. As they grew up, these children began to ask for a share of the Indian lands.

In 1824, the Sauk and Fox made their first cession in what is now Iowa. The small triangle between the Mississippi and Des Moines rivers was turned over to the half-breeds, and it became known as the Half-Breed Tract. The northern boundary of this tract followed the same line which John Sullivan had described as "the parallel of latitude which passes through the rapids of the river Des Moines." Of course, the Indians didn't know anything about parallels of latitude. They simply declared that the cession extended from "Ah-wi-pe-tuck" (the Head of the Rapids) to "Puck-e-she-tuck" (the Foot of the Rapids). "Ah-wi-pe-tuck" is now

Montrose, and "Puck-e-she-tuck" is now Keokuk.

A foothold had been gained, and white settlers began to move into the Half-Breed Tract. In 1820, Dr. Samuel Muir, an Army surgeon, had crossed into Iowa with his Indian wife and family. He had built a cabin at "Puck-e-she-tuck." A few years later, Moses Stilwell and Otis Reynolds moved into the Half-Breed Tract to become the neighbors of the Muir family. The Stilwells and the Reynolds were all white. Indeed, the daughter of Moses Stilwell was the first white child born in Iowa. The half-breeds allowed the white settlers to stay. They would have been driven out of the rest of Iowa.

THE GALLAND SCHOOL

Dr. Isaac Galland ventured further north. He built a home for his family at "Ah-wi-pe-tuck," the Head of the Rapids. Others soon joined him. Dr. Galland realized that the children of the little community could not go to school unless a schoolhouse and a teacher were provided. A log cabin had been built by a fainthearted settler who had decided not to stay. It became the first schoolhouse in Iowa. Dr. Galland persuaded Berryman Jennings, a young man from Kentucky, to be the teacher. School was held during the months of October, November, and December in 1830, and it was attended by less than a dozen children. The teacher was given board and room at the Galland home, and he was allowed to study the doctor's medical books. This was his total salary.

All of the boys and girls were taught in one room, regardless of grade level. The boys sat on backless benches along one side of the room. The girls sat on the same kind of benches along the other side. Sometimes the teacher put a boy on the girls' side, or a girl on the side with the boys. This was considered a worse punishment than being beaten on the palm of the hand with a ruler. Pupils were whipped not only for whispering, but also for poor spelling or reading.

The teacher sat at the front of the room, and the children stood before him when they did their reading. A blackboard, made of a wide plank and painted black, hung over the fireplace. The chalk was a piece of soft white limestone. The eraser was made of sheepskin. The older boys and girls used the blackboard to work their problems in arithmetic. The smaller children were not tall enough to reach it. The windows were covered with oiled paper, because glass was hard to get, and it was expensive. Oiled paper did not admit much light, but it was cheap. If it was broken, it could be replaced without much trouble.

The remains of the first schoolhouse in Iowa were flooded by the Mississippi when the dam was built at Keokuk. In 1940, the Schoolmasters Club of Lee County built a replica near the original location. The place was named Galland in honor of the doctor who was Iowa's first patron of education.

OTHER PIONEER INSTITUTIONS

Wherever settlers made their homes in small communities, teachers were brought into the Half-Breed Tract to instruct the children. A school was opened at "Puck-e-she-tuck," the Foot of the Rapids, only a month or so after Berryman Jennings began his brief term in the Galland school.

But teachers were not long content to work merely for room and board. "Rate schools" were established, and the teachers exchanged their services for whatever the settlers would give them. Old records indicate that one teacher gave a mother credit for $1.00 because she had washed his pants. Another entry shows that he accepted four bushels of potatoes as part-payment for tuition. Rates in money were indicated by such entries as "$8.00 for 120 days of schooling." At this rate, the boy whose mother washed the teacher's pants got 15 days of schooling for the job. Iowa was still a long way from the time when its people would be taxed for education, and teachers would be paid a straight salary.

In the pioneer community, the log schoolhouse served as a "meeting house" as well as a place where children could learn the Three R's. Preachers made the rounds of frontier settlements on horseback. If there was a meeting house, the building served as a church on Sundays or on weekday evenings. The preacher (or circuit rider, as he was called) took his meals with the people who invited him and slept wherever there was room. He was paid little in cash for his ministry, but like Father Marquette before him, his life was dedicated to God. Money was not important to him.

Money was important to the storekeeper, because he needed it to stock his shelves. In the early days of Iowa, the store was not called a "grocery" as it was in later times. This name was reserved for the place where liquor was sold for drinking on the premises. (The word "saloon" had not yet come into use.) Since the storekeeper noticed that the "grocery" was a popular meeting place, he provided the same attraction in *his* place of business. The use of whiskey became so common that the storekeeper kept a barrel handy with a dipper hanging beside it. Any man who made a purchase in the store could help himself to a dipperful of whiskey. This kind of refreshment finally turned out to be a public nuisance, and temperance groups were organized.

The Sons of Temperance, a nationwide organization, had members in the Half-Breed Tract as well as elsewhere. They signed declarations in which they agreed that "no brother shall make, buy, sell or use as a beverage any spiritous or malt liquors, wine or cider." The part about "use as a beverage" excused any brother who might take a spoonful of whiskey for an ailing stomach or a healing dram for snakebite.

The Indians, of course, had been trading their furs and lead for whiskey wherever they could get it. They were not invited to sign any temperance pledge. Fifteen million acres of land had been lost while their chiefs were too drunk to know what they were doing. When they "touched the goose quill" in St. Louis, it was too late for temperance.

But there was one among them who thought there was still time to stop the advancing tide of white settlement. He would *fight* to protect his ancient heritage. In our next chapter, we shall see that it was also too late to fight. ★ ★

9.
THE BLACK HAWK WAR

For over a hundred years, the brief resistance of a tough Sauk warrior to the overwhelming military might of the United States has been called "The Black Hawk War." The chasing of a few hundred Indians and their families by thousands of white soldiers can hardly be called a "war." The whole sorry business lasted less than three months. And the leader of the Indians wasn't even a chief. Black Hawk was simply a man of strength and courage who didn't like to be pushed around.

His Indian name was "Ma-ka-tai-me-she-kia-kiak," but white men couldn't take the time to pronounce anything like that. Can you imagine

BLACK HAWK's portrait, on which this sketch is based, hangs in the Iowa Department of History and Archives in Des Moines.

a scout running into the fort shouting, "Ma-ka-tai-me-she-kia-kiak is coming!"? It didn't take nearly as long to yell, *"Black Hawk!"* and to bolt the door of the stockade.

AN ENGLISH ALLY IN SAUKENUK

The Sauk warrior was born in 1767 in the Indian village of Saukenuk. His birthplace was located on the Rock River, near the point where this Illinois tributary flows into the Mississippi. His boyhood was filled with tests of daring and bravery, and he had his full share of fighting before he grew to manhood. The various Indian tribes in the Mississippi Valley were a long way from being a big happy family. One tribe was always getting "in the hair" of another tribe, and much of this hair was taken home for the scalp collection.

The British made no effort to disturb these fierce people. Instead, they promised to help them hold their land if they would fight for England against the hated Americans. This idea made sense to Black Hawk. As long as anybody could remember, Saukenuk had belonged to the earth people. The honored dead of many generations were buried there. It was sacred soil, and the British respected the rights of the Sauks to their ancient heritage.

By contrast, the Americans had obtained the title to Saukenuk and all the rest of the Indian land in Illinois without explaining the treaty to the Indians. Black Hawk promised his people that the Americans wouldn't get away with this kind of thievery, and that he would do something about it as soon as he got a chance.

He got his first chance when he was 42 years old and, as we read earlier, he made life so miserable for the soldiers in Fort Madison that they finally set fire to it and left the country.

In 1814, when he was 47, Black Hawk dealt the Americans another blow. Not far from Saukenuk, there was an island in the Mississippi which had been a trading post in the days of the fur trade. It was called Credit Island. On September 14, 1814, Zachary Taylor and 334 American soldiers landed on it to punish the Indians for an attack on another island, six weeks earlier. A force of about fifty British redcoats and nearly a thousand Sauks and Foxes led by Black Hawk defeated the Americans. The only reason Zachary Taylor and his badly beaten soldiers got away was that the British ran out of ammunition.

The word "led," which was often used to describe the activity of Black Hawk, simply meant that he was a natural leader. If there were chiefs around in times of crisis, they gave way to his military genius, even though he was never a chief himself.

EXODUS FROM ILLINOIS

When peace came to the Mississippi Valley after the War of 1812, white settlers moved into the old Indian lands east of the river in ever-increasing numbers. Keokuk left Saukenuk and moved his band of Sauks across the river into Iowa in 1829, but Black Hawk refused to budge. Finally, in 1831, a detachment of troops was sent up the river from St. Louis, and this body of Army regulars, plus the Illinois militia, forced Black Hawk to follow Keokuk across the Mississippi. The Illinois militia promptly burned Saukenuk to the ground.

Black Hawk camped on the Iowa River, not far from the village Keokuk had built. But he was not happy. His women wept because their corn and pumpkins at Saukenuk had been destroyed. The braves cried for vengeance on the invaders of their ancestral home. Black Hawk waited impatiently for the return of Neapope, a Sauk chief who had gone to Canada to ask the British for help.

Nobody knows if the British ever promised Neapope anything, or if he even talked with any British agents. The important thing is that when Neapope got back from his trip, he told Black Hawk that their old friends of the War of 1812 would send all the guns and ammunition they would need. Moreover, Neapope said that the Winnebagoes and the Pottawattamies would help Black Hawk if he moved back to Saukenuk.

This was all the encouragement Black Hawk needed. He and his braves went to Keokuk's village. They set a war post in front of Keokuk's lodge and began a war dance around it. Keokuk's men soon joined in the dance and struck their tomahawks into the post as a declaration of war and as a token of their willingness to follow Black Hawk.

Keokuk watched the dance for a while. Then he walked calmly to the post. He did not strike it. Instead he began to speak. Irving H. Hart has told us what Keokuk said, in his *Stories of Iowa:*

"Brothers," said Keokuk, "I have heard you demand to be led forth upon the war path against the pale-faces. Their cabins are as plenty as the trees of the forest, and their soldiers as the grass on the prairies. All we can hope for is to fight and fall, when fall we must, with our faces to the enemy. It is my duty, as your chief, to be your father in the paths of peace, and your leader in the paths of war. You have decided to follow the paths of war, and I will lead you forth upon these paths; *but upon one condition:* that we first put our wives and children, our aged and infirm, gently to sleep in that slumber that knows no waking this side the spirit land. For we go upon the long trail that has no turn. This sacrifice is demanded of us by the love we bear those dear ones."

Black Hawk Returns to Illiniois

Keokuk hoped that the condition he had made would win back his own warriors, as well as some of Black Hawk's band, and it did. But it had no effect on Black Hawk. The next morning, the stubborn old warrior and four hundred Sauk braves prepared to cross the river and reclaim their land. The date was April 6, 1832. Black Hawk was 65 years old.

The Sauk rebels, with their wives and children, crossed the Mississippi to the Illinois side. As the canoes entered the Rock River, the Indians beat their drums and sang loudly to show the Americans that they were not afraid. There was no opposition as the party journeyed up the river, but news of Black Hawk's return had spread far and wide.

General Henry Atkinson mustered six companies of United States regulars, and Governor Reynolds ordered out the Illinois militia and called for volunteers to put down the uprising. Among the volunteers was a young man named Abraham Lincoln, who never fired a shot at an Indian but who would receive Iowa land in recognition of his "war" service.

Black Hawk learned about the mobilization from scouts who were keeping watch on the white soldiers. But where were the guns and ammunition the British were going to send him to fight the Americans? And when were the Winnebagoes and the Pottawattamies going to join his four hundred warriors? His people were hungry. Their fields and stores of food at Saukenuk had been burned. Too late, Black Hawk realized that Neapope had given him only false promises. There was no sign of any British aid, and it became clear that the Winnebagoes and the Pottawattamies were not going to help him.

There was only one thing to do. He sent a flag of truce to the nearest battalion of white soldiers. If the Americans would allow him to pass unmolested down the Rock River, he would return to Iowa.

Unfortunately, the white soldiers were not regulars who knew the rules of war. They were militiamen who had been called into service with very little training, and they thought the white flag was just an Indian trick. The militia opened fire on the truce delegation, and three of Black Hawk's men were killed. A Major Stillman and his 275 untrained soldiers set off in pursuit of the rest of the delegation.

Black Hawk did not have his warriors organized for battle. He had not expected an attack on a truce party. Only about fifty of his braves were in the neighborhood. Although greatly outnumbered, the Indians fired on the advancing troops with such furious effect that Stillman's men turned tail and ran for their lives. It was the opening engagement of the so-called Black Hawk War. Stillman's defeat took place on May 14, 1832.

The militia had retreated, but Black Hawk knew there were seasoned Army veterans who would now be after him in earnest. Instead of trying to get back to the Mississippi the way he had come, he decided to lead his people north. Perhaps there would be an unguarded spot in northern Illinois or southern Wisconsin where he could cross the river into Iowa again.

Four hundred Sauk warriors and their families were pursued by ten thousand white soldiers. Several times the soldiers caught up with the Indians, but on almost every occasion they were outmaneuvered and outfought by Black Hawk. However, the outcome was never in doubt. Black Hawk had too small a force to wage effective warfare. His pathetic little group was constantly dwindling. Indian women and children, as well as braves, were killed by gunfire. Many died of starvation. The survivors of the long march finally reached a little stream in Wisconsin called the Bad Axe River.

At the place where the Bad Axe flows into the Mississippi, Black Hawk saw a steamboat named "The Warrior." He knew the captain of this boat. "Surely," he said, "an old friend will recognize me and my flag of truce and let us give ourselves up." But, again, the white flag was ignored. Captain Joseph Throckmorton turned a cannon on his old friend and his followers. Twenty-three Indians were killed in what Throckmorton later described as "the battle."

Black Hawk saw that he couldn't help his people by staying with them. He told his followers that they might try to cross the river, again, the next day. Maybe they would succeed if he wasn't in the crowd. Black Hawk took sorrowful leave of his friends and started for Chippewa country.

On August 2, the starving Indians made their last effort to cross the Mississippi. This time, the soldiers surrounded them and fired from all sides. One hundred and fifty Sauk men, women, and children were shot down. And that was the "glorious victory" which ended what the United States government called The Black Hawk War.

Black Hawk, the Man

There remained a humiliating personal surrender by Black Hawk, who turned himself in to a trusted Indian agent at Prairie du Chien. The old leader was put in chains. A young Army officer named Jefferson Davis took him to St. Louis and locked him in the barracks.

But he was still a man of great dignity. President Andrew Jackson wanted to see the Indian who had thrown the United States Army into confusion for three months. When the old Sauk warrior was taken to Washington, he stood before the President and held out his shackled hands. "I am a Man!" he said proudly.

"You are absolutely right!" replied the President. Turning to the guard, Jackson said, "This man is no wild animal. Take off his chains!"

Black Hawk left Washington a free man. His last years were spent in Iowa, where he wrote his autobiography. He died in 1838, but even in death the white man would not leave him alone. A quack doctor removed his body from the grave and made it an exhibit in his medicine show. The skeleton was finally recovered, and it was placed in a museum in Burlington. When the museum was destroyed by fire, there was nothing left of the old warrior but dust and ashes.

The Black Hawk Purchase

In the treaty which followed The Black Hawk War, General Winfield Scott forced the Sauk and the Fox to give up the eastern third of Iowa "for their failure to restrain one of their chiefs from making an unjust war upon the unoffending white settlers." The history books call this treaty The Black Hawk Purchase. ★ ★

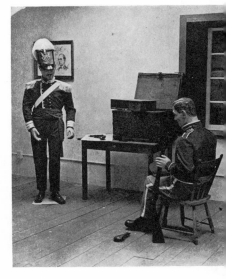

10. PROTECTING THE FRONTIER

In the treaty of September 21, 1832, General Winfield Scott demanded and got the eastern third of Iowa from the Sauk and Fox nation. As a reward for his loyalty to the United States, Keokuk was allowed to keep a strip of land along the Iowa River, later known as the Keokuk Reserve. The chief who had refused to take part in the so-called Black Hawk War pointed to these four hundred sections of land as evidence that the Great White Father had taken care of the *good* Indians!

As it turned out, the "good Indians" were allowed to stay in the Keokuk Reserve for only four years. A new treaty was signed on September 28, 1836, and Keokuk was pushed a little farther west. In nine more years, Keokuk would find himself pushed all the way into Kansas, wondering what had hit him.

What had caused this, of course, was an overpowering tide of white immigration. As soon as the eastern third of Iowa was opened for settlement, homesteaders descended upon the rich prairie as though they had dropped out of the sky. By 1836, when the Keokuk Reserve was unreserved, there were over ten thousand white people living in the area acquired by the Black Hawk Purchase.

Although the Indians were paid annuities whenever their land was

55

DRAGOONS, resplendent in full dress uniforms, forever prepare for inspection in this display at the Fort Atkinson Museum.

"purchased," the money was soon spent, and the treaties which had caused them to lose their homes and hunting grounds left a bitter aftertaste. The settlers were aware of this bitterness, and they feared that there might be an Indian uprising.

THE CAVALRY APPEARS

In 1834, three companies of dragoons were sent to the Iowa country under the command of Lieutenant Colonel Stephen W. Kearny. The government had suddenly realized that Iowa had been a political orphan for thirteen years—ever since 1821, when Missouri had been admitted to statehood. On June 28, 1834, Congress attached the orphan to the sprawling Territory of Michigan. This made it possible to divide the Black Hawk Purchase into counties and to civilize the country in other ways. One of the civilizing influences was the assignment of the dragoons to the lands west of the Mississippi. These dragoons were soldiers who rode horses. In later years, the soldiers on horseback would be called the cavalry.

Some kind of quarters had to be provided for both the men and the horses, so Kearny sent a force of workmen ahead of him to find a place for a camp. Lieutenant George Crossman, who was in charge of this advance party, fought his way through the Mississippi River rapids from Puck-e-she-tuck to Ah-wi-pe-tuck, and decided he had gone about as far as he could go.

An old Indian settlement named Cut-Nose, in honor of departed Chief Cut-Nose, looked like a suitable place for the camp. It was not far from the little cabin which Dr. Isaac Galland had converted into a schoolhouse. Crossman began cutting trees and laying the logs for the camp buildings. Lieutenant Colonel Kearny arrived on September 25, 1834. Among the officers in his three companies were Captain Nathaniel Boone, a son of Daniel Boone, and Lieutenant Albert M. Lea, who would be the first man to put the name of Iowa into print.

The quarters for the dragoons were a long way from being completed, and the stables for the horses hadn't even been started. The soldiers put on their work clothes and tried to get the shelters finished before the first of November. But the job of building weather-tight barracks for over a hundred officers and men was too big to be completed by that date. The dragoons lived in "air conditioned" quarters all winter. They were too cold to do much of anything except chop wood and care for their horses.

Kearny wrote to the Secretary of War. After describing his quarters as being "less comfortable and of meaner appearance than those occupied by any other portion of the Army," he asked what his three companies were expected to do. Also, what was his

"camp" to be called? (His dragoons had given it all kinds of names during the winter, but he didn't think any of them would be suitable.)

THE FIRST FORT DES MOINES

The Secretary of War answered the second question, first. "Let the post be called Fort Des Moines," he said. Evidently, the rapids of the River Des Moines had gained a reputation as far east as Washington. Kearny was considerably surprised to have his log camp called a "fort." There were no blockhouses and no stockade. The crude barracks had been built only to keep his men and horses out of the weather. The Indians had moved out when eastern Iowa was opened for settlement, and there was no longer any need for a fort in this part of the country. But, being an obedient officer, he christened his colony of cabins "Fort Des Moines." Then, Kearny gave his attention to the rest of his orders.

The dragoons were not to perform garrison duties. They were to ride over the Indian lands west of the Mississippi and show the Indians that the military power of the United States was ready to protect the rights of the settlers. There was to be no fighting, unless the dragoons needed to defend themselves. The main purpose of the march was to be a friendly display of strength and determination.

As soon as the early summer of 1835 turned the prairies green, Kearny and his dragoons left their camp on the Mississippi. The Secretary of War had ordered Kearny to follow the Des Moines River to the Raccoon Fork in search of a suitable location for a military post. Then, he was to march to Wabasha's village in Sioux country. From there, the dragoons were to seek out the headwaters of the Des Moines, and follow this river along the right bank all the way back to their base.

The long column of mounted soldiers began moving across the prairie on June 7, 1835. The countryside was beautiful. Wild strawberries were ripe, and somebody discovered that there was a milker among the beef cattle which the dragoons had taken with them for fresh meat. The streams were full of fish. Deer were plentiful, and there were still a few buffalo to give variety to their meat diet. There was other wildlife, too. One night, after an officer had pitched his tent, four rattlesnakes had to be put out before he could go to bed.

For some reason, Kearny missed the Raccoon Fork on his first try, so he turned northeast and marched to Lake Pepin. Wabasha and his Sioux were living near the present city of Winona, Minnesota. The three companies of mounted soldiers arrived at the Indian camp on July 19. The journal for that day reported: "We have seen but few of the Sioux, and those we have seen give us a poor idea of this tribe. They are mostly a dirty, thieving race living in the most abominable filthy manner. The Sauks, on the contrary, are cleanly and decent in their appearance."

Having carried out his orders to visit Wabasha, Kearny headed west until he crossed the Des Moines, then followed the west bank of the river until he reached the Raccoon Fork. He didn't think much of it as a place for a fort. For one thing, the Des Moines River was so shallow that he didn't think large boats could use it to deliver military supplies. For another, there didn't seem to be any point in building a fort at this particular location. The Sauks and the Sioux were at peace, and no military barrier was needed to keep them apart. Besides, the Sauks objected to the idea of a garrison at the Raccoon Fork, because white soldiers would drive off what little game was left in their country.

To confirm his belief that the Des Moines River was unsuitable for heavy transportation, Kearny sent Lieutenant Albert M. Lea down the stream in a canoe. Lea took soundings of the depth of the river and proved that it was every bit as shallow as Kearny thought it was. All of this had no effect on the Secretary of War. He decided to build a fort at the Raccoon Fork anyhow.

THE BOOK THAT GAVE IOWA ITS NAME

Kearny had completed his mission, so he led his three companies of dragoons back to Fort Des Moines. The round trip was completed on August 19, 1835, after an absence of

nearly three months and a journey of eleven hundred miles.

Lieutenant Albert Lea had seen so many interesting places that he decided to write a book about them. He resigned from the Army, but, by the time he had finished writing his description and drawing his map, Michigan had become a state, and Iowa had been made a part of the Territory of Wisconsin. The title of Lea's book had to be changed from *Notes on the Michigan Territory* to *Notes on the Wisconsin Territory*. The full title was pretty long for a book that had only 53 pages. It was *Notes on the Wisconsin Territory; Particularly with Reference to the Iowa District.*

This was the first time the name "Iowa" had appeared in print. Where did Albert Lea get it? In his first chapter, he wrote: " . . . from the extent and beauty of the Iowa river, which runs centrally through the District and gives character to most of it,

RESTORED SYMBOLS of the early government of the Wisconsin Territory enjoy close-clipped park-like surroundings probably unknown in the rough early years. These two buildings in Belmont, Wisconsin, were used in 1836 by the supreme court (left) and the council (right).

the name of that stream, being both euphoneous and appropriate, has been given to the District itself."

He didn't say how the stream got its name, but it is generally believed that the river was called the "Iowa" because the Ioway Indians had lived along its banks in early times. And, perhaps, the Ioways got their name from the Indian ancestor who crossed the Mississippi and greeted his new home by calling it "Ayooez," or "beautiful land."

Iowa or Ioway, Lea or Lee?

Several years after his book was published, Albert Lea said that the name of the Iowa District should have been spelled "Ioway" instead of "Iowa," because he had heard it pronounced like that when he was a lieutenant in the dragoons. His second thoughts on the matter were a little late. By the time he tried to correct his original spelling, the word Iowa had become a part of the American language. The only time it is pronounced Ioway, now, is when people sing *The Iowa Corn Song*.

Albert Lea, Minnesota, was named in honor of the literary lieutenant, but there is no Albert Lea, Iowa. The lieutenant insisted to his dying day that Lee County was named after him, even though the county name is spelled "L-e-e."

The only evidence in support of Albert Lea's claim is contained in a letter written by Lea, himself. In it, he wrote: "Starr (the man who drew up the bill naming the county) and I slept in the same room when he drew up that bill, and he put my name down for the first county, in consideration of my having mapped, described and named the area now known as Iowa and Minnesota. It is easy to see how the spelling was changed, as my mode of writing the final 'a' was unusual; and as I disappeared mainly from that theatre, and Captain Robert E. Lee had come upon it, the name was naturally attributed to him."

Albert Lea and Robert E. Lee had more in common than the credit for the name of Lee County. Both left the Union when the Civil War began, and both served for four years in the Confederate Army.

But the Civil War was still a quarter of a century in the future when Albert Lea wrote his book about the Iowa District. In 1836, the year in which Iowa became a part of the Wisconsin Territory, the government decided that Fort Des Moines was no longer needed. A town had grown up around the barracks, and the Indians were long gone. The frontier had moved farther west. The dragoons whose terms of enlistment still had some time to run were sent to Fort Leavenworth.

The new town at the head of the rapids was called "Mount of Roses" because of the wild roses which covered the hillsides. This name was later shortened to "Montrose."

There would not be another Fort Des Moines until 1843, when a military post would be established at the Raccoon Fork in spite of the difficulties of river transportation. By that time, Iowa would be a territory in its own right.

★ ★

11. A NEW TERRITORY

WHEN Iowa became a part of the Wisconsin Territory in April of 1836, the future state was just the bottom layer of the huge territorial cake. The territory extended from Lake Michigan on the east to the Missouri River on the west, and from the state of Missouri on the south to the Canadian border on the north. It included all of the future states of Wisconsin and Minnesota, parts of North and South Dakota, and all of Iowa.

Of course, most of this big tract of land was still Indian country. Only the part of the territory near the Mississippi had been cleared of Indian titles, and this was where the white settlers lived.

The first Territorial Assembly met in the frontier village of Belmont, in what is now Wisconsin. Eighteen of the members came from the western side of the river; nineteen from the eastern side. Belmont provided few comforts or necessities. The lawmakers had to carry sandwiches to

work with them if they wanted to eat during the day. Bread crusts and cookie crumbs attracted the mice, and there was a "gnawing conviction" that the capital should be moved to a place where lodging and dining would be less primitive. Jeremiah Smith, a member of the council who lived west of the river, invited the Territorial Assembly to meet at a place which had all the "modern conveniences."

FLINT HILLS

The high ground recommended to the War Department by Lieutenant Zebulon Pike in 1805 had never been fortified, so it had never qualified for a name such as Fort Madison or Fort Des Moines. The fur traders had called it Flint Hills. This was a translation of the Indian name "Sho-ko-kon."

When the eastern third of Iowa was opened by the Black Hawk Purchase, Flint Hills immediately at-

58

tracted people who wanted land of their own. On June 1, 1833, the first day of legal settlement, twenty-five heads of families crossed the river from Illinois and staked out their claims. Lawyers, surveyors, millers, ferrymen, and merchants followed in ever-increasing numbers.

One of the pioneer merchants thought the name of his boyhood home in Vermont would sound more civilized than Flint Hills. Somebody else offered Catfish Bend as a possible substitute. Another liked Pin Hook. But a majority of the residents agreed with the man from Vermont. The new settlement was called Burlington. This was the town to which Jeremiah Smith invited his fellow legislators, early in 1837.

The invitation was not accepted merely because Burlington was a bigger town than Belmont. Jeremiah Smith promised that he would put up a suitable building for the legislature *without cost* to the territory. It is not surprising that the Territorial Assembly promptly passed an act which located the seat of government at Burlington.

The two-story capitol was completed during the summer. (Note that the *building* occupied by a legislative body is spelled with an "o." The *town* in which the Assembly meets is spelled with an "a.") When the members of the legislature assembled in November of 1837, they were pleased with both the building and the town.

Burlington showed promise of becoming a busy river metropolis, and its new prestige as capital of the territory made its prospects even brighter. It had grown so fast that nobody thought about having a Fire Department until the night of December 12, 1837. After everybody had gone to bed, an overheated chimney set Jeremiah Smith's new building afire. Since there was no fire-fighting equipment, the flames quickly spread over a whole block on the riverfront. By the morning of December 13, seven wooden structures had burned to the ground.

Smith had put up the building for the legislature at his own expense. He had no insurance claim on the territory, and he lost his entire investment. But he had been successful in getting the capital of the territory moved to a location west of the Mississippi, and this would hasten the time when Iowa would have an identity of its own.

Meanwhile, the legislature had to find other quarters to continue its business. The council, or senate, held its meetings in a room above the newspaper office. The house of representatives moved into a large room above a store.

THE TRICK THAT ESTABLISHED A TERRITORY

Even before Jeremiah Smith's building had been destroyed, a group of delegates from the counties west of the river had been holding a convention in Burlington to discuss the division of the territory. Everybody, including the people who lived east of the river, agreed that the Wisconsin Territory was too large. It was their considered opinion that the Missisippi should be a political as well as a natural dividing line. Names such as Washington and Jefferson were suggested for the western part, but the name used by Albert M. Lea in his book about the Iowa District was finally adopted.

A petition for the establishment of the Territory of Iowa was sent to the United States Congress. It was presented in the House of Representatives in Washington by George W. Jones, the delegate to Congress from the Wisconsin Territory.

After much debate, a bill to establish the territorial government of Iowa was passed by the House of Representatives on June 1, 1838. But it still had to be passed by the Senate, and Senator John C. Calhoun of South Carolina was against it. He felt sure that in a few years Iowa would upset the balance between the free and the slave states by entering the Union as a free state. Thus, it might become "The Lion of the West". But Iowa was not yet a state. Indeed, it was not even a territory.

Congress was getting ready to adjourn, and Delegate Jones decided that he would need to work fast. It happened that Anna Calhoun, the Senator's daughter, was a good friend of Jones. She thought her father was being unreasonable in opposing her friend's bill. Jones played on her sympathy.

"Miss Calhoun," he said, "I'm going to ask Senator Clayton to introduce my bill in the Senate, today. It won't pass if your father makes a speech against it, because he has a great deal of influence over the other senators. So, if you will sit in the gallery, I'll give you a signal when Senator Clayton is ready. Then, you come down to the main floor, send your card to your father, take him to the library, and keep him there until I call for you." She agreed to follow his directions.

As soon as Calhoun was safely out of sight, Jones nudged his friend, Senator Clayton, and the bill was offered for adoption. Only six senators, all of them from the South, voted against it. Jones went to the library and joined the Calhouns. "What has been going on, young man?" asked the Senator. "Well, sir," replied the delegate from Wisconsin, "the bill to create the Territory of Iowa has been passed, and the Senate has adjourned."

The Senator turned to his daughter. "Anna, you bad girl," he said. "You have prevented me from making a speech to oppose that bill, as I would have done and done successfully." But it was too late now, and Calhoun accepted his defeat gracefully. President Martin Van Buren signed the bill into law on June 12, and Iowa became a territory on July 4, 1838.

Van Buren appointed Robert Lucas, a good Democrat and a former governor of Ohio, as the governor of the new territory. William B. Con-

ROBERT LUCAS looked like this when he began his term of office as Iowa's first territorial governor. This sketch is based on a portrait by Leonard Good which hangs in the governor's residence in Des Moines.

the answer for that question. It could meet in the new Methodist Church he was building. Money for construction was running a little short, and the rental of the church by the territorial government would help to get the job done.

Doctor Ross was a remarkable man. He had come to Burlington when the settlement was still known as Flint Hills. In 1833, he had brought the first stock of merchandise to the little colony of cabins and had become the first storekeeper. He was also the first postmaster, the first justice of the peace, and the first clerk of court. In addition to this list of firsts, he was the first bachelor among the settlers to get married. Since there was no church or preacher in town, he hired a boat, took his bride-to-be across the river and was married in an open field by a preacher from Monmouth, Illinois.

When the newlyweds got back to Burlington, the bridegroom said, "We're going to have to make weddings easier than that! People who want to get married can't always cross the river for the ceremony. How can they be sure there will be a preacher in that field over there?"

OLD ZION

Doctor Ross made arrangements with a circuit-riding preacher, the Reverend Mr. Barton H. Cartwright, to conduct Methodist services in his cabin. But the town really needed a church, and, with his usual energy,

way was appointed as secretary, and three justices for the territorial supreme court were chosen to complete the official roster. The Territory of Iowa was now in business.

Burlington was chosen by Governor Lucas as the capital, since it was at the center of population in the territory. Now that the old Wisconsin Territory had been divided, the representatives of the counties east of the Mississippi went back to Wisconsin and met in their new capital at Madison.

Where was the Iowa Territorial Assembly going to meet? A Burlington doctor named William Ross had the good doctor did something about that, too. In 1836, he bought two lots on Third Street for one hundred dollars, and paid seventy-two dollars for digging the basement.

By 1838, the Methodist congregation had grown large enough to have a resident pastor, and a fund-raising campaign was launched. Money came in slowly, but the building of the church was begun. It was to be a brick structure—the first brick church in the Iowa Territory. It would not have the honor of being the first church building in Iowa. This distinction had been won by a log chapel erected by the Methodists in Dubuque in 1834.

The rental of the church (on week-days) by the territorial government speeded the completion of the building. The Legislative Assembly was scheduled to meet in November of 1838, and the church was ready in time. The main floor was assigned to the house of representatives, because it had more members than the senate and therefore needed the larger space. The front part of the basement was used by the senate. The back part was partitioned into offices. (The Iowa Territory thus began its activity in government with the lower house of the legislature upstairs, and the upper house in the basement.)

In territorial days, the building was known only as the Methodist Church. In 1851, *The Burlington Telegraph* noted that the church was in need of repairs. Remembering that

the site of the temple in Jerusalem had been called Zion, the editor of the newspaper headed his appeal for funds with the words: "Old Zion Needs A New Roof." The name stuck, and the church was known thereafter as Old Zion. In 1881 the Methodists moved to a larger building. The property on Third Street was sold, and Old Zion was torn down to make room for a theatre. In time, the theatre was torn down, too, and the historic site of Iowa's first territorial government is now a parking lot.

But all of this was still in the future. Before the church achieved its famous name and passed into oblivion, it would be the scene of many exciting events. We shall recall some of them in our next chapter.

★　★

12. TERRITORIAL ADVENTURES

CONGRESS had a general idea of the size and shape of the Iowa Territory when the bill to establish a territorial government was passed, but no congressman had ever seen any accurate maps of it. There was a good reason for this. There weren't any. Albert M. Lea had made a map of parts of Iowa and Minnesota when he published his *Notes on the Wisconsin Territory*, but there was more to it.

In 1836, a French geography expert named Joseph Nicollet had been hired by the fur merchants of St. Louis to explore and map the upper Mississippi. Henry Schoolcraft had found the true source of the great river in Lake Itasca in 1832, but Nicollet determined the exact latitude and longitude of the headwaters four years later. This professional job made such a favorable impression in Washington that Nicollet was given the assignment of making a survey and map of the Iowa Territory. The War Department ordered a young Army lieutenant named John C. Fremont to accompany him.

The expedition set out in the spring of 1838. All along the way, Nicollet and Fremont took careful notes and compass readings of the precise locations of lakes, rivers, and other geographical features. The job took three years, but the Nicollet map gave the first reliable information about the true size and shape of the Iowa Territory.

63

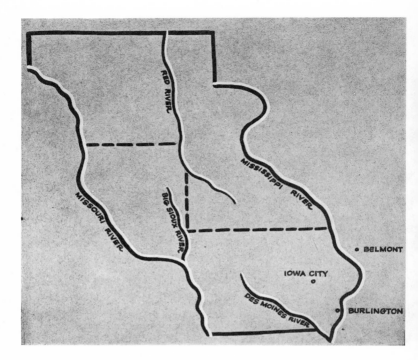

MONEY AND MONKEY BUSINESS

Governor Robert Lucas had been governor of Ohio for two terms, but he didn't know much about the wild country west of the Mississippi. Before taking over the full duties of his new office, he decided to visit the river counties where most of the white people in the territory lived. He took a steamboat from Keokuk as far north as Dubuque and talked with the people he met at the landings.

It was not until the Governor had visited several towns in the territory that he selected Burlington as the capital. President Van Buren had given him the authority to pick any town he wanted as the seat of government. As we noted earlier, Burling-

ton was his choice because he considered it to be nearest the center of population.

If you look at a map of the Iowa Territory, you will wonder how a city in the southeast corner could be at the center of anything. We must remember that the Indians were considered to be little more than wild animals. The center of population was determined by the density of *white* settlement.

The Territorial Assembly began its deliberations in the Methodist

Church at Burlington in November of 1838. The senate had thirteen members. The house had twenty-six.

Travel in Iowa was not a simple matter in those days. Some of the legislators who lived along the Mississippi made the trip to Burlington by steamboat. Others came by stagecoach over the winding roads that connected the frontier settlements. Still others came on horseback. A few came on foot, because they couldn't afford any other kind of transportation.

But when it came to spending government funds, the members of the legislature soon used up the entire appropriation voted by Congress and even ran into debt. This was contrary to the advice given by Governor Lucas. He had recommended thrift, but since the government in Washington was paying most of the bills, the lawmakers decided to get all they could for their home counties.

Henry Sabin, in his book, *The Making of Iowa*, reports the experience of Robert A. Roberts, a representative from Cedar County who spent most of his time visiting with fellow members and paying no attention to the business of the house. Whenever a bill came up for a vote, he would call out: "Mr. Speaker, if Cedar is in that bill, I vote yea; if not, no."

One day a bill was presented as a joke, depriving Cedar County of any representation in the house. As usual, the representative from Cedar hadn't been listening. The bill came up for adoption, and Roberts, having been assured that "Cedar is in that bill," voted for it. When he discovered that he had voted himself out of a job, he begged that the action be reconsidered. The other members assented and, thereafter, Representative Roberts listened carefully before he voted.

Laws, Lines, and Border Disputes

But legislation in the Territorial Assembly was not all fun and games. Over six hundred pages of laws were passed in the first session. Governor Lucas was an executive with experience and ability, and his tactful guidance of the legislature resulted in measures which are still a part of the Code of Iowa.

The first territorial governor had to be tough as well as tactful, however. Among the many problems which he had to solve was a boundary dispute with the state of Missouri. The trouble dated back to the boundary line drawn by John C. Sullivan in 1816. Sullivan didn't know it at the time, but his line wasn't straight. It didn't follow a parallel of latitude. He had forgotten that the compass needle does not point to the actual North Pole; it points toward the *magnetic* North Pole. In this part of the country, the magnetic North Pole is several degrees *west* of the North Pole.

Sullivan failed to make the necessary correction in his compass readings and, as a result, the line which he drew veered toward the north instead of going straight east. When extended across the southeast corner of Iowa, it went through Ah-wi-pe-tuck, the Head of the Rapids, better known today as Montrose.

Nobody knew about Sullivan's mistake, and it made no difference to anybody until settlers began to move into northeastern Missouri. Many of the markers left by Sullivan had disappeared, and people living near the border didn't know whether they lived in Missouri or Iowa.

As a result of the Sullivan survey, the Constitution of Missouri defined the northern boundary as "the parallel of latitude passing through the rapids of the river Des Moines." In 1837, a surveyor named J. C. Brown was hired by the legislature of Missouri to resurvey the line, using the reference to the rapids as his guide.

Brown didn't know that "the rapids of the river Des Moines" were in the Mississippi, so he looked for rapids in the Des Moines River. He found a "riffle" in the Great Bend of the Des Moines near the present town of Keosauqua. This, he decided, was the eastern end of the boundary. It was actually nine miles north of the point where Sullivan had ended *his* survey.

Brown ran a line straight west from the "rapids" in the Des Moines River, and the Missouri legislature immediately adopted this line as the true boundary. By doing so, Missouri

claimed twenty-six hundred square miles of land which belonged to Iowa.

Sheriffs from northern Missouri counties began collecting taxes from settlers in the southern part of the Iowa Territory. What was even worse, Missourians cut down three of the "bee trees" on which the Iowa settlers depended for their "sweetenin'." Sugar was almost unknown as an item of merchandise, and sorghum cane was equally rare. The wild honey stored in hollow trees was prized as a special luxury. When the bee trees were cut down, the Iowa settlers appealed to Governor Lucas to do something about it. What he did has been called "The Honey War."

Protests to Governor Boggs of Missouri were rejected. Angry words finally led to the calling of the militia on both sides of the line in 1839. The Missouri militia camped at Waterloo, Missouri, ready to invade Iowa. Governor Lucas ordered the territorial militia to be ready for action, and more than a thousand Iowans marched toward the border.

Everybody who had saved a sword from the War of 1812 was an officer. The Iowa militia had four generals, forty colonels and majors, and eighty captains and lieutenants.

DISPUTED BOUNDARIES between Iowa and Missouri are shown on this map. The U.S. Supreme Court finally ruled that the Sullivan line was the legal boundary.

The foot soldiers were armed with pitchforks and squirrel rifles. There was a great deal of straggling along the line of march, and only five hundred members of the Iowa militia finally reached Farmington, across the Des Moines River from Waterloo.

By the time the Iowa militia was ready for battle, the Missouri militia had grown tired of waiting and had gone home. "The Honey War" ended without the firing of a single shot. The dispute was carried through the courts all the way to the highest tribunal in the United States. At long last, the Supreme Court ruled that the Sullivan line, crooked though it was, would remain the legal boundary between Iowa and Missouri.

Irving H. Hart, in his *Stories of Iowa,* quotes the reaction of one of the settlers who lived in the disputed territory. He said: "I'm sure glad the *Soo*preem Court decided that I live in Ioway. I'm a farmer, and I never did want to farm in Missouri. That Missouri land ain't near as good as ours!"

THE CAPITAL MOVES TO IOWA CITY

The tide of settlement in the Iowa Territory had moved west, as well as south. The legislature decided that Burlington was no longer the center of population and that the capital should be moved farther west. Every town in the territory wanted the honor of being the new capital, but a compromise was finally reached.

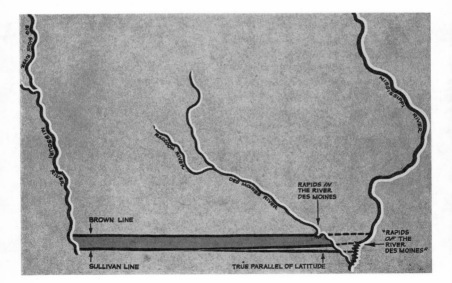

Three commissioners were appointed. They were told to meet on May 1, 1839, and "proceed to locate the Seat of Government at the most eligible point within the present limits of Johnson County."

Johnson County, at that time, was "unoccupied public land"— which meant that it was unoccupied by white men. There were about a thousand Sauk and Fox Indians occupying it, but they didn't count. The commissioners found an attractive site on high ground overlooking the Iowa River, and they proceeded to locate the seat of government at the place which was to become the "City of Iowa," or Iowa City. Poweshiek was the Sauk and Fox Chief in this part of the country. He made a speech when his "unoccupied lands" were taken.

"Soon," he said, "I shall go to a new home, and you will plant corn where my dead sleep. Our towns, the paths we have made, and the flowers we love will soon be yours. I have moved many times and seen the white man put his feet into the tracks of the Indian and make the earth into fields and gardens. I know that I must go away, and you will be so glad when I am gone that you will soon forget that the meat and the lodge-fire of the Indian have been forever free to the stranger, and that at all times he has asked for what he fought for—the right to be free."

This was a good speech, and the white men gave it their polite ap-

THE OLD STONE CAPITOL in Iowa City is now the administrative center of the University of Iowa. Built to serve as the territorial capitol, it was also used as Iowa's first state capitol building. Its Doric porticos on the east and west fronts open into a cool, high-ceilinged interior dominated by a handsome hanging spiral staircase.

plause. Then, they returned to the business at hand. The cornerstone of the new capitol building was laid on July 4, 1840, by Governor Robert Lucas. But it took a long time to build a stone capitol. In 1841, a man named Walter Butler built a frame hotel which was used for the first meeting of the Territorial Assembly in Iowa City in December of 1841.

THE FIRST GOVERNOR IS FIRED

By the time the territorial government moved to the new capital, Governor Lucas had been moved out of his job. William Henry Harrison, a Whig, was elected President of the United States in 1840. On Inauguration Day in 1841, he stood in the rain too long and got pneumonia. He died a month later. His one month as President gave him time enough to dismiss Democrat Robert Lucas and to appoint John Chambers, a member of his own party, as governor of the Iowa Territory.

Robert Lucas built a house in a grove of wild plum trees near the new town of Iowa City and called it Plum Grove. Here, he spent his years of retirement as the honored elder statesman of Iowa. The house is still standing. It reminds us of a man of strength and character who provided wise leadership at a time when the local government of Iowa was established.

PLUM GROVE, on Kirkwood Avenue in Iowa City, was built by Governor Robert Lucas for his years of retirement. Today its brick walls, faded to a soft rose color, shelter rooms restored to their original appearance.

★ ★

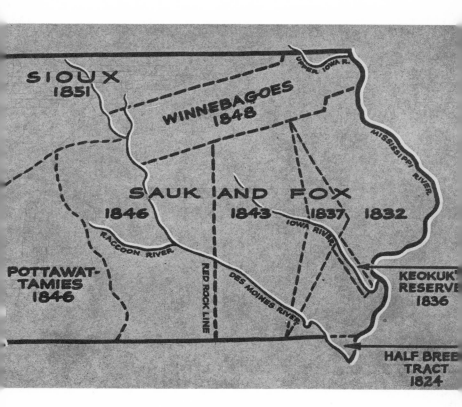

13. MOVING THE INDIANS

As EARLY AS 1825, the United States government realized that keeping the peace in Iowa was not just a matter of avoiding fights between white men and Indians. The Indians were constantly fighting among themselves. When the Sioux looked at the Sauks and Foxes, they saw red. The same thing was true when the Sauks and Foxes looked at the Sioux.

In an effort to keep these tribes from fighting, the Indian agent called

all the tribes of the Upper Mississippi Valley to a Great Council at Prairie du Chien in 1825. After entertaining his guests at a big barbecue, the agent got out his map of the Upper Mississippi Valley and drew a line on it from the mouth of the Upper Iowa River to the upper fork of the Des Moines River.

Pointing to the map, he suggested that the Sioux stay north of this line, and the Sauk and Fox stay south of

INDIAN LANDS became smaller and smaller until the Red Man was finally moved out of the state.

it. The chiefs thought this was a good idea, and they went back to their hunting grounds west of the Mississippi. The trouble with the agreement was that when the Indians looked for the line in Iowa they couldn't find it. The raids and scalpings started all over again.

THE NEUTRAL GROUND

Of course, the soldiers at Fort Crawford couldn't do much about this Indian fighting, because they never knew where it would break out next. So the Indian agent at Prairie du Chien tried diplomacy a second time. The Indians were invited to another council in 1830. At this council, he persuaded the Sioux to give up a strip of land, twenty miles wide, on the north side of the 1825 boundary. The Sauks and Foxes gave up an equal strip on the south side of the line. The Indian agent then told the chiefs that everybody must keep off this Neutral Ground.

It would seem that a buffer zone forty miles wide and two hundred miles long should have been big enough to keep things quiet, but it wasn't. As long as one side kept hunting in it, the other side didn't feel bound by its promise to stay out, either.

Fort Atkinson is Built

Then Black Hawk threw the Army into a dither by returning to Illinois after the government had thought he was out of the way. By the time the so-called "Black Hawk War" had been won by the United States, somebody thought up a solution of the Neutral Ground problem. The Winnebago Indians in Wisconsin had given sanctuary to Black Hawk. Why not punish the Winnebagoes by moving them into the Neutral Ground? This would set up a human barricade between the Sioux on the north and the Sauks and Foxes on the south. Besides, white settlers wanted the Winnebago land in Wisconsin.

The Winnebagoes didn't like this idea at all, so General Henry Atkinson was ordered to move them into the Neutral Ground whether they liked it or not. Soldiers escorted the reluctant Indians across the Mississippi. The military force established a camp on the Turkey River and called it Camp Atkinson in honor of their commander.

In the summer of 1840, while Governor Robert Lucas was laying the cornerstone of the new capitol in Iowa City, barracks were built on a hill overlooking the Turkey River, and the new post was named Fort Atkinson. A company of dragoons was assigned to it for both garrison and patrol duty.

The Winnebagoes were not happy in Iowa, even though an imposing fort had been built to protect them from their Sioux and Sauk and Fox neighbors. They had reason to fear these neighbors. It had not been their idea to come to Iowa in the first place; but now that they were here, they were occupying some of the favorite hunting grounds of the Sauks and Foxes. It made no difference that the Sauks and Foxes had promised to keep off the Neutral Ground. Other Indians were now on it, and there were rumors that the Sauks and Foxes were going on the warpath to reclaim their land.

The garrison at Fort Atkinson was strengthened by more soldiers from Fort Crawford. Stone blockhouses and a stone powder magazine were rushed to completion. A high stockade fenced the hilltop, and a military road was built from the bastion on the Turkey River all the way to the Mississippi for quick movement of additional troops from Fort Crawford, if they should be needed. By the time Fort Atkinson was completed, the United States had spent $90,000 on it.

The War Department had learned a lesson at Fort Madison. This time, no Indians could climb a ridge overlooking the fort and shoot at the soldiers inside the stockade as Black Hawk had done at Fort Madison. Fort Atkinson had been built on the highest ridge the Army could find.

The promised raid by the Sauks and Foxes never took place. The Neutral Ground remained neutral. The only fort ever built by the United

THE ORIGINAL POWDER MAGAZINE at Fort Atkinson was built with double walls and roof to keep the powder dry. The stockade is part of the restoration undertaken by the State Conservation Commission.

States to protect Indians from Indians was never attacked. The dragoons passed the time by riding over the prairies on patrol, watching for trespassers and chasing whiskey peddlers out of the Winnebago villages. The Sioux, except for an occasional outlaw, stayed at a safe distance, and the Sauks and Foxes did no visiting, either.

The Winnebagoes gave the dragoons more trouble than anybody else, because they missed no opportunity to go back to Wisconsin. Whenever this happened, they had to be brought back by force. In 1848, the government decided to move them to a new Indian Reservation in Minnesota, and the Winnebagoes left the Neutral Ground for good. No Chamber of Commerce ever got much comfort out of the Winnebagoes' opinion of Iowa. It was no "Beautiful Land" to them.

"Goodbye to Bedbugs"

There was no longer any reason to keep a company of soldiers at Fort Atkinson and, in February of 1849, the remaining officers and men marched away and left the barracks and parade grounds to the wildlife of the prairie. The caretaker found a parting message tacked to one of the bunks. It said: "Farewell to bedbugs." The property on the hilltop was sold at auction in 1853 for $3,521. You will remember it had cost $90,000. (It was therefore an early example of "War Surplus.")

Fort Atkinson is now maintained as an historic monument by the State Conservation Commission. The stone blockhouses and powder magazine could still be used in case of need, but the possibility of an Indian uprising is now remote. Part of the north barracks building has been converted into a museum which preserves relics of the Neutral Ground. Foundations of other buildings indicate the size and plan of a frontier fort which effectively preserved the peace in a time of turmoil.

THE SAUKS AND FOXES GO WEST

Fort Atkinson remained in service throughout the years in which the Sauks and Foxes were dispossessed of their Iowa land. Some of this land had been lost before the fort was built, but the Indians living near the Neutral Ground did not leave until the pressure of white settlement forced them to move farther west. The first big segment of Sauk and Fox land was acquired by the government as a result of the Black Hawk Purchase in 1832. "Keokuk's Reserve" was the next to go, in 1836. A tract of a million acres, just west of the Black Hawk Purchase was obtained in 1837.

Although the money paid to the Indians for all this land looked big at the time, it didn't last long. Many of them, including Chief Keokuk, had become fond of whiskey, and the whiskey peddlers were waiting to sell it to them whenever the annuities were paid. Dishonest traders cheated the Indians out of the rest of their money by selling them cheap merchandise at extremely high prices. When ready cash was not available, the Indians bought what they needed on credit. In a few years, the Sauks and Foxes had debts amounting to hundreds of thousands of dollars.

How could they pay these debts? The government had a quick answer for that question. The Indians could sell the rest of their land in Iowa. In October of 1842, a council was held at Agency City, about six miles east of the present city of Ottumwa. John Chambers, the Governor of the Iowa Territory, represented the government. He arrived in the glittering uniform of a Brigadier General, which made the bright feathers and blankets of the Indians look pale by comparison. The interpreter for the Governor was Antoine LeClaire. He had also been the interpreter for General Winfield Scott at the time the Black Hawk Purchase was made. LeClaire was part Indian himself, and the Sauks and Foxes trusted him.

The council in Agency City lasted for several days, but everybody knew how it would end. On October 11, 1842, the Sauks and Foxes agreed to give up the rest of their land in Iowa. The government promised to pay their debts to the traders, plus about $40,000 a year, which, of course, had to be spread out over the entire membership of the Sauk and Fox nation. The total of the debt payments and annuities amounted to a little over a million dollars.

RED ROCK BLUFFS on the Des Moines River gave the "red rock line" its name.

The Red Rock Line

Of course, the Indians couldn't pick up their baggage and leave the country the next day. A plan of moving was worked out. There were some unusual red rock bluffs on the Des Moines River, about seven miles north of Knoxville. They were chosen as a boundary because they were well known to the Indians. It was agreed that the Indians would move west of a line drawn north and south through these bluffs by May 1, 1843. By October 11, 1845, they were to be out of the rest of the territory.

After the council ended, the Sauks and Foxes had less than six months to remove themselves and their belongings from all the land east of the line, but they made it. Settlers crowded into the vacated area so rapidly that dragoons had to patrol the border to keep the white men from going *beyond* the Red Rock Line in advance of the date specified in the treaty.

Despite the dragoons, many settlers were able to slip across the line to study the land and pick sites for future homesteads. They believed in the old pioneer maxim, "Git a-plenty while yer gittin', and git the best!"

On October 11, 1845, men in covered wagons, buggies, and on horseback found positions along the line and waited for midnight when the firing of guns would signal the beginning of the race for new land. The dramatic event was described by an eyewitness in an early history of Marion County:

"As it neared midnight, settler after settler took his place on the border with his bunch of sharpened stakes and a lantern or blazing torch. Precisely at midnight, there were loud reports of firearms which announced that the empire of the red man had ended forever. Answering reports rang for miles around, and all understood that civilization had commenced her reign in central Iowa. . . . Throughout the country, thousands of acres were laid off in claims before dawn."

END OF AN EMPIRE

And where were the Sauks and Foxes while all this land-grabbing was going on? They had kept their part of the bargain and were now on an Indian reservation in Kansas. The Pottawattamies, who *thought* they were living on an Indian reservation in southwest Iowa, discovered they were mistaken. They were also removed to Kansas in 1846. As we noted earlier, the Winnebagoes were escorted from the Neutral Ground to a reservation in Minnesota in 1848.

The only Indians remaining in Iowa were the Sioux. They sold their lands in 1851 and moved to the Dakota Territory. It had taken only nineteen years for the government to

"persuade" all the Indians to leave Iowa.

Some of the Indians would come back. Of these, some would challenge the rights of the white settlers to occupy their former lands, and the Spirit Lake Massacre would leave a permanent stain on the honor of the Sioux nation.

Some of the Foxes would buy a part of their old hunting grounds and would establish the peaceful Mesquakie Settlement near Tama. Keokuk's body would be brought back from Kansas to lie in Iowa soil. But, with these few exceptions, the long history of the Indians in Iowa had come to an end.

14. AFFAIRS OF STATE

Iowa REMAINED a territory for several years after the capital had been moved to Iowa City. The people were in no great hurry to take on the responsibilities of statehood. In 1840, two years after the territory was established, Iowa had 42,000 settlers, and the legislature asked them to vote on the question of Iowa becoming a state. There wasn't much enthusiasm about the idea, and less than four thousand took the trouble even to vote on the issue. When the ballots were counted, 937 had voted for statehood, and 2,907 had voted against it.

The general feeling was that the laws of the United States and the territory were good enough. There was no sense in paying the salaries of the governor, the secretary and the judges of the supreme court, as long as the federal government paid the territorial expenses.

In 1842, the population had nearly doubled. Again, the territorial legislature asked the people to vote on statehood, and again they turned it down. By 1844, however, the people who wanted Iowa to become a state were in the majority, and a constitutional convention met in Iowa City to draw up a constitution and decide upon the boundaries of the new state.

The convention was held in the stone capitol, where the territorial legislature had been meeting since 1842. This beautiful building, which is now the administrative center of the University of Iowa, was designed by John Francis Rague. Despite the fact that Rague was clearly identified in the archives of the territory as the architect, the credit for designing the capitol was given to another man. This man was a Dominican missionary named Father Samuel Mazzuchelli.

It is not hard to understand how the legend began. Father Mazzuchelli was a man of many talents, and one of his talents was architecture. He designed the church in Dubuque which was later consecrated as a cathedral. He designed the courthouse in Fort Madison, which is still admired for its impressive Tuscan columns. He conducted services for the Roman Catholics in Iowa City, and his reputation as an architect was coupled with the gleaming stone structure that was to be the home of the territorial government. But, beyond the fact that he saw a well-designed capitol being built in Iowa City, Father Maz-

UPSTAIRS ROOM in the Old Stone Capitol in Iowa City was used by both the territorial and state legislatures. Today it is the scene of meetings and lectures.

zuchelli had no connection with it. John Francis Rague drew the plans, and his name was inscribed on the scroll which was placed in the cornerstone of the building.

BOUNDARIES FOR A NEW STATE

The 72 men who met in the stone capitol in October of 1844 didn't care much, one way or the other, whether Father Mazzuchelli or John Francis Rague had designed the building. They had problems of much greater difficulty to solve. The greatest of these was the problem of boundaries.

The eastern, western and southern boundaries drawn by the conven-

tion were practically as they are today. The northern boundary was drawn to follow a line from the mouth of the Big Sioux River northeast to the Minnesota River and then to the Mississippi. These boundaries had first been proposed in 1839 by Governor Robert Lucas, who had begun talking about statehood soon after the Territory of Iowa was established. The boundaries were therefore called the "Lucas Boundaries."

Augustus Caesar Dodge was the territorial delegate representing Iowa in Washington. When he submitted the constitution to Congress, there was an immediate outcry that the Lucas Boundaries would make the state too big. Congressmen from the South didn't want Iowa admitted to the Union in the first place, because this would upset the balance between the free and the slave states. To offset the advantage to the free states, a bill was introduced to admit Florida as a slave state, but Congress still objected to the size of Iowa.

"Make the western boundary a line passing north and south along the meridian of longitude seventeen degrees and thirty minutes west of Washington, D.C.," Congress declared. This would have put the boundary about forty miles west of where Des Moines is today, and it would have made the state only half as wide as it is now. The western boundary suggested by Congress was based on the surveys by Joseph Nicollet of the ridge which divided the

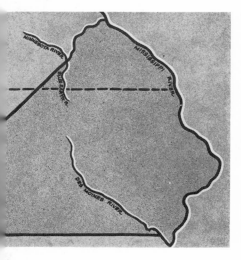

SHADED PORTION of the map indicates the size and shape Iowa would have taken had Congress accepted the proposed Lucas boundaries.

Congress finally got around to passing the bill which granted statehood to Iowa, and the bill was signed by President James K. Polk on December 28, 1846. On that day, Iowa officially became the twenty-ninth state in the Union.

ELECTION BEFORE STATEHOOD

But the people of Iowa hadn't waited for Congress and the President. As soon as the constitution had been ratified in August, the governor of the territory called for a general state election. Ansel Briggs was elected as the first governor of the state. Briggs was a Democrat who lived in Andrew, where he had been running a stagecoach line and carrying the mail. Cyrenus Cole observed in his *Iowa Through the Years* that Briggs was a "diligent and honest man who had absorbed a great deal of horse sense while driving stagecoaches." He was a bachelor, and the governor's salary of eight hundred dollars a year made it possible for him to live in comfort and style during the four years of his administration. Under the first constitution, governors were elected for a four-year term.

Ansel Briggs was inaugurated on the same day that the first state General Assembly met in Iowa City. Both the election and the inauguration had

waters running into the Mississippi and Missouri rivers. The "Nicollet Boundary" was voted down in Iowa by a resounding majority.

Nothing much happened after that until May of 1846, when the convention assembled again. A new constitution was submitted to Congress. It had some new features, but it called for the old Lucas Boundaries. Stephen A. Douglas, chairman of the Committee on Territories, proposed the Missouri and Big Sioux rivers as the western boundary and the parallel of latitude forty-three degrees and thirty minutes north as the northern boundary. The convention in Iowa City accepted the boundaries suggested by Douglas and wrote them into the constitution. This constitution was ratified by the people of Iowa on August 3, 1846.

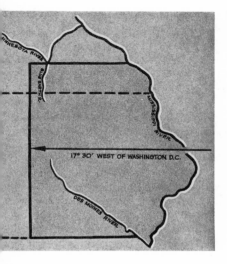

THE NICOLLET BOUNDARY, shown by the shaded area, was rejected by the people of Iowa. The dotted lines indicate the boundaries proposed by Stephen A. Douglas and accepted by all in 1846.

THE HAWKEYES

The people of Iowa were sentimental about names. As early as 1838, when James G. Edward published the first issue of the *Fort Madison Patriot,* he suggested that the name "Hawkeyes" be adopted by the people of Iowa. As he said, it would "rescue from oblivion a memento, at least, of the name of the old chief." The "old chief" was Black Hawk, who had been released from his prison chains and had come back to Iowa to die. When Edwards moved his newspaper to Burlington, he called it the "Hawkeye," and it still bears this name. The word "Hawkeyes" has become a synonym for "Iowans."

OUR LIBERTIES WE PRIZE

The first General Assembly adopted the official motto, "Our Liberties We Prize and Our Rights We Will Maintain." The motto was placed on the Great Seal of Iowa in 1847.

The constitution written in 1846 guided the General Assembly in making its laws. This made legislation on banking a very simple matter, because the constitution stated that there were to be no banks. The only bank in Iowa during the years of territorial

taken place before the state had come into legal existence. By the time President Polk signed the bill which admitted Iowa to the Union, the state government was in full swing.

S. C. Hastings and Shepherd Leffler had been elected as members of the House of Representatives in Washington, and they promptly reported for duty. Getting senators to Washington wasn't quite as easy. In those days, the senators were chosen by state legislatures. The General Assembly couldn't agree upon men to serve as senators, and for the first two years of its history as a state, Iowa didn't have *any* senators in Washington. It was not until 1848 that Augustus Caesar Dodge and George W. Jones were chosen to represent Iowa in the United States Senate.

ANSEL BRIGGS was the state of Iowa's first governor. The sketch is based on an old photograph.

land but very little cash. The per capita money in circulation, for a population of about 100,000, was only $1.11. Of course, this made a good political issue for the party out of power. The Whigs blamed the "poverty of the people" on the Democrats, because many Democrats had insisted on keeping banks out of Iowa. But the constitution said *no banks,* and the constitution wasn't going to be amended as soon as someone tried to make a political issue out of it.

The time would come when the constitution of 1846 would be amended and banks would be allowed in Iowa, but for the first ten years of its history as a state, Iowa prized its liberties by maintaining only "banks of earth." And, since these banks were well filled with rich, black deposits, the farmers, at least, were content.

government had failed and banks in other states issued paper money which could not be redeemed in gold or silver. The men who wrote the constitution therefore decided that they would have no banks at all.

Ansel Briggs even made a speech about it. "No banks but banks of earth," he said, "and those well tilled." Since a till was a drawer in which a banker kept his change, the reference to "banks of earth . . . well tilled" was a pretty good pun for a governor who was just getting started.

When Iowa began its existence as a state the people had plenty of

THE COUNT ON COUNTIES

Iowa didn't have 99 counties at the beginning of its history as a state. In 1846, it had only 44. The first General Assembly carved seven more from the lands which had been occupied by the Pottawattamie and Winnebago Indians. This made a total of 51.

In 1851, the third General Assembly divided the rest of the state into 50 counties, making 101 in all. A later General Assembly combined the counties of Risley and Yell, and since nobody wanted either of the original names, the new combination was called "Webster." Bancroft County was united with Kossuth County, and this union retained the name of "Kossuth." The total was thus reduced to 99, which is the number of counties we have today.

NAMING OF THE COUNTIES

Many of Iowa's county names were inspired by the Indians who lived in Iowa before the white man came. Some of the counties took their names from statesmen of the East or South who won renown far from Iowa, but who were gratefully remembered by the settlers in the new state. Counties which were organized after Iowa was admitted to the Union honored battles or heroes of the Mexican War. The county names of Iowa therefore represent a roll call of historic places and personalities in the story of the nation as a whole.

ADAIR COUNTY took its name from General John Adair, who fought in the War of 1812 and was the sixth governor of Kentucky.

ADAMS COUNTY was named in honor of John Adams, the second President of the United States.

ALLAMAKEE COUNTY got its name from Allan Makee, a trader who bargained with the Indians along the upper Mississippi. Somewhere along the line, "Allan Makee" was changed to "Allamakee." Clerks who copied items of this kind for

official records often skipped a letter or changed the spelling because of poor penmanship on the original entries.

APPANOOSE COUNTY took its name from a Sauk chief. The county seat was named for William T. Senter, a Tennessee preacher. The Iowa legislature thought somebody had misspelled "Senterville" and changed it to "Centerville."

AUDUBON COUNTY recalls the Iowa visit of John James Audubon when he was gathering material for his great book on *Birds of America*.

BENTON COUNTY paid a neighborly compliment to the state of Missouri by adopting the name of its famous senator, Thomas Hart Benton.

LOCOMOTIVE WHEEL monument marks the site of Jesse James' famous train robbery—the first in the west—near Adair in Adair County.

BLACK HAWK COUNTY was never visited by the most widely known of all the Sauk warriors, but it took his name anyhow.

BOONE COUNTY could have picked Daniel Boone as its inspiration, but it chose instead to honor his son, Colonel Nathan Boone, who explored central Iowa with Kearny's dragoons.

BREMER COUNTY was one of two counties in Iowa to be named for famous women. The honoree in this case was Fredrika Bremer, a Swedish traveler and writer.

"OLD SLAVE HOUSE" in Cass County was used by abolitionist John Brown as a station on the Underground Railroad.

BUCHANAN COUNTY was named for James Buchanan, the fifteenth President of the United States.

BUENA VISTA COUNTY was named in celebration of the victory at Buena Vista in the Mexican War.

BUTLER COUNTY also took note of the war with Mexico by naming itself after General William O. Butler.

CALHOUN COUNTY was originally known as Fox County, but a member of the Iowa legislature in 1853 was an ardent admirer of John C. Calhoun, the fiery senator from South Carolina, and he persuaded the General Assembly to change the county name to Calhoun.

CARROLL COUNTY singled out a name from the list of signatures on the Declaration of Independence: Charles Carroll.

CASS COUNTY honored Senator Lewis Cass of Michigan. The county seat was thought to be halfway between the Atlantic and Pacific oceans, so a coin was flipped to decide whether to call it Atlantic or Pacific. Pacific won, but it turned out to be an overworked town name in the Middle West, and Atlantic was chosen instead. Lewis, in the western part of the county, was an active station on the Underground Railroad.

CEDAR COUNTY was named for the Cedar River, which crosses the southwestern corner of the county.

CERRO GORDO COUNTY recognized the importance of the battle of Cerro Gordo in which General Winfield Scott was victorious in the Mexican War.

CHEROKEE COUNTY didn't care for the Indian names that were native to the state, so it picked the name of a southern Indian tribe.

CHICKASAW COUNTY was really named for a southern Indian nation—and not for the prairie chicken, though legend has it that a party of white surveyors sent their Indian guide in search of wild game. He returned with excited news about a flock of prairie chickens he had discovered. "Chick I saw! Chick I saw!" he shouted. Since he may have had a southern accent, he probably said "Chick ah saw!" It is even possible that he was a Chickasaw Indian in the first place and was only reciting his qualifications as a hunter.

CLARKE COUNTY was named for James Clarke, the third governor of the Iowa Territory.

CLAY COUNTY was created after the Mexican War. It is therefore believed to have been named in honor of Henry Clay, Jr., who fell in the battle of Buena Vista, rather than his famous father, Henry Clay, the senator from Kentucky.

CLAYTON COUNTY was created by the Wisconsin Territorial Assembly and was named for Senator John Middleton Clayton of Delaware. The shelf of St. Peter Sandstone which crosses the state is exposed as a tall bluff in Clayton County.

CLINTON COUNTY also reflected the influence of eastern statesmen, because it took the name of DeWitt Clinton, the fifth governor of New York.

DRUM-LIKE DRYERS remove moisture from sand mined at the St. Peter sandstone cliffs in Clayton County.

CRAWFORD COUNTY was named for Senator William Harris Crawford of Georgia.

DALLAS COUNTY decided that Vice Presidents were not given enough recognition, so it honored Vice President George Mifflin Dallas, who was being overshadowed by President James K. Polk.

DAVIS COUNTY is often thought to have been named for Jefferson Davis, but local historians declare that the honor was bestowed upon Garrett Davis, a congressman from Kentucky.

DECATUR COUNTY took its name from Captain Stephen Decatur, a naval hero in the War of 1812.

DELAWARE COUNTY settlers had no personal recollections of Lord Delaware, but they fondly remembered their old homes in Delaware County, New York.

DES MOINES COUNTY was originally a part of Demoine County, the southern segment of the Wisconsin Territory. The northern segment was called Dubuque County. When the present limits of the county were established in 1836, it kept its name, even though it no longer had any contact with the Des Moines River.

DICKINSON COUNTY reflected the eminence of Senator Daniel S. Dickinson of New York.

DUBUQUE COUNTY honored Julien Dubuque, the first settler in what is now Iowa.

EMMET COUNTY brought the name of Robert Emmet, a famous Irish patriot, into the melting pot of the state.

GREY STONE WALLS and gothic arches of the chapel and refectory of the Trappist monastery of New Melleray bring a touch of the Old World to Dubuque County. The tall hedge surrounds the abbey cemetery.

FAYETTE COUNTY added the last part of a distinguished French name to the Iowa roster—the name of the Marquis de Lafayette.

FLOYD COUNTY historians are divided on the source of their county name. Some trace it back to William Floyd, one of the signers of the Declaration of Independence. Others believe that Sergeant Charles Floyd of the Lewis and Clark expedition was closer to their roots, and they offer the name of Charles City, the county seat, in further evidence.

FRANKLIN COUNTY was named for Benjamin Franklin, whose achievements were greatly admired by the early settlers.

FREMONT COUNTY took its name from John Charles Fremont, who helped to map the Iowa territory.

GREENE COUNTY recognized the valor of General Nathaniel Greene, a hero of the Revolutionary War.

GRUNDY COUNTY was named in honor of Felix Grundy of Tennessee, rather than Mrs. Grundy, the prudish character in the play *Speed the Plough* by Thomas Morton.

GUTHRIE COUNTY honored the memory of Captain Edwin Guthrie, an Iowa volunteer in the Mexican War.

HAMILTON COUNTY acknowledged the eminence of William W. Hamilton, who presided over the Iowa senate in 1857.

HANCOCK COUNTY proudly took the name of John Hancock, the President of the Continental Congress, whose name led all the rest on the Declaration of Independence.

HARDIN COUNTY paid tribute to Colonel John J. Hardin of Illinois, who was killed in the Mexican War.

HARRISON COUNTY was named for William Henry Harrison, the ninth President of the United States.

HENRY COUNTY picked the first, rather than the last, name of General Henry Dodge, Governor of the Wisconsin Territory.

HOWARD COUNTY would have had spelling trouble if it had picked the first name of General Tighlman Howard of Indiana, so it settled on his last name.

HUMBOLDT COUNTY has a name of German origin, inspired by the travels and scientific research of Baron Frederick Alexander von Humboldt.

IDA COUNTY was named on the recommendation of a surveyor who saw Indian fires on the hill overlooking the present town of Ida Grove. They reminded him of the Greek legend of Mount Ida, where sacred fires could be seen by true believers in the gods of antiquity. Both the county and the county seat therefore have Greek names.

IOWA COUNTY took its name from the river which crosses it.

JACKSON COUNTY honors Andrew Jackson, the seventh President of the United States.

JASPER COUNTY recalls the name and fame of William Jasper, a sergeant in the Revolutionary War. The washing machine industry is centered in Newton, the county seat.

EARLY WASHING MACHINES are preserved in the Maytag factory at Newton. The model in the center went on the market in 1907.

JEFFERSON COUNTY was named for Thomas Jefferson, the third President of the United States.

JOHNSON COUNTY was named in honor of Vice President Richard Mentor Johnson. Although he never became President, as did both of the later Vice Presidents with the same last name, Richard Mentor Johnson was the only Vice President who was ever elected by the United States Senate. No candidate received a majority in the Electoral College in 1837, and the choice had to be made by the upper house of Congress.

JONES COUNTY was named for George Wallace Jones, the delegate in Congress from the Wisconsin Territory who succeeded in obtaining territorial status for Iowa.

KEOKUK COUNTY preserved the pride and prestige of Chief Keokuk of the Sauk nation.

KOSSUTH COUNTY added the name of the Hungarian patriot, Louis Kossuth, to the list of nationalities represented in the Hawkeye State.

LEE COUNTY seems to commemorate the military fame of Robert E. Lee, but it was really named in honor of Albert M. Lea, who mapped the Iowa District of the Wisconsin Territory. Somebody made a mistake in copying his name, and the county has been Lee ever since. The court house in Fort Madison, the county seat, is believed to be the oldest in the state.

TUSCAN COLUMNS dominate the facade of the Lee County courthouse at Fort Madison. Father Samuel Mazzuchelli, pioneer priest and architect, designed the building in the Greek Revival style popular at the time.

LINN COUNTY was named for Dr. Lewis F. Linn, a United States Senator from Missouri.

LOUISA COUNTY was the first of the two counties in Iowa to be named in honor of a woman. It honored Louisa Massey, who shot her father's assassin.

LUCAS COUNTY took the name of Robert Lucas, the first territorial governor of Iowa.

LYON COUNTY paid homage to Brigadier General Nathaniel Lyon, who led the Union attack at the battle of Wilson's Creek.

MADISON COUNTY was named for James Madison, the fourth President of the United States. When names for the county seat were being considered, somebody suggested Summerset. Another member of the committee, shivering with cold, cried out in protest. "Summerset!" he exclaimed. "You'd better name it Winterset!" The majority of the committee agreed, and it has been Winterset ever since.

MAHASKA COUNTY preserved the name of Chief Mahaska of the Iowa nation. On a visit to the "Great White Father" in Washington, Chief Mahaska thought the window of his second floor hotel room was a door. He walked through it and broke his arm.

MARION COUNTY remembered the War of Independence and named itself in honor of Francis Marion, a hero of the Revolution. Knoxville, the county seat, was the home

IOWA STATE FLAG designed by Mrs. Dixie Cornell Gebhardt is on display in a museum in Knoxville, Marion County.

of Mrs. Dixie Cornell Gebhardt, who designed the Iowa state flag.

MARSHALL COUNTY was determined to be a monument of law and order. It took the name of John Marshall, the fourth Chief Justice of the United States Supreme Court.

MILLS COUNTY established itself as a continuing memorial to Major Frederick Mills of Burlington, who was killed in the Mexican War.

MITCHELL COUNTY respected and admired the defiance of the Irish. It took the name of John Mitchell, a refugee from British rule in Ireland.

MONONA COUNTY was one of the last outposts of Indian residence in western Iowa, and it acknowledged this fact by retaining an Indian name.

MONROE COUNTY was originally named Kishkekosh, in tribute to a popular sub-chief of the Sauk and Fox Indians, but this became a hazard for poor spellers and the county adopted the name of President James Monroe instead.

MONTGOMERY COUNTY went all the way back to the Battle of Quebec when looking for a name. It settled upon General Richard Montgomery of the Continental Army in making a choice.

MUSCATINE COUNTY adopted the name of the Mascoutin Indians and changed the Indian spelling. The city of Muscatine, which is the county seat, became famous in the fresh-water pearl button industry.

O'BRIEN COUNTY had a warm regard for the heroes of the Irish independence movement. It selected William Smith O'Brien as its patron.

OSCEOLA COUNTY was named in honor of a famous southern Indian chief whose wife was Oskaloosa, "the last of the beautiful."

PAGE COUNTY was named in memory of Captain John Page, who was killed in the first battle of the Mexican War.

PALO ALTO COUNTY commemorated the battlefield in southern Texas where General Zachary Taylor won the first victory in the war with Mexico.

PLYMOUTH COUNTY was named for the first settlement of the pilgrims who came to America in the Mayflower.

POCAHONTAS COUNTY gratefully acknowledged the help of the Virginia Indian princess who saved the neck of Captain John Smith.

POLK COUNTY, which was organized in 1846, took note of the signature of President James K. Polk on the bill which admitted Iowa to the Union in that year.

POTTAWATTAMIE COUNTY remembered the Indian tribe which briefly occupied its land before being moved to Kansas. The visit of Abraham Lincoln in Council Bluffs, the county seat, is recalled by a monument in his honor.

POWESHIEK COUNTY was named in honor of a wise and temperate chief of the Sauk and Fox.

RINGGOLD COUNTY, which pronounces both of the middle letters, paid its respects to Major Samuel Ringgold, who was killed in the Mexican War.

SAC COUNTY couldn't decide upon a favorite chief among the Sauk Indians, so it honored the whole nation. However, it used the French rather than the Indian spelling and pronunciation.

SCOTT COUNTY was the setting for The Black Hawk Purchase. General Winfield Scott was the chief arm-twister for the government, and the county acknowledged his ability by taking his name.

SHELBY COUNTY honored a hero of the Revolutionary War. The settlers from the South may have remembered, also, that General Isaac Shelby was the first governor of Kentucky.

SIOUX COUNTY took the name of the last Indian nation to leave the state.

STORY COUNTY was named for Joseph

ABRAHAM LINCOLN viewed the valley of the Missouri River from this point in Pottawattamie County. It is believed that this visit in 1859 influenced him in designating Council Bluffs as the eastern terminus of the Union Pacific Railroad. This monument commemorating the visit is at Point Lookout in Council Bluffs.

Story, an Associate Justice of the United States Supreme Court.

TAMA COUNTY prophetically took the name of Tai-mah, a Fox chief. The Fox Indians, reverting to their historic identity as the Mesquakies, came back to the county and purchased land for tribal ownership.

TAYLOR COUNTY was named for Zachary Taylor, victorious general in the Mexican War and twelfth President of the United States.

UNION COUNTY was to have been named in honor of Judge Charles Mason, but a compromise on the slavery issue in 1850 offered hope that the Union would be preserved, and the name was changed to Union.

VAN BUREN COUNTY was named in honor of President Martin Van Buren, who signed the bill which created the Iowa territory.

WAPELLO COUNTY fondly remembered Chief Wapello of the Fox Indian nation. The chief was buried beside his friend, General Joseph Street, near the town of Agency.

WARREN COUNTY took its name from General Joseph Warren, who was killed during the battle of Bunker Hill.

WASHINGTON COUNTY was first named Slaughter, in tribute to a secretary of the Iowa territory. In 1839, the territorial legislature decided to honor the first President of the United States instead, and the name was changed to Washington.

WAYNE COUNTY was named for General Anthony Wayne, who won glory in the Revolutionary War.

WEBSTER COUNTY echoed the distinction of Daniel Webster, the statesman from Massachusetts. Fort Dodge, the county seat, took its name from the military post which guarded the frontier.

WINNEBAGO COUNTY remembered the brief and reluctant residence of the Winnebago Indians in Iowa.

WINNESHIEK COUNTY was carved out of the Neutral Ground. Its name was inspired by a chief of the Winnebagos.

WOODBURY COUNTY was named for Levi Woodbury, an Associate Justice of the United States Supreme Court.

WORTH COUNTY honored General William Jenkins Worth, a veteran of both the War of 1812 and the war with Mexico.

WRIGHT COUNTY was named for Silas Wright, the twelfth governor of New York.

CHIEF WAPELLO lies buried beside the tracks of the CB & Q Railroad near Agency.

15. THE MORMONS MOVE WEST

WHEN the calendar was turned to 1846 in Iowa, nobody realized what an eventful year it would be. Shortly before the end of December, Iowa would become a state. The Pottawattamie Indians would follow the Sauks and Foxes to Kansas. The constitution would be adopted by popular vote, the first election for state officers would be held, and the Mexican War would begin. But the most dramatic event of the year would be the movement of 15,000 Mormons across the southern part of the Iowa territory.

In some respects, the Mormons were like the Sauk and Fox Indians. They, too, were being driven from one home to another.

In 1830—the same year in which Dr. Isaac Galland started the first school in Iowa—a young man named Joseph Smith started a new religion in New York state. He claimed that an angel had appeared to him in a vision and had told him to dig in the earth at a certain place near his home.

Smith did as he was told and he found a set of golden plates covered with strange inscriptions. He took the plates home with him, translated them into English, and buried the originals again. The translation was called the Book of Mormon.

On the strength of the revelations made to him, Joseph Smith organized the Church of Jesus Christ of Latter-Day Saints. Because of the reliance of the members of this church upon the Book of Mormon, the Latter-Day Saints were usually called "The Mormons."

AN IOWAN BEFRIENDS THE MORMONS

As William J. Petersen has pointed out in *The Palimpsest* for November, 1956, "the Mormons, from their very inception, met with rebuff and persecution wherever they formed a settlement, partly because of their claim that they alone were the chosen people."

JOSEPH SMITH organized the Church of Jesus Christ of Latter-Day Saints. This drawing is based on an old painting in the church archives.

In 1831 they moved from Fayette, New York, to Kirtland, Ohio, where they built a temple. But they were not permitted to stay in Ohio very long. In 1833, while settlers were moving into Iowa's Black Hawk Purchase, the Mormons were trying to establish a settlement in Independence, Missouri. "The Prophet," as Joseph Smith was known, had told them that this would be the New Jerusalem, where Christ would receive His chosen people at His Second Coming. The people of Missouri didn't like the Mormons because the Latter-Day Saints were opposed to slavery. The idea of being considered outside the circle of salvation didn't appeal to the Missourians either, and, in less than six years, the Mormons had been driven out of the state.

Dr. Isaac Galland, a convert to the new faith, helped the fugitives to find temporary homes in the Half-Breed Tract. The doctor owned a section of land in Hancock County,

Illinois, which included the village of Commerce. In 1839, he sold all of this land to Joseph Smith, who changed the name of the village to Nauvoo and started the building of a new city for his followers.

By 1844, Nauvoo had a population of 12,000. It was the largest city in Illinois—even Chicago was smaller. But, with increasing prosperity and power, the Mormons were heading for trouble, again. They voted as a bloc, and their control of politics was so strong that Joseph Smith announced his intention to become a candidate for President of the United States. The church was gaining converts all over the country, and Smith knew he could count on the vote of every member of his faith.

The gentiles, as the Mormons called the people who didn't belong to their church, decided upon drastic action. The Latter-Day Saints were charged with crimes ranging all the way from petty theft to arson and murder. Joseph Smith and his brother were arrested, and, while they were awaiting trial in Carthage, a mob stormed the jail on June 27, 1844, and the Prophet and his brother were murdered.

EXODUS

Brigham Young became the leader of the church, and, for a time, order was restored. But the Mormon elders knew their days in Nauvoo were numbered. A group of ninety Mormons known as the Emmett party crossed the Mississippi and started west in August of 1844. They spent the winter on Mormon Ridge near Marshalltown, where they suffered much hardship from cold and hunger. After wandering through western Iowa and the Dakota territory in search of a New Zion, they finally rejoined Brigham Young.

The new head of the church had appealed to the governor of Illinois for protection from hostile neighbors, but the persecution continued. Young decided that the Mormons could find freedom to worship only by leaving the United States. He proposed that the Latter-Day Saints make one more move. This would be a long one. It would take them beyond the Rocky Mountains into land owned by Mexico. Here, he believed, they would be safe.

Preparations were made to leave Nauvoo "so soon as grass would grow and water run" in the spring of 1846. Wagons were built for the long jour-

ney. Tents, farming tools, cooking utensils, and provisions were assembled. Comfortable homes would be abandoned. The Mormons would be living in their wagons and under the open sky for over a year, and only the necessities for their physical and spiritual survival could be taken with them.

The winter was mild, and the first family crossed the Mississippi on February 4, 1846. The grass was not yet growing, but all signs pointed to an early spring. Of course, there was no bridge across the river. The wagons, people and stock had to be ferried from the Illinois to the Iowa side. On February 15, Brigham Young and his twelve apostles crossed into Iowa, and the whole company moved inland about nine miles and established their first "Camp of Israel" at Sugar Creek in Lee County. There would be fourteen more of these Camps of Israel across southern Iowa.

The hopes for an early spring suddenly collapsed. Snow began to fall, and the temperature dropped to twenty below zero. Many families had rushed out of Nauvoo without bringing enough blankets and warm clothing with them. Despite the warnings of the leaders, they had neglected to provide themselves with enough food for their own needs and the needs of their stock, and they were obliged to ask the Iowa settlers for help.

The Mormons were no strangers to these pioneers. Many had lived in

Iowa until they joined Joseph Smith in Illinois. Governor Lucas had described them as "industrious, inoffensive and worthy citizens."

By early March, the Mormons were able to resume their journey. For a time, they followed the general course of the Des Moines River. The deep mud of the prairies broke some of the wagons, and part of the group had to stay behind to repair them. Meanwhile, the others moved on to a new camp near the present town of Keosauqua. They crossed the Des Moines River at a point in what is now Lacey-Keosauqua State Park. The crossing was named Ely's Ford in honor of one of the Mormon leaders.

Wherever one party stopped, seeds were planted. The exodus from Nauvoo continued over a period of several months, and, as the later travelers followed the Mormon Trail, they found vegetables ready to eat.

The Mormons who were at the head of the procession soon discovered that oxen were needed to pull their heavy wagons through the mud, and the horses were exchanged for the slower but stronger animals. Even so, during the first month of the journey, they were able to average only three miles per day.

The slow progress was discouraging, but the Saints did not lose their faith in God. Prayers were offered daily, and a brass band kept up the spirits of the pilgrims with lively music. Indeed, the band was so popular in the frontier communities that the

settlers hired the musicians to play for their dances. The money earned for this kind of service helped to pay the bills for supplies along the way.

SETTLEMENTS ARE ESTABLISHED

On April 23, the Mormons came to a place which they named Garden Grove. Here, Brigham Young decided to establish a more permanent settlement. He picked several men and their families to build log cabins, fence in a large field, cultivate crops, and take care of the Mormons who would be coming along later in the summer. Garden Grove was one of the most important Camps of Israel to be established in Iowa. It provided a place where the faithful could restock their supplies and find shelter after long weeks on the open prairie.

Another important camp was located on the bluffs overlooking the Grand River in what is now Union County. The Mormons named this camp Mount Pisgah after an ancient peak in Palestine. A mill was built; granite boulders were chipped to serve as burrs, and horses were used for power. A spring furnished water for the camp, a tabernacle was built, and crops were planted on 1,500 acres plowed with the aid of cows. All that remains of this bustling settlement today is a limestone shaft erected in memory of the Mormons who died at Mount Pisgah and were buried there.

Each of the settlements reduced the number of Saints moving westward, but there were new groups leaving Nauvoo at intervals through-out the summer. They were strung out across the entire width of Iowa until September 17, when the last of the Mormons left Nauvoo. According to Dr. Petersen, "in July of 1846, fifteen thousand Mormons were said to be encamped or toiling westward along the Iowa trails, with three thousand wagons, thirty thousand head of cattle, horses and mules, and a vast number of sheep."

Brigham Young reached the Missouri River on June 14. It had taken him five months to travel the three hundred miles across Iowa. The settlement at which he and his followers stopped had been known as Hart's Bluff, because a man named Hart had operated a fur trading post there. When the Mormons arrived, the name was first changed to Miller's Hollow in honor of a Mormon elder. The families remaining in the town to help the later Saints on their way toward the west changed the name to Kanesville in tribute to Thomas L. Kane, an Army officer who was friendly to the Mormons. It was not until 1853 that it took its present name, Council Bluffs.

The Mormons built a ferry boat at Miller's Hollow, and, during the summer of 1846, the "chosen people" were ferried across the Missouri River to an encampment which became known as Winter Quarters. In April of 1847, Brigham Young led the first group of Mormons on the second stage of the long journey. After trav-

MOUNT PISGAH monument in Union County marks the burial site of hundreds of Mormons who died at this Camp of Zion during the historic Mormon crossing of Iowa.

eling a thousand miles across Nebraska, Wyoming, and part of Utah, the leaders entered the Valley of the Great Salt Lake through Emigration Canyon on July 24, 1847.

THE MORMON BATTALION

One group of Mormons which began the trip with Brigham Young didn't get to finish it on schedule. While the Saints were crossing Iowa, the Mexican War began. An Army officer was sent to the Mormon camps to see if he couldn't get the young men to enlist. He didn't get much encouragement at first. There was an understandable lack of enthusiasm about helping a government which had done nothing to protect the Mormons while they were being persecuted in Missouri and Illinois. But the Saints were in need of money, and when the officer promised to pay a bounty of $20,000 for a full battalion of young men, Brigham Young approved the idea, and 500 volunteers were sent to California for military service.

These 500 Saints made up "The Mormon Battalion." They were good soldiers, and they were mustered out with honor at the close of the war. But, when the Mexican War ended, the territory which the Mormons had marched so many miles to reach became a part of the United States. Brigham Young had tried to get his followers out of the U.S.A., and, ironically, his young men had helped get them back into it!

THE REORGANIZED CHURCH

Not all of the Latter-Day Saints followed Brigham Young to Utah. The wife of the Prophet and the son of Joseph Smith did not accept Young's new leadership. Shortly before the Prophet was imprisoned and murdered, he had declared that he wanted his son to be his successor. The boy was too young to assume the leadership of the Saints when his father became a martyr, but he and

his mother and a group of loyal retainers decided to stay in Illinois. In time, this group established the Reorganized Church of Jesus Christ of Latter-Day Saints. They moved their headquarters from Plano, Illinois, to Lamoni, Iowa, in 1881. Joseph Smith III became the president of the Reorganized Church.

The numbering of the Joseph Smiths is often confusing, because the Joseph Smith who started the Mormon Church in the first place was Joseph Smith II. *His* father was Joseph Smith I. To keep them straight, the first Joseph Smith is usually called the Patriarch because he was the veteran of the family. Joseph Smith II, who was the most famous of the three, is known as the Prophet.

For twenty-five years, the Reorganized Church had its headquarters in Lamoni. "Liberty Hall," the house built for Joseph Smith III, is still standing. In 1906, the administration of the church moved to its world headquarters in Independence, Missouri. The New Jerusalem had been regained.

LIBERTY HALL, near Lamoni, was built as a residence for Joseph Smith III, president of the Reorganized Church of Jesus Christ of Latter-Day Saints.

THE HANDCART BRIGADES

Ten years after Brigham Young and his Latter-Day Saints had crossed southern Iowa on their way to the Valley of the Great Salt Lake, the railroad had reached Iowa City. Mormon missionaries had traveled as far as Europe in search of new converts. An emigration fund had been set up to pay the expenses of these European converts across the Atlantic and as far west as the railroad would carry them.

But how were they to go the rest of the way to their New Zion? They had no money to buy Conestoga wagons or oxen. Brigham Young had the answer. He said: "Let them come on foot, with handcarts or wheelbarrows; let them gird up their loins and walk through, and nothing shall hinder or stay them."

It sounded as though it would be an exciting adventure, and everybody would get a lot of healthy exercise in the open air. The converts from Europe set up a camp just across the Iowa River from the state capital. There was a sawmill at the place where Coralville is located today, and, here, the Mormons built their two-wheeled carts—one cart for every five persons.

In accordance with the directions given by Brigham Young, the carts were made entirely of wood, to keep them from being too heavy. They were built large enough to hold only one change of clothing and the necessary food for five people. Even the food was carefully rationed to avoid excess weight.

During the summer of 1856, fifteen hundred converts came to the camp. The first group started west on June 9. The fifth and final group for the year of 1856 left during the last week of July. It took each of the groups about a month to walk from Iowa City to Council Bluffs. The rest of the journey was the hard part, because the country west of the Missouri River was still wild and very largely unsettled.

The groups which left Iowa City in early summer completed the trip to Salt Lake City before snow fell in the mountains, but the later groups endured unbelievable hardships. Hundreds of the migrants froze to death or died of starvation. The ones who made it all the way had the satisfaction of knowing that they had walked 1300 miles, pulling their meager possessions in handmade, two-wheeled carts.

The years between 1856 and 1860 marked the only period in history during which the handcart was used for mass migration. Nearly 3,000 men, women, and children marched to their Promised Land on foot. But the toll of human life had been heavy, and the handcart expeditions were discontinued after 1860.

★ ★

16. MISSIONARIES AND MISSIONS

THE HISTORY of salvation in Iowa actually began with the arrival of Father Marquette in 1673. This Jesuit missionary was no ordinary explorer. He was not interested in claiming new lands for France. His only goal was the winning of converts to Christ among the Indians who lived along the Great River. Other missionaries of the Roman Catholic Church followed Father Marquette into the country which would become the state of Iowa.

EARLY CHURCHES AND "HUMMER'S BELL"

The first church building in Iowa was built by the Methodists in the summer of 1834, four years before Iowa became a territory. A circuit rider named Reverend Barton Randle had been sent into the newly opened Black Hawk Purchase in 1833 by Peter Cartwright, a famous frontier evangelist.

The Reverend Mr. Randle decided that Dubuque, with its growing population of miners and merchants, needed a church more than any other place on his circuit. He obtained contributions for the building from seventy men and women of different creeds, nationalities, and colors. The amounts ranged from $25 contributed by Woodbury Massey to 12½ cents contributed by Caroline Brady. (In those days, the 12½-cent coin, or "bit," was in common use. We still use the expression "two bits" for 25¢, even though the "bit" is no longer coined.)

The church was built of hewn logs. It was 20 feet wide, 26 feet long, and one story high. There was no steeple. It looked very much like the first schoolhouse at Galland. Indeed, the church was used as a schoolhouse and community center during the week. On Sundays, the Methodists shared it with other denominations, since the $255 which had been raised to build it had come from people of several different creeds.

As we noted earlier, the first *brick* church in Iowa was also built by the Methodists. It was used by the territorial legislature and was known as "Old Zion." But the brick church in Burlington was not completed until 1838. The second church in Iowa was a stone building erected in Dubuque by the Roman Catholics. It was designed by Father Samuel Mazzuchelli, a Dominican missionary who had created the diocese of Dubuque. When the building was completed in 1837, it was named St. Raphael's Church. St. Raphael's became the Cathedral of the Territory of Iowa in 1839. This was the year in which Mathias Loras became the first Bishop of the Dubuque diocese. Father Mazzuchelli had been offered the bishopric, but he had declined it in order to remain a missionary.

The diocese of Dubuque extended from the state of Missouri to the Canadian border and from the Mississippi to the Missouri River. When Bishop Loras arrived in Dubuque, the diocese had only three Roman Catholic churches: St. James Chapel in Lee County; a combination church, school, and dwelling in Davenport; and St. Raphael's in Dubuque. Roman Catholics who lived in more sparsely settled parts of the territory were served by missionaries.

Other Protestants besides the Methodists were also building churches in Iowa. A church had been built by the Presbyterians in Iowa City, and the belfry of this church contained the first bell which had been brought into Iowa. But it didn't stay there long. The Reverend Michael Hummer and his people had a disagreement about the pastor's salary, and Reverend Hummer decided he would take the bell in payment of the amount which the congregation owed him.

He climbed into the belfry and lowered the bell to a friend who was standing at the foot of the ladder, but at this point it changed hands. An alert group of Presbyterians had arrived. They removed the ladder (with the pastor still in the belfry), loaded the bell on a wagon, and drove out of town with it. By the time another ladder had been found and the Reverend Mr. Hummer had descended from the belfry, the bell had disappeared. It was found, many years later, in Salt Lake City. "Hummer's Bell" had been buried near the Iowa River, and a friend of the Mormons had found it and sent it to Brigham Young as a present.

THE IOWA BAND

In 1838, the Reverend Asa Turner, a Congregational minister, made the long trip from New England to a little settlement called Haystack, nine miles from Fort Madison. In later years, it would take the name of Denmark. Turner, who was a graduate of the School of Theology at Yale, was delighted with Iowa and described it as a country "so beautiful that there might be an unwillingness to exchange it for the paradise above."

But it was a big country, and he wrote to his mission board again and again for missionaries to supply the growing territory. Eleven men, all members of the 1843 graduating class of Andover Theological Seminary, heard the call. They decided to give up the comfortable New England parishes that awaited them and go instead to the "Macedonia" which was still a wilderness.

The group met in Denmark, Iowa, in November of 1843 and organized what is now known as the "Iowa Band." Under the guidance of Asa Turner, they selected individual fields of labor throughout the territory. Their slogan was: "Each to found a church; all a college," for they made education a basic principle of their ministry.

The Iowa Band of Congregationalists practiced what it preached. The young ministers conducted services under the trees and in rooms over saloons. But each of them founded at least one church, and all of them combined their efforts to establish the school which ultimately became Grinnell College.

"OLD PIONEER," on the campus of Iowa Wesleyan College, Mount Pleasant, is the oldest college building in Iowa.

OTHER CHURCH COLLEGES

Meanwhile, the Methodists had also been active in education. One of the oldest colleges west of the Mississippi had been founded by them at Mount Pleasant in 1842. It was destined to become Iowa Wesleyan College. "Old Pioneer," the original building, is still standing on the Iowa Wesleyan campus.

In 1851, Elder George Bowman, a Methodist circuit rider, stopped his horse on the crest of a long hill about sixty miles north of Mount Pleasant. Inspired by the beauty of the scene, he dedicated the spot to Christian education. The hill was given the name of Mount Vernon. Plans to build a college were immediately begun, and the new school opened in 1853 as the Iowa Conference Male and Female Seminary. It was renamed Cornell College in 1855.

Many other church colleges would be established in the years to come, but Grinnell, Iowa Wesleyan, and Cornell were among the first in Iowa.

THE CIRCUIT RIDER

A traveling preacher like Elder Bowman was called a "circuit rider" because he rode on horseback from place to place, bringing the gospel to widely separated communities. His journeys might take him on a circuit of two or three hundred miles before he got back to his starting point. The preacher could not visit any single cabin or schoolhouse more than once every six weeks, or even longer intervals. He carried all of his personal belongings in the saddlebags which he strapped to the back of his horse.

The circuit rider seldom received more than board and lodging in exchange for his services. One of the traveling preachers kept a record of the money given to him over a period of six years; it amounted to less than $100. But, like the other missionaries who made their rounds in all kinds of weather to unite couples in marriage, baptize infants, comfort the sick, and bury the dead, the circuit rider believed that he was an apostle of Christ, and this belief rewarded him more than any material contributions.

As more and more people came into Iowa, villages and towns grew large enough to build their own churches and to hire pastors who could give all their time to local ministries. In addition to Methodist, Roman Catholic, Presbyterian, and Congregational churches, there were Baptist, Episcopalian, Christian, Lutheran, Quaker, and Mormon churches in the state.

A man named Abner Kneeland, who was an atheist, felt so crowded by all the churches being built in Iowa that he tried to start a town where no one would be allowed to build a church. This town in Van Buren County was called Salubria. Few people wanted to live in a godless community, and Salubria didn't last long.

THE CISTERCIANS

An entirely different community was established near Dubuque in 1849. Here a group of Cistercian monks built a monastery and gave their full attention to prayer and penance. Not only did these monks pray for their own souls, but also for the souls of the people who lived outside the monastery walls. They were devoted to a strict observance of the Rule of St. Benedict, and their total life was dedicated to prayer, spiritual reading, and manual labor. Even as they worked in the fields to exercise their bodies and raise their food, they observed the rule of silence in order to keep their thoughts on God.

But the voices of the monks did not become rusty through disuse. They spent six hours in their chapel every day, chanting the canonical hours from two o'clock in the morning until seven o'clock at night. Then they went to bed.

Although the Cistercians were new in Iowa, their order had been old in Europe for hundreds of years. It was founded at Citeaux, France, in

1098. The Latin word for Citeaux is "Cistercium." The monks were therefore known as the Cistercians. They were also called Trappists, because one of the early French abbeys had been built at LaTrappe. The French Revolution wiped out the monastery at LaTrappe, and the Trappists found refuge in Ireland, where the abbey at Mount Melleray was built.

THE TRAPPISTS COME TO IOWA

In the middle years of the nineteenth century, a potato famine in Ireland caused great hardships, and Bishop Loras of Iowa offered the monks a tract of land in his diocese. A group of Cistercians from Mount Melleray accepted the offer, and *New* Melleray was founded in 1849, only three years after Iowa became a state.

The monastery is still in existence. It is located near Peosta, about twelve miles southeast of Dubuque. The monastery is now called the Abbey of Our Lady of New Melleray. The prayers of the monks are addressed to Our Lady, the Mother of Christ, who brings them to the attention of her Son.

Only two of the wooden buildings erected by the monks in 1849 are still standing. The white stone abbey which the visitor at New Melleray sees today was built in the years following 1875. It is constantly being enlarged as new members join the order.

The concrete highways of modern Iowa are beyond the horizon. The abbey stands remote and silent among the farm lands from which the monks obtain their food. Only the sounds of the chapel bell, the chanting of prayers, and the singing of birds break the stillness. The guest in the abbey feels that he has been transported back to the Middle Ages. Here, only a few miles from the roar of traffic and the clatter of industry, he can stand in the quiet groves where the monks and missionaries walked when Iowa was young.

WEATHERED SIDING covers one of the original monastery buildings at New Melleray. Formerly alive with the busy, silent life of the abbey, the old structure is now used only for storage.

17. THE CITY OF REFUGE

THE MISSIONARIES and monks who had come to Iowa in the early years of statehood were dedicated to serving God. The missionaries and circuit riders moved from place to place establishing churches. The monks, who had built their monastery in eastern Iowa, stayed on their monastery grounds but they believed that their prayers and penance were making the world a better place in which to live. They could have offered these prayers in Ireland as well as in Iowa, but the potato famine in Ireland had made it necessary for them to move.

The Trappists were not the first people from the Old World who had come to live in the new state. Freedom of worship and freedom of opportunity had brought many Europeans to America, and the cheap land west of the Mississippi had attracted hundreds of immigrants to Iowa. In a short time, these people from other lands learned to speak English, and, as they adopted the customs of their neighbors, they became indistinguishable from other Americans.

However, there are some communities in Iowa where the German, Norwegian, Danish, Czech, or Dutch language is still spoken fluently. This does not mean that the people in these villages are unable to speak English. It means only that they have not forgotten the country from which their grandparents or great-grandparents came. Their roots are meaningful to them, and the language of their ancestors reminds them of their origins.

Many immigrants established their homesteads in localities which had no associations with the countries of their birth. Others made the long trip across the ocean together and decided to set up counterparts of their home communities in colonies where

DOMINIE SCHOLTE and his followers sought religious freedom in Iowa. This sketch of the Dutch leader is based on a portrait in the family home in Pella.

their native language and customs could be preserved.

THE DUTCH

The first of the large immigrant groups to settle in Iowa came from Holland. This group had a long heritage of religious freedom. Under William of Orange, the Dutch had successfully resisted the efforts of Spain to make Holland a Roman Catholic nation.

In 1608, the Separatists from the Church of England had found refuge in Holland, where they were permitted to worship God as they pleased. Later, these Separatists crossed the ocean in a small ship called the "Mayflower." William Bradford had spoken of himself and his followers as "pilgrims and strangers upon the earth," and the founders of the Plymouth Colony were there-

fore called the Pilgrims.

The Dutch had treated the Pilgrims kindly, but the people from England wanted their children to remain English, instead of growing up in Holland and learning the Dutch language and the Dutch ways of life. This determination to preserve their own identity had led them to America.

Two hundred years later, the tolerant manners of the Dutch had change considerably. After the war with Napoleon, the state took over the church. Anyone who dared to preach the separation of church and state went to jail.

A popular young minister named Dominie Henry Peter Scholte could not tolerate these restraints upon his freedom. The title, Dominie, was given to a clergyman or pastor, and Dominie Scholte considered it to be no empty title. As a Dominie, he believed it to be his duty to preach the gospel as his conscience revealed it to him.

When the government told him what he could say and what he could not say from his pulpit, Scholte left the state church, and his entire congregation walked out with him. This, of course, was a defiance of the king, and the unfrocked pastor and his outspoken followers were fined and imprisoned. After they had served their terms in jail, Scholte decided he and his people could no longer remain in Holland. The king was glad to be rid of the troublemakers, and he gave them permission to go. They sold their houses and lands, put all their gold in a big iron chest, and sailed for America. The year was 1847.

Americans liked the Dutch. They were clean and thrifty, and they expected charity from no one. Wherever Dutch immigrants had settled in the United States, they had improved the land and established prosperous communities. Dominie Scholte and his 800 Hollanders were given a warm welcome when they arrived in St. Louis. Illinois tried to get them to settle in Nauvoo, which the Mormons had just left. The people of Missouri also tried to keep the group in their state, but the Dutch didn't like the idea of slavery which Missouri accepted.

Scholte had heard of the new state of Iowa, and he decided to explore its possibilities. Taking five men of his company with him, he

IRON CHEST, in which Scholte and his 800 followers kept their money on the long journey from Holland to Iowa, can still be seen in Pella.

went to Fairfield, where the land office was located. The land agent was favorably impressed by the delegation from Holland, but his maps extended no further west than Fairfield, and all of the large tracts of land in his area had been claimed.

END OF THE SEARCH

While the Hollanders were in Fairfield, the daughter of the land agent died. Scholte believed that his presence as a minister might help to comfort the grieving parents, and he stayed for the funeral. On his way back to town from the cemetery, he fell into conversation with a Baptist circuit rider, who had also assisted in the burial service.

When Scholte told him that he was trying to find land for his 800 companions, the Baptist preacher said, "I know just the place for you. It is on high ground in Marion County, and I am sure the Yankees who are now living on the land will be glad to sell it. They want to move farther west."

Guided by their new friend, Scholte and his party journeyed northwestward and found the land to be just what they wanted. The settlers were willing to sell their claims, and the Hollanders bought 18,000 acres before the Yankees could change their

ARCHITECTURE in Pella followed the styles of the Old Country. This two-story building, which combines characteristics of Holland and mid-19th century Iowa, served for many years as an historical museum.

minds. Even at the bargain price of $1.25 per acre, the outlay in gold for 18,000 acres proved that the Dutch were not exactly paupers. They still had a substantial amount of money left after the real estate deal had been closed.

There was only a single claim cabin at the place where Dominie Scholte decided to build his City of Refuge. The pastor asked the Yankees to put up a few extra cabins which his people might occupy until they could build their own homes. The Yankees promised to do this, and the Hollanders began their journey back to St. Louis. As a final gesture, they drove a pole into the ground and nailed a shingle to it. The crude signpost bore a single word: "Pella." Before they had left Holland, the immigrants had agreed that this would be the name of their new home. The original Pella was a free city in Palestine which offered sanctuary to people in trouble. It was an appropriate choice, for Pella, Iowa, would become a sanctuary for strangers in a strange land.

News of the land purchase was greeted with joy by those who had been left behind in St. Louis. The 800 refugees made the journey to Keokuk by steamboat. Here the Hollanders disembarked and bought oxen, wagons, and supplies for the passage inland. The oxen didn't understand the Dutch language, and they refused to budge until an obliging settler spoke to them in round frontier English. Having learned the necessary vocabulary, the travelers began their three-day trip up the Des Moines River valley.

The Yankees had left Pella without building the shelters they had promised, and there was only the single cabin to greet the new landowners on their arrival. By common consent, Dominie Scholte and his family were given the use of the cabin. The rest of the company slept in (or under) their wagons until better accommodations could be provided.

The day after they arrived, the Hollanders dug holes in the ground, covered these pits with a lattice of poles, and piled straw on top of the makeshift rafters. The covered dugout were the first homes in the Dutch community. Pella was called "Strawtown" by travelers who passed through the village in the early days of settlement.

But the people from Holland were industrious and enthusiastic. Sturdy houses were built within a short time, and the town quickly took shape. The house built by Dominie Scholte is still standing. It has been occupied by Scholte descendants for more than a hundred years, and many of the original furnishings are still preserved.

The motto "In Deo Spes Nostra et Refugium" (In God Is Our Hope and Refuge) was placed on the city seal. It expressed the faith which had carried the settlers from their old home in the Netherlands to a new dwelling place in Iowa.

CITIZENSHIP AND SCHOOLING, TROUBLE AND TRIUMPH

Although the Dutch immigrants continued to use their old language and customs, they were proud of their new identity as Americans. They immediately applied for permission to take the oath of citizenship and, two weeks after their arrival in Iowa, a representative of the government came to Strawtown. All of the adults in the community made their pledge of allegiance to the United States of America. The law required five years to elapse before the final papers could be issued, but for all practical purposes, the Dutch were Americans in less than a month after they arrived in Iowa.

There were many children and young people in the new community and Dominie Scholte was determined that they should have a good education. He offered land, a suitable building and a solid endowment for the establishment of a college in Pella. The Baptist Church accepted the offer, and Central College was founded in 1853. It remained a Baptist college until 1916, when it was transferred to the Dutch Reformed Church.

The early years of settlement involved many of the hardships which were common on the frontier. The

Dutch-Americans were often home-sick, but they prized the freedom of their new land more highly than the oppression of the old country, and they faced the future with courage and confidence.

Two years after Pella was built, the Gold Rush to California began. Thousands of the Forty-Niners passed through the well-stocked farming community in Marion County and paid high prices for the produce and cattle raised by the Dutch farmers.

Dominie Scholte advertised the colony in the Netherlands, and hun-dreds of Hollanders came to Iowa to share the freedom and prosperity of the pioneers. Land became so expensive around Pella that the new arrivals looked for cheaper land in northwest Iowa, which was still beyond the frontier of heavy settlement.

Henry Hospers was the trail blazer of the Dutch who established Orange City and other towns in Sioux County. The Pella Tulip Festival and the Orange City May Festival are annual reminders of the resourceful immigrants who came to Iowa and built their cities of refuge.

18. THE IRON HIGHWAY

DOMINIE SCHOLTE and his refugees from Holland made the journey from Keokuk to Pella in wagons drawn by oxen. There were no railroads in Iowa when the Dutch arrived in 1847. Steamboats afforded passage up and down the rivers of the state, but cross-country travel was possible only by using wagons, stagecoaches, ponies, or by walking. The "Iron Horse" did not enter Iowa until 1855.

In 1853, a meeting was held in Davenport to discuss the possibility of building a railroad across the state. Representatives of the Chicago and Rock Island Railroad Company told the city fathers of Davenport that their line would soon be completed to the east bank of the Mississippi. Did the people of Iowa want a bridge to cross the river and bring the railroad into their state?

Antoine LeClaire, a leading citizen of Davenport, immediately said "Yes!" LeClaire had served as interpreter for General Winfield Scott at the time of the Black Hawk Purchase. In return for this service to both the government and the Indians, LeClaire had obtained the land on which the city of Davenport was built. As a result, he was now a man of considerable wealth and influence. Among other things, he operated a ferry between Rock Island and Davenport. Instead of opposing the bridge, which would certainly put his ferry out of business, he put his full weight behind the project. Since he weighed 300 pounds, this proved to be solid encouragement.

IRON TRACKS TO THE CAPITAL

LeClaire lost no time in organizing a company which would extend the railroad from the Iowa end of the bridge all the way across the state.

ANTOINE LE CLAIRE knew the Indian language, and frequently served as interpreter. This sketch was made from a contemporary portrait.

LE CLAIRE'S HOUSE in Davenport served as Iowa's first railroad station. This frame building located on Brady Street was a later home of Le Claire. It is no longer standing.

Agents were sent out to sell the idea of an iron highway from Davenport, through Iowa City, to Council Bluffs.

Many of the settlers had never seen a railroad. Moreover, they had no wish to see one. God had made the world without railroads, they said, and it was against the Lord's will to lay a path of iron across good farm country. God had made the world without wagons and stagecoaches, too, but the settlers didn't object to them. The wagons and stagecoaches were pulled by horses instead of smoke-snorting engines. Horses had been good enough in grandfather's time, and they were good enough today!

Of course, not all of the people of Iowa took this view. At a meeting of citizens in Council Bluffs, an agent for the railroad made an eloquent plea for local support. One of the settlers arose and faced his neighbors. "My friends," he said, "I believe we should give this project a fair trial. I still have doubts about it, but, one of these days, we will see the locomotive coming across the prairies with its head and tail up like a bedbug."

A small railroad company had been organized in Iowa City as early as 1850. It was interested only in laying a track from Davenport to the state capital. The line was surveyed, but before any grading was begun the original company sold its right-of-way to Antoine LeClaire's Mississippi and Missouri Railroad Company. The transfer of ownership was made in 1853, and the M and M promised to have the line from Davenport to Iowa City completed by January 1, 1856.

Work on the roadbed was started at once, and the track began inching its way toward the west. In the summer of 1855, the first locomotive was ferried across the Mississippi River. The wooden railroad bridge from Rock Island to Davenport was being built, but it was not yet ready for traffic. This first locomotive was named the *Antoine LeClaire* in honor of the largest stockholder in the company. The LeClaire house became the first depot.

Muscatine was closer to Davenport than Iowa City, so a branch line to the neighboring town was soon completed. The main track was another story. Sixty miles of prairie had to be graded, thousands of wooden ties had to be firmly grounded, and heavy iron rails had to be carefully gauged and spiked to the crossties.

The Irish workmen who had been brought into the state were strong and skillful, but time was running out. In order to finish the track to Iowa City by New Year's Day of 1856, volunteers from the capital joined the railroad crews so that work would continue around the clock.

The temperature dropped to twenty below zero, and huge bonfires were built along the right-of-way to keep the workmen warm and to furnish light during the hours of darkness. By pushing the job day and night, the last mile of track was finished on schedule. The first train made a triumphal entry. It was greeted by the booming of cannon, and a great feast was served in the stone capitol.

THE STEAMBOAT FIGHTS BACK

The bridge from Rock Island to Davenport was also completed in 1856. A locomotive pulling a string of empty cars crossed the bridge from the Illinois to the Iowa side on April 21. It was the first time the channel of the Mississippi had ever been spanned. But there were people who took a dim view of this achievement. Even though the bridge had a section which could be opened for river traffic, the steamboat men complained that it obstructed their use of the river.

Only fifteen days after the bridge was opened, the steamboat "Effie Afton" crashed against the draw-span pier. It burst into flames, and burned both the steamboat and the draw-span of the bridge. Some observers declared that the "Effie Afton" had run into the bridge on purpose, in order to burn the whole thing down. Of course, this could not be proved, and the owners of the steamboat promptly brought suit for damages against the bridge company.

A lawyer from Illinois was hired by the Chicago and Rock Island to defend the company in court. His name was Abraham Lincoln. Lincoln argued that the right to navigate a stream was no more fundamental than the right to cross it, but the first jury disagreed. The case was not settled until the Iowa supreme court ruled that a navigable stream may be spanned by a bridge if it does not materially obstruct navigation. To this day, however, boats have priority, and bridges are opened promptly at their approach. The historic wooden bridge between Rock Island and Davenport is long gone. A steel bridge replaced it in 1873. Only a part of one stone pier of the first bridge is still standing. It is preserved as a memorial on the Rock Island Arsenal grounds.

RAILROADS CROSS THE STATE

It was in 1856, shortly after the M and M railroad completed its line to Iowa City, that the Mormons made their historic Handcart Expedition. Even while the Mormon handcarts were pushed across Iowa, railroad construction was continuing.

Communities donated money, and townships and counties levied taxes and issued bonds to get the railroad companies to give them the benefit of their service. The General Assembly had asked Congress to make land grants for railroad construction, and the grants were made. The total amounted to more than four million acres.

But the Civil War stopped railroad expansion in Iowa when only five hundred miles of track had been laid. Four rival companies were trying to be first in crossing the state with their lines, but not one of them got the job done before the war began. The Chicago and Northwestern finally won the race to the Missouri River in 1867. Two years later, the Chicago and Rock Island also reached Council Bluffs. The Burlington lines were laid across the state in the same year, and, in 1870, the Illinois Central arrived in Sioux City. By that time, the four east-and-west trunk lines had three thousand miles of track in Iowa.

The man in Council Bluffs who had been willing to give the Iron Horse a fair trial had seen his prophecy come true. The locomotive now huffed and puffed its way across the prairie with its "head and tail up like a bedbug." Like the bedbug, it was not an unmixed blessing, but it was faster than any other form of transportation which · man had yet devised. The Iron Highway, stretching from coast to coast, had made the United States "one nation, indivisible."

★ ★

19. MILLS AND MACHINES

THE RAILROAD was a great help in moving raw materials from farm to factory and in delivering finished goods to the best markets. But the industrial growth of Iowa began with mills rather than railroads. The first mills were built long before the Iron Horse entered the state, and their wheels were turned by water power.

A sawmill was built on the Yellow River before the land west of the Mississippi was opened for settlement. Federal troops from Fort Crawford were ordered to build a dam across the river, and the mill was erected in the summer of 1831. Oak and pine trees grew in abundance in the Yellow River forest, and the big logs were sawed into beams and dimension lumber for use at the fort. The sawmill operations were under the immediate command of Lieutenant Jefferson Davis, who later became the president of the Confederate States of America. Travelers in northeast Iowa who look for the "Jeff Davis" mill today will not find it. Iowa's first sawmill burned to the water's edge after a brief but productive career.

THE GROWTH OF MILLS

As we noted earlier, the region west ᵒᶠ the Mississippi River was opened to white settlers on June 1, 1833. The pioneers needed mills for the sawing of logs and the grinding of grain. But needing a mill and having one were two different things.

First, it was necessary to build a dam which would assure a steady flow of water for the mill wheel. Then, the inside of the mill had to be equipped with sawing· or grinding machinery, as the case might be. The same water power was often used for

PINE CREEK MILL stands quietly in Wildcat Den State Park, Muscatine County. Restored by the State Conservation Commission, it was once a busy center of activity and typical of the many water-powered mills that dotted the river banks of Iowa in the 19th century.

both, in a combined sawmill and grist mill. But all of this took more time, skill, and money than the average settler could spare. Most of the pioneers hewed and shaped their logs with axes and most of the grinding of grain was done with hand mills–coffee mills or homemade crushers and grinders.

In time, however, men arrived who had confidence in their ability to build and operate mills at a profit, and their business talent enabled them to succeed. A man erected a grist mill at the mouth of Catfish Creek in Dubuque County in 1834. Settlers from as far as 100 miles away crossed the prairie and forded the streams in order to wait their turn at the mill and have their grain made into flour.

By 1838, when Iowa became a territory, other mills had been built, and it was obvious that some kind of legal controls had to be established. The first Territorial Assembly decided that a milldam could be built only if a franchise had been obtained. Among the franchises granted by this first assembly was one giving authority to Benjamin Nye to build a dam across Pine Creek in Muscatine County. The grist mill which made use of this dam is still standing. It was restored by the State Conservation Commission in 1932, and it is a popular tourist attraction in Wild Cat Den State Park.

Flour mills flourished in the middle decades of the nineteenth century, but grasshoppers and chinch bugs finally convinced the farmers that Iowa was not good wheat country, and corn became the main crop. The mills turned their attention to the manufacture of cornmeal instead of flour. As time went on, newer machinery was introduced and special cereals were processed. The Quaker Oats Company in Cedar Rapids became the largest milling industry of its kind in the world.

OTHER IOWA INDUSTRIES

But all of Iowa's early industry was not limited to mills. In 1848, two brothers from Germany put up a stone building in Henry County and established the Melcher Pottery. Since it was located on the Agency Road, which connected Burlington with the Indian Agency near Ottumwa, a great deal of traffic passed the pottery, and business was good. The Melcher brothers turned out thousands of milk pitchers and pickle jars, as well as jugs and churns. The community in which the Melchers operated their pottery was named Lowell, but outsiders called it "Jugtown." The fine deposits of clay at Lowell provided plenty of raw material, and, until glass containers became common, the handmade jugs and sauerkraut jars were widely used on the frontier. Jugs made at the old Melcher Pottery are now prized as collectors' items.

The Shot Tower

The city of Dubuque was the center of the lead industry for over a hundred years. The Old Shot Tower on the river front is an empty monument now, but it is still an impressive symbol of business enterprise in the mid-nineteenth century. It was built in 1856 to make shot from the lead mined in the Dubuque area. Molten lead was poured through a large colander on the top floor of the 150-foot tower. As the hot lead streamed through a tube extending to the bottom floor, it was broken into pellets by air resistance and surface tension. These pellets dropped into a tank of water at ground level, where they cooled and hardened into shot.

Rival interests in St. Louis bought the shot tower and stopped its operations. In return for the substantial price paid for it, they required the former owner to sign an agreement that he would not build another shot tower within a hundred miles of Dubuque. After the agreement was signed, the buyers from St. Louis returned to Missouri in the confident belief that there would be no more competition from Dubuque. But the former owner of the shot tower hadn't given up yet. He looked around until he found an old mine with a shaft 150 feet deep. He placed his big colander across the top of the mine shaft and his tank of water at the bottom, and went back to the business of making shot. The St. Louis people tried to stop him, but, since he had not built another tower, there was nothing they could do about it.

Feather Dusters

Iowa has become famous for its eminence in manufacturing oatmeal, fountain pens, buttons, washing machines, and other products. It also has the distinction of being the Feather Duster Capital of the world. The Hoag Duster Company of Monticello was founded on the idea that turkey feathers, if bound together and attached to a handle, would pick up dust. Although mechanical and electrical dust collectors have generally replaced the earlier model, more than a hundred thousand feather dusters are still turned out every year. The idea came to the inventor in 1870, and his heirs have been "cleaning up" ever since.

FOOT-POWERED LATHE built by John Boepple in 1891 was used to cut fresh-water pearl buttons. It is now on display in a Muscatine museum.

Fresh-Water Buttons

The history of the fresh-water pearl button industry began in Muscatine in 1890. In that year, a German farm laborer named John F. Boepple cut his foot on a clamshell while wading in the Mississippi. Boepple had made buttons from horn in Germany, but he believed that the clamshell would be better than horn, because it had both hardness and natural beauty. He gathered a few shells, rigged up a foot-power lathe in his home, and proceeded to cut a dozen buttons, all of which he sold to a Muscatine store for a total amount of ten cents. These buttons were the first fresh-water pearl buttons to be made in the United States.

Boepple was a poor business man and he never became rich. But there were others who did get rich on Boepple's idea, and, until the Keokuk Dam halted the free movement of clams

along the bed of the river, Muscatine opened the "pearly gates" to industrial fortune. The lathe on which Boepple cut his first buttons is now preserved in the Muscatine Public Library.

Washing Machines

The washing machine business put Newton on the map in 1898, when an incubator factory added a sideline of ratchet-slat washers. In 1904, Fred H. Bergman, the owner of the incubator firm, took out a patent on a machine which made it possible for the housewife to avoid the drudgery of bending over a washtub. His success in selling this first washing machine led to the formation of the One-Minute Manufacturing Company.

Fred L. Maytag, the "Washing

Machine King," also got into the business by the back door. He owned a quarter-interest in the Parsons Band Cutter and Self-Feeder Company, which employed an inventive genius named Howard Snyder. Maytag and Snyder decided that the sales of the band cutter and the self-feeding accessory for threshing machines were too seasonal so they would make washing machines to offset the loss of income during the rest of the year.

With Snyder as the inventor and Maytag as the promoter, the company turned out a new kind of hand-powered washer in 1907. An electric motor was added in 1911. These first washers worked on the principle of sloshing clothes through water by means of a wooden dolly located at the top of the tub. In 1922, Snyder reversed this idea and developed an aluminum agitator which worked on the bottom of the tub. This "gyrofoam" action revolutionized the washing machine industry. In fifty years, ten million washers had been sold by the Maytag Company alone.

Fountain Pens

The world's first lever self-filling fountain pen was invented in 1908 by Walter A. Sheaffer, a Fort Madison jeweler, who founded and gave his name to the W. A. Sheaffer Pen Company. The worldwide reputation of the Sheaffer pen, plus the fact that the factory is a neighbor of the Iowa State Penitentiary, has given Fort Madison the name of "The Pen City."

Lithograph City

But it would be a mistake to assume that all of the industrial enterprises of Iowa were successful. Some of them were launched with hope and confidence, but they sank without a trace. One of these failures was Lithograph City.

In 1910, a geologist discovered some unusual stone along the Cedar River in the northern part of Floyd County. Laboratory tests convinced him that it was the same kind of porous limestone which was believed to exist only in Bavaria. Lithography, the method of printing pictures from stone, had originated in Europe, but it had also been adopted in America to replace the cumbersome process of printing pictures from woodcuts or steel engravings. In 1914, the geologist decided to build a town where he could prepare and market the Iowa stone for lithograph work. World War I had begun in Europe, and Bavarian stone could not be imported at any price. By 1915, a thriving community had been built, fourteen miles northwest of Charles City, and the stone polishing plant was in full operation.

But a stroke of fate suddenly cut off the bright hopes of Lithograph City. Shortly after the town began to prosper, printers discovered that zinc and copper could be used for printing pictures by a process known as photoengraving. The demand for lithograph stone collapsed, and Lithograph City died completely. Its existence was so brief that it didn't even have time to establish a post office. There is only an empty field on the site of Lithograph City today. The town was literally plowed under.

Most of the industrial ideas which took root in the state were not blighted by such quick disaster. Although they did not all survive, a substantial number grew and flourished, and Iowa has many factory products which are as famous as its corn and hogs.

★ ★

20. PAVING THE WAY

IN THE previous chapters, we have followed the early citizens of Iowa along the roads to settlement and statehood. These "roads" were often rough and hard to travel, but rough roads were an old story in Iowa. The people of the state accepted primitive highways as a fact of life. Everything else moved along fairly fast, but road building proceeded only under pressure. The first mile of concrete highway was not laid until 1913, 67 years after the state was admitted to the Union.

THE EARLIEST ROADS

There were, of course, no highways of any kind when Iowa was young. The hunters and trappers who crossed the Mississippi to explore the western prairies followed Indian trails or the paths of wild animals.

When the Black Hawk Purchase was opened for settlement, the soldiers assigned to the frontier soon discovered that they could not move military supplies inland without some kind of a road. As long as the white population had remained along the river, the Mississippi had been used for transportation. But the tide of settlement was moving westward. In 1839, the Iowa Territorial Assembly decided to locate the seat of government at a new site in Johnson County.

Congress appropriated $20,000 to build a military road from Dubuque to Iowa City. This was to be no paved highway such as the one that connects the two cities today. It was to be nothing more than a cleared and graded dirt road, wide enough for horses and wagons to travel.

A man named Lyman Dillon hitched his oxen to a breaking plow and cut a furrow across the prairie all the way from Dubuque to Iowa City. He followed high ground as much as possible and avoided the low places, where sloughs and marshes might bog down the army wagons. This furrow served as the guideline for the road builders who followed.

If a plow could be used to mark a military road, a furrow could also be used to guide settlers who needed to go long distances for their supplies. In the early 1850's, it was not uncommon for travelers crossing the western prairies to lose their way. A man named Alexander McReady decided to do something about it. In 1856, he and his son set out from Sioux City with oxen and plow to mark the trail between Sioux City and Fort Dodge. Winding across the country to avoid hills and uneven places, McReady and his son kept going until they reached the county seat of Webster County. On the return trip, they plowed a parallel furrow, sixty to ninety feet from the first. Thereafter, travelers needed only to remain between the furrows in order to stay on the trail. In time, the dirt between the furrows was packed hard by wagon traffic, and the path marked by the McReadys came to be known as "The Great Road."

There were no bridges on the early roads. Streams could not always be avoided, and the people who marked the trails tried to find places where the water was shallow enough to be forded. If a river was too deep for fording, a boat was used to ferry wagons and passengers across the stream. The owner of the ferry was paid for this service, and, on a well traveled road, the operation of a ferry could be a profitable business.

But crossing a stream by ferry was a slow process, and wagon drivers had to wait their turns to be taken from one side of the stream to the other. Some ferry owners decided that they could collect more tolls per day if they built bridges to replace the cumbersome ferryboats. There would be no waiting; travelers could take themselves across the stream, and all the bridge owner had to do was sit in his tollhouse and collect the money.

Many of the covered bridges in Iowa were originally toll bridges. Putting a roof over the span almost doubled the cost of a bridge, but the builders figured that the wooden beams would last a long time if they were protected from the weather, and that the extra expense would be justified. They were right. Twelve of the old covered bridges are still standing in Iowa. There are seven in Madison County alone.

As bridges made travel more convenient, many of the early roads in Iowa were used as routes for stage lines. Ansel Briggs, the first governor of Iowa, was a stage driver in Jackson County. We shall note, also, that the state officers were given a free ride

COVERED BRIDGES may still be seen crossing some of Iowa's streams. This is the interior of one of seven still in use in Madison County. Note how the arches of the "burr truss" have been stiffened by timber bracing and how both have been protected by the siding and roof.

the fare was five cents a mile. In rainy seasons or during the winter when travel was more difficult, the fare went up to seven cents a mile.

The Plank Road

The first organized effort to get Iowa out of the mud was made by the Burlington and Mount Pleasant Plank Road Company. Timber was plentiful in the Hawkeye State, and, in 1851, more than five million feet of oak lumber were used to build a plank road, thirty miles long, between Burlington and Mount Pleasant. The road had a sixty-foot right-of-way and a thirty-foot grade. One side of the road was planked. The other side was dirt. Empty coaches or wagons had to yield to those which were loaded.

The plank section was laid on heavy stringers. Planks were three inches thick and eight feet long. Tollgates were set up every four miles. A four-horse coach was charged three cents a mile to use the road. A one-horse buggy or a two-horse wagon was charged two cents a mile.

The plank road was a resounding success for six years, but when train service began between Burlington and Mount Pleasant in 1857, the toll highway was doomed. The entire project was written off as a failure in 1858. Carpenters and farmers tore up the planks of the highway. Some of the lumber went into fences and farm buildings. Broken planks were sawed into short pieces for boardwalks in

in the coaches of the Western Stage Company when the seat of government was moved from Iowa City to Des Moines in 1857.

Before the coming of the railroad, the stagecoach was the bus of early Iowa. But it was not "such a comfort to take the bus" as it is today. Because of the condition of the roads, the average speed of a coach was no more than three to four miles per hour. When going up a hill, passengers often had to get out and walk in order to spare the horses. When the coach was hub-deep in mud, they helped to push it out. In dry weather, the towns along the road. Only the Jimtown Inn, a mile west of Danville, remained as a landmark of Iowa's first "paved" highway.

DIRT, DUST, AND GRAVEL

The railroad solved the transportation problem for long hauls between cities, but mud and dust continued to be the rule on town streets, just as they were on country roads. Many kinds of paving materials were tried. Blocks of swamp pine were brought in from the South. They were imbedded in sand and covered with tar, but the blocks rotted in the ground. Pavements made of soft brick were not much better. The bricks crumbled under heavy wagon traffic, and the red brick dust was as much of a nuisance as the yellow dust of raw clay.

Railroad tracks were laid in the streets, and cars were pulled by horses. Later, electric power was applied to these cars by means of an overhead wire with a trolley wheel to bring the current to the street-car motor. In Sioux City, one of the first lines to be electrified was an elevated railroad from the business district to Morningside, where a college was founded in 1894. The track on stilts lifted transportation above both the mud and the dust.

"Riding High" had been popular in America since the high-wheel bicycle had been displayed at the Centennial Exposition in Philadelphia in 1876. But there were few roads in Iowa on which it was safe to ride a high-wheeler. The invention of the "safety bicycle" in 1889 made travel on two wheels less dangerous. The rider then sat between two wheels of equal size, rather than at the top of a high wheel with a small trailer wheel behind him. If he got himself stuck in a rut, he didn't have as far to fall as he did from the earlier model.

At first, bicycles were given scant courtesies on the roads. The man with a horse and buggy or a team and wagon refused to turn out for the man on two wheels. To protect their rights, the bicyclers organized the League of American Wheelmen. In Iowa, the members of the league called on the General Assembly for help. The lawmakers paid no attention to their pleas, so the wheelmen built gravel and cinder paths along some of the main roads at their own expense.

Since the beginning of settlement in Iowa, the farmers had needed reliable roads more than anybody else. Grain had to be taken to the mill, supplies had to be brought to the farmstead from town, and farm produce had to be hauled to market. When prices were highest, the prairie trails might be closed by mud. The plank road from Burlington to Mount Pleasant had been so successful that farmers had hoped other plank roads would be built. But the coming of the railroad had put an end to all plans for any more plank roads. The farmers thought rail service was all right as far as it went, but it did not reach all the places they wanted to go.

In the eastern states, which many Iowa settlers had left in search of better farm land, the soil was thin, and rock was plentiful. This was not the case in Iowa. Limestone was quarried for building purposes, but most of the material for all-weather farm-to-market roads had to be dug out of the gravel beds of streams and lakes. Not all of the gravel was used to the best advantage, but roadbeds which were carefully graded in advance and graveled only after a good base had been prepared are still being used in many parts of the state.

CONCRETE HIGHWAYS

The first concrete highway in Iowa was only a mile in length. It was laid west of Mason City on a stretch of deep sandy road which had long been a bottleneck for farmers. By 1915, the concrete had been extended into Mason City. In 1918, the full distance of eleven miles between Mason City and Clear Lake had been paved, and the first interurban highway was completed. Dedication ceremonies were held, with speeches in Mason City and a grand finale in which decorated bicycles, buggies, wagons, and automobiles were strung out in a triumphal parade to Clear Lake.

At the half-way point, a mound of earth had been carefully piled on the highway. The parade came to a halt, and officials of the two towns joined forces in a "ground-removing" ceremony to show that the dirt road between Mason City and Clear Lake was a thing of the past. It would have been easier to stretch a ribbon across the highway and to have the mayors cut the ribbon in the time-honored manner, but shoveling the dirt off the concrete made much more sense as a dramatic symbol.

The automobiles in the parade were also symbolic. Although farmers had been in need of hard roads for a long time, it was not until city folks bought automobiles that the demands for better roads were finally heeded. The income from a state tax on gasoline and the sale of automobile licenses provided millions of dollars for road construction, and by gradual degrees, Iowa became a state in which highway travel was possible in wet as well as dry seasons.

21.

UTOPIAS IN IOWA

WHEN Dominie Scholte and his 800 followers from Holland put their money in a single iron-bound chest, they had no intention of sharing all they owned in common, thereafter. A careful accounting was made, just as though the money had been deposited in a bank. When the Hollanders arrived in Pella, they withdrew the gold they had put into the chest before they left the Old Country. Some took out more than others, but this was because they had *put in* more than the others in the first place.

Three groups of immigrants *did* come to Iowa with the intention of sharing all they owned in common. They came from different countries. One group came from Germany. Another came from Hungary. The third came from France. Community ownership was not inspired by the same reasons, but all three groups tried it. The first group proved that the idea was practical. The other two couldn't make it work.

THE INSPIRATIONISTS

The group from Germany was deeply religious. Away back in 1714, a Lutheran preacher named Eberhard Ludwig Gruber and a preacher's son named Johann Friedrich Rock had organized a new sect. They reasoned that since God had spoken to His prophets in Biblical times, His voice could still be heard by those who knew how to listen. The original Inspirationists were sure that God spoke

CHURCH at Homestead is typical of those built in the Amana colonies. There are two entrances: one for men, the other for the women. The meeting room is between the two entrances.

to them in dreams, and that His Divine Will was thus made known to His children. Gruber and Rock attracted a large following, but after they died the sect fell apart.

The idea of God speaking through prophets instead of ordained ministers came up again, a hundred years later. Christian Metz, a carpenter in the German province of Hesse, declared that he was a "Werkzeug," or prophet. A new congregation of Inspirationists accepted his leadership, and, as in the case of Dominie Scholte and his Hollanders, the rebels against the established church were persecuted by both the religious and political rulers of Germany. Barbara Yambura, in her book, *A Change and a Parting,* tells how, "in the midst of despair, the Lord revealed a plan [through Metz] for leading his people towards the West." According to the revelation, God promised to guide Christian Metz to land which was still open to him and to the people of his faith.

Metz and three other men immediately booked passage for America and were guided to the old Seneca Indian Reservation near Buffalo, New York. The year was 1842. Convinced that they had been led by the hand of God, they bought the five thousand-acre tract, and sent word to the Inspirationists that the Promised Land had been found. By 1843, 800 immigrants (the same number that had followed Dominie Scholte) had come from Germany to occupy the new land and to lay out five villages. The total community was organized as the Ebenezer Society.

In 1846, a constitution set up the principle that all property should be owned in common. It was based upon the words of the Apostle Paul in the Book of Acts, Chapter 2, verses 44 and 45: "And all that believed were together, and had all things common; and sold their possessions and goods and parted them to all men, as every man had need."

The people thought this was all right, back in St. Paul's time, but they didn't think much of it in 1846. The elders had difficulty enforcing the constitution until 1854. In that year, the Lord testified through Christian Metz that a curse would be put upon everybody who refused to take part in communal sharing. This did the job, and the communal system was adopted.

As Barbara Yambura has pointed out, the Inspirationist pattern of living was unlike Marxian Communism. It was controlled by religion. "The purpose of the communal system was to simplify the business of living so that members might have more free time for their larger calling of serving the Lord."

But the city of Buffalo was expanding closer to the Inspirationists in Ebenezer, and the temptations offered by their worldly neighbors were giving the elders a great deal of concern. A committee led by Christian Metz left Ebenezer to look for a more suitable location in the newly opened Territory of Kansas.

Nobody got excited about Kansas, but, in November of 1854, another committee went to the state of Iowa and found just what the Society wanted. Eighteen thousand acres of excellent farm and forest land were purchased along the Iowa River, and the move from New York to Iowa began.

The first village of the Iowa settlement was called "Amana," which means "Believe Faithfully." It was laid out in the summer of 1855. In the following ten years, the holdings in Ebenezer were sold at a profit, and all the members of the Society of True Inspiration were moved to Iowa. Five more villages were laid out. All of them were called Amana, but adjectives were added to keep them from being confused with the main village. Thus, the towns were named West Amana, South Amana, High Amana, East Amana, and Middle Amana.

A seventh village was acquired when the elders decided they needed a town on the railroad to move their products to market. Such a town had been built, south of the original Amana settlement, so it was bought outright by the Amana Society. The town had been given the name of Homestead by the railroad company. This is the reason why it is the only one of the seven villages in the colony which does not have the word Amana in it.

Communal Life in Amana

The broad freedom to live in isolation from the outside world enabled the members of the Amana Society to prove that communal ownership really worked. All meals were served in community kitchen houses, with as many as fifty people of the same neighborhood eating together. Families were assigned to individual houses which provided only bedrooms and a sitting room. The men and women worked at trades or crafts for which they were best qualified by temperament and training. Some used their skills to operate looms in the woolen mills; others worked the farm land, or built furniture, or baked bread, or prepared sausage.

Nobody worried about where the next meal was coming from, or what would happen in case of illness, or who would minister to the needs of old age, or how the expenses of a funeral would be paid. The Society took care of all its members in every emergency of life or death. And, at the center of all activity in each village, there was the church. As a rule, there were eleven services a week. Black clothing was worn to church by both men and women. The men sat on one side of the room, the women on the other, with the elders at the end of the room facing them. Thus, "all that believed were together, and had all things common"—their religion, in particular.

But strong influences outside the Amana colony finally forced a change in the pattern of community life. Visitors by the thousands were attracted to the quaint villages. The railroad, the automobile, the radio, and other modern conveniences excited the imagination of the younger members of the Society, and they became dissatisfied with the strict rules of community ownership.

The elders realized that they could not resist the pressures of the outside world forever, and a new Amana Society was formed. All members of the old Society were issued shares of stock in the common property, which they could sell or retain as they pleased. Spiritual and temporal affairs were separated. The Amana Church Society preserved the religious traditions of the founders. The new Amana Society became a modern business corporation operated for profit and authorized to pay salaries to its workers.

On June 1, 1932, the old order came to an end, and the new capitalist order had its beginning. The religious unity remained unchanged. It had protected the colony from disruption throughout the revolutionary changes that the twentieth century had forced upon it.

THE HUNGARIAN UTOPIA

Communal living was also tried by a group of Hungarian exiles led by Count Ladislaus Ujhazy. In 1850, the Count and his followers came to Iowa and rode over the prairies of Decatur County on their high-spirited

ICARIAN COLONY near Corning centered around this farmhouse which served as the community kitchen and dining center. The colony print shop was on the second floor.

horses in search of a place to establish New Buda. A site was found, and the Count built a log castle 50 feet long, with rooms in it reserved for the famous Hungarian patriot and statesman, Lajos Kossuth. Kossuth never came to Iowa, but his admirers were determined to have an American utopia ready for him in case he should ever come. They did everything but put their hands to the plow, and since plowing and manual labor were necessary to survival on the frontier, the whole project was foredoomed to failure. By 1875, the last remnant of New Buda collapsed, and its post office was transferred to Davis City. All that remains of the colony today is its name. It is still used by the township.

ICARIA

The third communal enterprise in Iowa was Icaria. It took its name from a book by Etienne Cabet called *Voyage en Icarie.* This was a story of a happy land where all property was held in common, and where each worked for all. France, the home country of Cabet, would not permit such a community to be established. Cabet therefore sent a group of men to the United States to set up an Icarian colony in the New World. The members of the party first tried to lay the foundations of Icaria in Texas, but many of the men died of fever. The rest became discouraged and went to New Orleans to await the coming of Cabet himself.

When the author of the book on Icaria arrived in 1848, he learned that the Mormons had been driven out of their homes in Nauvoo, Illinois, and he took his little company up the Mississippi and moved into the empty houses. The principle, "from each according to his ability, to each according to his need," gradually broke down as Etienne Cabet became a dictator. Cabet was finally expelled from the community.

In 1860, 235 Icarians left Nauvoo and settled on 3,000 acres of land which they had purchased in Adams County, Iowa, near Corning. Alexis Marchand was elected president of the new settlement. For a while, the dream of Icaria seemed to have come true, but disagreements arose and, in 1876, the property and funds were divided. One group of Icarians left the original settlement and established itself in another location nearby, which became known as New Icaria. In 1881, the old colony disbanded, and the members moved to California. By 1895, New Icaria was also dissolved.

At the present time, all that is left of Icaria is the cemetery, the schoolhouse, the community dining hall, the community cistern, and an old barn. The schoolhouse is closed, and the other buildings are now privately owned by local farmers.

Why did Icaria fail while Amana succeeded? Irving H. Hart has given the answer in his *Stories of Iowa.*

"Icaria was founded on a philosophy; Amana was founded on a faith. There was nothing in the philosophy of Icaria which would conquer the selfishness which is too often the controlling passion of the human heart. The religion of Amana did this to a degree almost unmatched in our day."

22. THE CAPITAL MOVES WEST

As EARLY AS 1846, when Iowa entered the Union, the General Assembly recognized the fact that the seat of government should be located near the center of the state. Iowa City was too far east to serve the total population, but a lot of money had been spent on the stone capitol, and it seemed a shame to leave it while it was still practically new.

The clamor for moving west became more insistent each time the legislature was in session. Clarence Ray Aurner, in his *Iowa Stories,* reports that "the people endeavored to make their wishes known through petitions—more than twenty having been presented during a single session. These did not all favor one locality. Fort Des Moines, Pella, Oskaloosa, and Red Rock were among the favored spots. Indeed, Oskaloosa was mentioned about as often as Fort Des Moines in those days, and, if the number of petitioners should be considered, the former city was far in the lead."

The fifth General Assembly took action on the matter in 1855 and decided that the capital should be moved to a place within two miles of the Raccoon Fork of the Des Moines River. Pella, Oskaloosa, and Red Rock were all more than two miles from the Raccoon Fork, so it was obvious that Fort Des Moines had been chosen.

A NEW CONSTITUTION

While it was in the moving business, the fifth General Assembly decided that the constitution of 1846 had some things in it which ought to be moved *out*—notably the law prohibiting banks in Iowa. The legislature could not take direct action on this, but it could call for a vote of the

people on the question of holding a constitutional convention, and it did.

The election was held, the voters approved the idea, delegates to the convention were chosen, and a new constitution was drafted early in 1857. It was ratified in a special election, and the revised constitution went into effect by proclamation of the governor on September 3, 1857. This constitution of 1857 has remained the fundamental law of the state of Iowa ever since.

DE MOYEN AND THE CAPITOL BUILDING

All of this took place before the government got itself seated on the Raccoon Fork. The fifth General Assembly had unquestionably chosen a place near the center of the state.

The interior region had been called "de moyen" by the early French fur traders, and the words meant "the middle." The name was first applied to the river which ran through the "middle valley." Lieutenant Zebulon Pike translated "riviere de moyen" to mean "The River of the Monks," but there is no record that any monks ever did any missionary work on it.

The first Fort Des Moines had been built by Stephen W. Kearny, and was located on the Mississippi River at the head of the Des Moines rapids. The *second* Fort Des Moines had been built at the Raccoon Fork of the Des Moines River in 1843. It had served as a dragoon post and as an agency for the Sauk and Fox Indians. The new capital of the state took its name from the second fort, but it went through several variations, such as "De Moyen," "De Moin," and even "Demon," before it settled upon the present spelling–Des Moines.

After the legislature had passed a law to locate the capital in Des Moines, the governor was authorized to name five commissioners to select the site of the statehouse. Not only the land for the necessary building, but also the building itself, had to be provided without expense to the state. Getting all of this for nothing was not as big a chore as it seemed to be. The cities interested in becoming the capital had offered many attractive inducements, including free sites and buildings, and Des Moines was no exception.

The commissioners selected a hill on the east side of the Des Moines River as the most suitable location. In later years, it was said that all but one of the commissioners owned land adjoining the new site and made a handsome profit on it because of the rise in property values. Whatever the reason for the choice may have been, it proved to be a *good* choice. The elevation gave the statehouse a commanding view of the city.

The first state capitol in Des Moines was not the building which is in use today. After the location had been decided, a three-story brick building, sixty by one hundred feet in size, was erected at the place where the Soldiers and Sailors Monument now stands.

At the time it was built in 1857, the new capitol stood in the midst of heavy woods, with squirrels, wild turkey, and deer darting in and out of the thickets. Henry Sabin described the site, in his *Making of Iowa,* as having "no sidewalks near the capitol. Hazel brush was dense. Not far off was a pond containing muskrats. The only bridge across the river was a pontoon structure. The East Side, the side on which the capitol was located, had about thirty houses. Muddy lowland stretched between the capitol and the river."

All of this didn't look very promising, but Des Moines' was still a frontier community at that time, and Governor James W. Grimes had faith in its future. He issued a proclamation approving the state house for the use of the legislature and the state officers. Then the fun began!

Moving to Des Moines

The railroad extended no further west than Iowa City, and moving the state offices with all their furniture turned out to be a tremendous job. The road to Des Moines was not the interstate highway that it is today. There was a prairie road which was used by the coaches of the Western Stage Company, but it wound its crooked way for a distance of one hundred and twenty miles between Iowa City and Des Moines. It crossed streams which had no bridges and swamps which would not support heavy wagons unless the ground was frozen.

In November of 1857, the state officers were given a free ride to Des Moines by the Western Stage Company. Since the ground was hard with frost, the trip was made in only two days. Moving the office furniture was another story, and four massive safes created special problems for the teamsters.

The ground was frozen, but a heavy snowstorm overtook the ponderous wagons, and the biggest safe of all—the one belonging to the office of the state treasurer—was bogged down by snow drifts on the open prairie. It was only after farmers along the way rigged up a special sled and hitched it to ten yoke of oxen that the safe was finally delivered to the new capitol. The state officers were glad to see it

arrive, because it contained the gold to pay their salaries. (For a while, it had looked as though they might have only "frozen assets" on payday.)

The members of the official family settled in their new quarters, and the final act of putting the state government into operation took place on January 11, 1858, when the legislature held its first session in Des Moines.

The law for the removal of the capital had said that buildings for the use of the state should be provided without public expense. However, as Clarence Ray Aurner pointed out, "After years of discussion and petition from those who had put themselves in debt for this purpose, the State of Iowa repaid the amount. The State did what it should have done at first: namely, built its own buildings and thereby kept itself from obligations to individuals who had to borrow from public funds."

A PERMANENT CAPITOL

As the population of Iowa increased, it became obvious that a larger building would be needed to accommodate the expanding activities of state government. The construction of a permanent state capitol was authorized by the twelfth General Assembly in 1868. Even though the legislature wanted a large and impressive building, it appropriated only one and one-half million dollars to get the job done.

The architect was a Frenchman

named A. Piquenard, who had come to the United States with the Icarians in 1848. He was also the architect of the Illinois state capitol in Springfield. Piquenard did the best he could within the financial limits which had been set by the legislature, and construction was begun in 1871.

Governor Samuel Merrill laid the cornerstone on November 23, 1871, but the foundation walls crumbled during the hard winter which followed. The stone was removed, and the whole job was started again—this time, with better materials. The cornerstone, cut from a granite boulder obtained in Buchanan County, had been dated 1871, and the names of the capitol commissioners and the architect had been inscribed on it.

The next General Assembly directed that all of the inscriptions should be removed, and that only the word "Iowa" should appear on the stone. A stonecutter named J. G. Waers was hired to remove the original carvings and to alter the date to A.D. 1873, the year the new foundation was completed. The legislature had directed that only one word should be inscribed on the stone, but Waers was so proud of his handiwork that he cut his own name into the letters of "Iowa." It is still there, if you look closely.

Appropriations of additional funds were made by twelve separate General Assemblies. When the building was finally completed in 1884,

more than three million dollars had been spent on it. But the capitol building commissioners looked with satisfaction upon the giant they had created. It was 360 feet long and 245 feet wide. The height to the top of the finial on the dome was 275 feet. Twenty-nine different kinds of imported and domestic marble were used in the interior, plus many varieties of Iowa wood, such as walnut, cherry, catalpa, butternut, and oak.

The Most Elegant of Its Time

Although the building was Romanesque in architectural style, it was a symbol of American prosperity and progress. An architect who attended the dedication ceremony described it as "a beautiful contribution to the world of art," and the speaker of the day declared that it was "a splendid edifice" which represented the most elegant tastes of its time.

This is the point that must be brought to the attention of detractors who call it "the ugliest state capitol in the United States." Obviously, the Iowa state house does not resemble the streamlined skyscrapers which have been built in more recent years, because architectural design in the days of its construction favored the classic style. We must judge the building in terms of the traditions which were accepted at the time it was built.

The scorn that has been heaped upon it dates back to an incident which occurred when a young man had his picture taken while *standing on his head* in front of the capitol. He had been photographed in this position during a visit to each of the state capitols in the United States. Before he left Des Moines, he told a reporter that he thought the Iowa capitol was the ugliest of all he had seen. This flippant remark was printed in a national magazine, and the label stuck. Nobody ever bothered to ask why the opinion of a head-standing vagabond should be accepted as artistic authority. The statement had appeared in print, and it was accepted as the gospel truth.

If Iowa should decide to build a new capitol today, it would undoubtedly be built in the architectural style of the present. But as long as our 1884 structure continues to be in use, it should be regarded as a segment of Iowa history—a relic of our romantic past, when the new state was flexing its muscles and standing up to be counted.

23. THE INDIANS RETURN

WE HAVE SEEN that the removal of the Indians from Iowa began with the Black Hawk Purchase. The Sauks and Foxes gave up a strip of land about fifty miles wide, which extended from the Neutral Ground on the north to the state of Missouri on the south. This land was "purchased" by paying the Indians a token sum in annual installments called "annuities." The Indians were moved farther west as each "purchase" was made, and they collected their annuities at the agencies which the government set up for their "protection."

One of the best known of these Indian agencies was the one established by General Joseph M. Street. Street was assigned to the Sauk and Fox tribes in 1838. After consulting with chiefs Poweshiek and Wapello, he decided to locate the agency near the Des Moines River, about six miles southeast of the present city of Ottumwa. He built a large council house, a two-story home for his family, and several smaller buildings, including a mill in which the Indians were encouraged to grind their corn.

The Indians liked General Street because he always treated them fairly, but they had little interest in the white man's way of life, and the mill stood idle most of the time. There was only one thing made of corn which the Indians really wanted, and that was whiskey.

General Street knew that whiskey was the Indians' worst enemy and he banned whiskey peddlers from the agency grounds. But the Indians knew where the peddlers could be found, and, when the agent paid them their annuity, they quickly exchanged it for firewater.

General Street was not the only white man who tried to stop the whiskey traffic. Father Pierre-Jean DeSmet had come from Belgium to save the souls of his red brothers in America. He noted in his journal that he had seen fifty large barrels, "each containing 30 gallons of whiskey, rolled out of a Missouri River steamboat. When night came, the whiskey was in the stomachs of the Indians, and the annuities were in the pockets of the traders."

Territorial Governor John Chambers, in his message of 1845, said that, among the Indians, "the chase is almost abandoned, and the council fires, if kindled at all, seem only intended to light up the wretched scene of their drunkenness and debauchery."

The whiskey peddlers relentlessly followed the Indians across Iowa into Kansas, where most of the survivors of a once proud race died in despair and degradation.

THE MESQUAKIE LEAVE KANSAS

But there were some who saved the money paid them by the government. The Fox Indians in particular still felt some pride in their historic past. They even reclaimed their old name of "Mesquakie." The bare, flat land of the reservation in Kansas was alien to them. They remembered the grassy prairies and tree-bordered streams of Iowa, and a group of the Mesquakie decided to go back to their old hunting grounds along the Iowa River.

No white settlers were occupying the river land in Tama County, and, in 1856, the Iowa General Assembly passed a law permitting the Mesquakie to stay. It also urged the Indian Office in Washington to continue payment of their annuities. When the federal government refused to do this, the Mesquakie pooled the money they had saved and bought eighty acres of land at $12.50 per acre. The price had gone up since the government had "purchased" it from them at *ten cents* an acre.

The Mesquakie wanted the land to belong to the tribe, rather than to its individual members. This put the

FRAMEWORK of a wickiup on the powwow grounds of the Mesquakie Indian settlement near Tama. At powwow time in August, the frame is covered and the Indians live in the wickiup just as their ancestors did.

The word "reservation" should be used only when Indian land is set apart from the public domain by the government. The land in Tama County was *bought* by the Indians from private owners. It was, in no sense, given to them by the government. They had to buy it with their own savings, and it is therefore private property.

The Mesquakie are proud of their tribal antecedents, and they welcome the public to the annual Pow Wow in which they display their ancient ceremonies. At other times of the year, however, they wish to live in privacy. Since they do not occupy the public domain, they are fully entitled to this right.

THE SIOUX RETURN TO IOWA

The homesick Mesquakie were treated kindly by their white neighbors when they returned to Iowa. The Sioux were not so fortunate. They had been the last of all the Iowa Indians to sell their lands, but, in 1851, they, too, moved out of the state. Hunting parties wandered back from time to time, and, as long as they didn't molest the settlers, they were allowed to come and go in peace.

A whiskey peddler named Henry Lott took advantage of the Sioux by selling them cheap whiskey by day and stealing their ponies by night. A chief named Sidominadota trailed some of these stolen ponies to the Lott cabin on the Des Moines River. When

state of Iowa in a dilemma, but as Ruth A. Gallaher has reported in *The Palimpsest* for February of 1926, Governor James W. Grimes consented to act as trustee, and, on July 13, 1857, five Indians, on behalf of those then in Iowa, secured their first eighty acres. The deed was made out to James W. Grimes, Governor of the state of Iowa, and his successors in office, in trust, for the five Indians and their heirs.

Other purchases of land were made after 1857, and the Mesquakie now own over three thousand acres along the Iowa River in Tama County. The settlement is commonly called the "Tama Indian Reservation." It is not a reservation at all.

Lott saw the chief and his braves approaching, he slipped out of the back door and left his wife and son to take care of themselves.

While Sidominadota was beating Mrs. Lott because she wouldn't tell him where her husband was hiding, the son, Milton, escaped and started running toward Boone for help. It was a freezing winter night, and, after stumbling through the snow for several miles, Milton crawled into a hollow log to warm himself. Drowsiness overtook him. He fell asleep, and never awoke.

Meanwhile, Sidominadota had reclaimed his stolen ponies and returned to his camp. Mrs. Lott died of the beating she had received. Lott came out of hiding and went back to the business of selling whiskey. He did not blame himself for what had happened to his wife and son. Instead, he put the full blame on the Indians.

In 1853, his path crossed that of Sidominadota, again. The old chief was nearly blind by this time, and he didn't recognize Lott. The whiskey peddler invited him to go on an elk hunt, and, while they were alone on the prairie, Lott shot the chief in the back. Then, he disguised himself as an Indian, entered Sidominadota's lodge at night, and stabbed everybody in it—except two children who escaped the slaughter and reported the crime to Inkpaduta, the brother of Sidominadota.

Inkpaduta vowed to avenge the murders, and, in the spring of 1857,

he got his chance. He didn't have the satisfaction of killing Henry Lott, because Lott was an expert at running away from trouble, and this time he didn't stop until he got to California. Here, however, his luck ran out. Frontier justice finally caught up with him and he was hanged by vigilantes.

Inkpaduta was no monument of virtue either. He had been banished by the Sioux nation because he had killed his own father. There was no love lost between him and his brother, but the fact that Sidominadota had been shot down by a white man gave him an excuse to plunder the possessions of any white settler he could find.

The winter of 1856–57 had been severe in northwest Iowa. Inkpaduta and his fifteen Sioux outlaws had wandered from one settlement to another, begging for food. Wild game had been scarce. As long as the Indians were outnumbered by the settlers, they were polite and proper, but if they happened upon a lone cabin on the prairie, they took what they wanted. A single settler and his family could do nothing to resist a band of bullies, and, as Inkpaduta and his ruffians plodded through the snow toward Spirit Lake and East and West Okoboji, they became bolder and more brutal.

The lake region in Dickinson County was known as "Spirit Lake" from the Indian word "Minnie Waukon" which meant "Spirit Water." It has been said that Inkpaduta and his scavengers were particularly resentful toward the settlers who had built their cabins near the lakes, because the Sioux believed the Spirit Lake country to be sacred ground. It is hard to believe that Inkpaduta considered anything to be sacred. Most likely he was drawn toward the region because the cabins were widely separated, and he could therefore attack each family without danger of interference by neighbors.

THE SPIRIT LAKE MASSACRE

The Spirit Lake Massacre began on March 8, 1857. Inkpaduta went to the Gardner cabin, first. The family was at breakfast and, since the Gardners thought the Indians were merely in need of food, they freely shared their meager store of provisions. Rowland Gardner and his son-in-law, Harvey Luce, were alert to possible danger, however, and the efforts of the Indians to take all of the Gardner ammunition were stoutly resisted. Inkpaduta and his surly crowd were afraid to make an issue of it as long as there were two men in the house, and they left as suddenly as they had arrived. As soon as they were gone, Luce took a roundabout way to warn the neighbors.

Soon after, the Gardners heard shooting in the woods. It was Sunday, and they knew that none of their neighbors would be hunting on the Sabbath. Fearful that Harvey Luce had been killed, the door of the cabin

GARDNER CABIN at West Okoboji was the only dwelling to survive the Spirit Lake Massacre. A canopy has been built over the original log structure. This protects the old building, but the resulting higher roofline and surrounding "porch" effect have altered its appearance.

was barred, and Rowland Gardner vowed that he would defend his family with the two loaded guns still remaining in the house. When the Indians returned later in the day, demanding more food, Mrs. Gardner urged her husband to let them come in. She still believed that kindness would soften the mood of the savages. This was a mistake.

There was only one white man left in the cabin, now, and, as soon as Rowland Gardner turned to get some provisions for his unwelcome guests, the Indians shot him in the back. The women and younger children were beaten to death in order to save ammunition, and only fourteen-year-old Abigail was spared. She was dragged off as a captive. During the next few days, she watched in horror as every family in the lake region was wiped out.

Thirty men, women, and children were killed before the blood lust of Inkpaduta was satisfied. Abbie Gardner and three older women were forced to accompany the murderers. Mrs. Thatcher and Mrs. Noble died of brutal treatment along the way. Mrs. Marble and Abbie Gardner were released in early summer after ransoms had been paid by friendly Indians who returned them to the world of white men.

News of the massacre traveled slowly, but when the report of the tragedy reached Fort Dodge, a relief expedition was organized by Major Walter Williams. A hundred men started north on March 24. The snow drifts were deep, and they did not reach Spirit Lake until April 2, almost a month after the massacre. By this time, Inkpaduta was long gone.

On his way to the Dakotas, he had plundered the town of Springfield, Minnesota. Troops from Fort Ridgely arrived in Springfield the next day, but the commanding officer refused to give chase because he had no orders to do so. As a result, Inkpaduta got away and he was never punished.

The relief expedition from Fort Dodge arrived too late to overtake the assassins. There was nothing to do after the long march except to bury the dead.

In later years, Abigail Gardner married Cassville Sharp and returned to the lake country to make her home in the Gardner cabin. Her *History of the Spirit Lake Massacre* has been the principal source of information on this dark episode in Iowa history. The Gardner cabin is still standing on the shore of West Okoboji. Near it are the graves of the Gardner and Luce families, the tall Spirit Lake Monument, and a museum which tells the story of treachery and death on the frontier.

★ ★

24. THE UNDERGROUND RAILROAD

WHEN Iowa entered the Union in 1846, there was no question about where it stood on the slavery issue. It was admitted as a free state. In 1820, the Missouri Compromise had permitted Missouri to enter the Union as a slave state with the understanding that, thereafter, the southern boundary of Missouri—thirty-six degrees and thirty minutes north latitude—would be the dividing line between free and slave states west of the Mississippi. Iowa was far north of this line, and it was therefore a free state from the beginning. But Iowa would feel the effects of the struggle between the free and slave states long before the Civil War began. The Underground Railroad would cross the southern half of the state well in advance of the Iron Highway.

OSAWATOMIE BROWN

In 1854, Congress passed the Kansas-Nebraska Act which established the territories of Kansas and Nebraska. If the Missouri Compromise had been allowed to stand, there would have been no question about slavery in the new territories. However, the Act of 1854 had repealed the Missouri Compromise and established the principle of "popular sovereignty." This gave the settlers in new territories an opportunity to decide for themselves whether they wanted to enter the Union as free or slaveholding states. Congress had issued an open invitation to trouble, and it was promptly accepted.

Nobody worried much about Nebraska, because it was clearly in the

JOHN BROWN looked like this shortly before he was hanged for treason and murder. Brown did some of his recruiting for his Virginia raid in Springdale.

northern belt, but Missouri was determined to make its western neighbor a slave state. Hundreds of Missourians moved into the Kansas Territory to give it a southern majority. Immigrants from the northern states were equally determined to make Kansas a free state. The opposing factions were soon engaged in a "knock-down-and-drag-out" fight, and the Territory became known as "Bleeding Kansas." Nobody was more helpful in giving Kansas this reputation than "Osawatomie Brown," who didn't even live there.

John Brown was an ardent abolitionist whose home was in New York state. He had come to Kansas in 1855 to visit his five sons, who had settled

in Osawatomie. This little town was only eighteen miles from the Missouri border, and it was a constant target for border ruffians. After one of his boys had been killed and two others had been dragged through the streets in chains, John Brown got into the killing business too. A price was set on his head, and "Old Osawatomie" went into hiding in Tabor, a small community in southwestern Iowa. Here he found refuge in the home of the Congregational minister.

The Congregational Conductor

The Reverend John Todd was a "conductor" on the Underground Railroad. There was, of course, no actual railroad anywhere near Tabor, and no subterranean passage for a line of tracks. The Underground Railroad was a secret overland route along which runaway slaves could find their way to freedom. It took its name from a statement made by a southern slaveowner: "Negroes escape to Canada as easily as if they traveled on a railway which runs beneath the ground." Tabor was not far from the Missouri border, and it was often the first stop for slaves who had escaped from their owners in Missouri.

Helping slaves to escape was a violation of the law. The Fugitive Slave Act of 1850 made it a crime to aid the runaways, but, as Curt Harnack pointed out in *The Iowan* for July, 1956, "the friends of the slaves were often highly religious and felt it their moral duty to befriend the Negroes. . . . They looked to the Mosaic Law to justify their activities: 'Thou shalt not deliver unto his master the servant which is escaped from his master unto thee!' "

The Reverend Mr. Todd took tremendous risks by concealing runaway slaves in his home and helping them to the next "station" on the Underground Railroad. It is not surprising that the minister was also willing to help John Brown in spite of the danger in this association. Indeed, he was so dedicated to the abolition movement that he kept two hundred rifles hidden in his barn for an entire winter. They had been sent to Tabor by a committee in Massachusetts which wanted to assist in the cause of freedom. The rifles were to be used by "Free Soil" settlers in defending themselves and their property after they crossed into Kansas.

Another Use for the Tabor Rifles

But John Brown had another idea for the use of these rifles. He obtained written permission from the Massachusetts committee to take charge of the store of arms in Tabor. In August of 1857, he handed this order to the Reverend Mr. Todd. Then, he sent word to a group of his trusted followers in Kansas, requesting them to join him in Tabor. There was a great deal of drilling in the town park, and, in November of 1857, the John Brown party loaded the rifles into

wagons and drove out of town. The Reverend Mr. Todd thought the Free Soilers were going to Kansas. Instead they headed northeast, and, late in December, they arrived in the Quaker settlement of Springdale in Cedar County, Iowa. Springdale was a station on the Underground Railroad, and they were sure they would find friends there.

Brown had decided to spark an insurrection of the slaves throughout the southern states. This would force the slavery people to attend to their own affairs and leave Kansas alone. On the long trip from Tabor to Springdale, he had discussed an invasion of Virginia. He felt sure that,

THE TODD PARSONAGE in Tabor served as a station on the Underground Railroad. The two small windows under the eaves enabled runaway slaves hidden in the attic to watch for pursuers.

if an uprising of the slaves could be started in this hotbed of the slave traffic, a chain reaction would sweep the entire South.

It has often been said that John Brown was insane. If he was, it didn't bother the people who gathered around him. The Quakers in Springdale had been active in the Underground Railroad for a long time. When John Brown promised that he would soon free *all* the slaves, he sounded like a prophet. Besides, he looked like one. His long beard and piercing eyes gave him the appearance of having stepped right out of the Old Testament.

Brown and his party stayed in Springdale until the Spring of 1858. Plans were made in the utmost secrecy. Only a few of the people in the Quaker village–among them, brothers Edwin and Barclay Coppoc–knew what Brown had in mind. When the guests left Springdale, the Coppoc boys were told that they would be notified when and where to report for duty. The rest of the Quakers thought John Brown and his followers were going back to Kansas.

But Brown was not yet ready for the invasion of Virginia. To get some practice, he led his little company on a raid into Missouri, where he rescued eleven slaves and killed a slaveowner. The whole country became aroused about the boldness of John Brown. A large reward was offered by the state of Missouri for his capture, "dead or alive."

Harpers Ferry

By using the Underground Railroad, Brown stayed ahead of the United States marshal, who was hot on his trail. He stopped briefly in Tabor, in Lewis, in Grinnell, and in Springdale. Then, for a while, no one in Iowa knew where he was. In July of 1859, Edwin and Barclay Coppoc received word from Brown that he wanted them to join him in Ohio. Despite the forebodings of their widowed mother, the boys left at once.

October brought the news that "a crazy old man" with twenty followers had captured the arsenal at Harpers Ferry. The "crazy old man" was John Brown. He had hoped that this daring deed would cause the slaves of Virginia to throw off their chains and rush to the arsenal, where he could provide them with plenty of guns to blast their way to freedom. Not one slave showed up. But the United States Marines did. They quickly regained possession of the arsenal and took Brown and his followers to jail. The prisoners were put on trial for treason, and all were convicted. Barclay Coppoc escaped, but his brother Edwin was hanged. So was John Brown. The abolitionists were so impressed by the dramatic death of the old warrior that they made up a song about him:

"John Brown's body lies a-mouldering in the grave,
But his soul goes marching on."

THE LEWELLING HOUSE in Salem had hiding places for fugitive slaves in the basement and in a pit under the kitchen floor. The handsome old stone building is now a Quaker shrine.

WORKING ON THE RAILROAD

Meanwhile, the Congregationalists and Quakers in Iowa continued to operate the Underground Railroad. Mention has been made of the Reverend John Todd in Tabor. Another Congregational minister, the Reverend George B. Hitchcock, built a parsonage in Lewis which became known as "The Old Slave House." The Reverend Josiah B. Grinnell, who lived in the town named in his honor, was an active abolitionist. And the founder of "The Iowa Band," the Reverend Asa Turner, was so energetic in helping runaway slaves that he was accused of "Negro stealing" by the *Fort Madison Plain Dealer*.

The activity of the Underground Railroad could not be carried on without taking elaborate precautions. Even though Iowa was a free state, most of the people living in it regarded the abolitionists as troublemakers who were interfering with something that was none of their business.

Small out-of-the-way towns were safest as stations on the Underground Railroad, and little-traveled roads were used for moving the fugitives from one station to another. Even so, the conductors hid the slaves under layers of straw in their wagons, or disguised them as sacks of potatoes or barrels of apples.

A small Quaker town in Henry County had been laid out soon after eastern Iowa was opened for white settlement. Quaker families from towns called Salem in New Jersey, Ohio, and Indiana moved west and established their homes in the new community. To the surprise of no one, the town was named Salem.

Like the Friends in Springdale, the Quakers of Salem were dependable allies of runaway slaves. The Lewelling House, which is still standing, has a hidden trapdoor in the kitchen through which a slave could enter a pit below the floor. Runaways often had to remain in cramped quarters like that for days, until they could be safely moved to another station. The moving was usually done at night or during a storm, when neighbors and bounty hunters were not likely to be watching. The danger of discovery could never be overlooked. Even in towns where the abolitionists were in the majority, there was always someone eager to collect a reward, and the penalties for breaking a federal law were severe.

But the risks of fines and imprisonment were taken with as much composure as the threats of personal violence. A slaveowner once brought a cannon from Missouri and gave the Lewellings a choice of returning his slaves or having their house blown off its foundations. There was no surrender. After storming around town for a while and making no impression on the Quakers, the slaveowner packed up his cannon and went home without firing a shot.

Cannonballs would not fall on Iowa soil until the Civil War began. But that is another story, which will be told in our next chapter.

★ ★

25. WAR BETWEEN THE STATES

MONUMENT in Croton commemorates the Battle of Athens, fought on the Missouri side of the Des Moines River. Cannonballs aimed too high crossed the river and landed in Croton.

ONE YEAR after John Brown was hanged for his raid on Harpers Ferry, Abraham Lincoln was elected President of the United States. The South was so angry about the election of Lincoln that it decided to withdraw from the Union and set up a government of its own. The War Between the States, or Civil War, began when southern troops attacked Fort Sumter off the coast of South Carolina, and captured it.

The dispute between the North and the South had been given an entirely new dimension. Only a minority of the people in Iowa had been opposed to slavery. Many of the settlers in Iowa had come from states where it was common to own slaves. As long as they didn't have to live with the institution of slavery themselves, they had no more objection to it than they had to the eating of hominy grits, or to any other custom peculiar to the South. But splitting up the United States was another story. The majority of the people in Iowa agreed with President Lincoln that the southern states had no right to secede. Having different customs was one thing. Breaking up the Union was something else. It was the general opinion in Iowa that the hotheads who were trying to set up the Confederate States of America had to be stopped.

THE CALL FOR VOLUNTEERS

On April 16, 1861, four days after the first shot had been fired at

Fort Sumter, Governor Samuel J. Kirkwood received a message from the War Department. It called for one regiment of militia for immediate service. The governor was stunned. He doubted that he could raise one thousand men for a regiment, but he hopefully issued a call for volunteers. To his great surprise, he got enough men for *ten* regiments.

Kirkwood was proud of the patriotism of his state, but he was also at a loss about what he could do with ten thousand volunteers. His Iowa soldiers were willing to fight, but he had no guns, no ammunition, no uniforms, and no supplies for them. "Send us arms," he wrote to the Secretary of War on April 29. "I ask for nothing but arms and ammunition. We have the men to use them."

On May 6, 1861, the First Regiment of Iowa Infantry was ordered into camp at Keokuk. The government thought this one regiment was enough, but Governor Kirkwood was so besieged by impatient volunteers that he mobilized another thousand men. This was the Second Iowa Regiment. The First Iowa was sent down the river to St. Louis, but the volunteers of the Second Iowa were arriving in Keokuk, and still no arms were being received.

The Battle of Athens

Finally, the governor got some action from the War Department. On August 1, 35 tons of supplies, including rifles and ammunition, arrived in

Keokuk. The news of this shipment traveled fast, and it came to the ears of an unorganized group of Missouri rebels. These guerrillas were led by an officer named Martin Green.

Green decided that he would attack the town of Athens, where Colonel David Moore had set up a Union recruiting base. Athens was on the Missouri side of the Des Moines River. Directly opposite Athens, on the Iowa side of the river, was the little railroad town of Croton. Green planned to capture Athens, cross the Des Moines River to Croton, and take the railroad from there to Keokuk, where he would confiscate the entire shipment of arms. It didn't work out that way.

Rumors of the rebel plan spread quickly. A company of volunteers named the Keokuk Rifles learned about the impending attack. The men of this local militia took the train to Croton, waded across the Des Moines River, and joined Colonel Moore's recruits. On the morning of August 5, the rebels arrived on the outskirts of Athens, planted two cannons on the bluffs behind the town and began blazing away. The cannons were aimed too high and the cannonballs flew all the way across the river and landed in Croton. Fortunately, no spectators on the Iowa side were hit, but there was a lot of excitement until the rebel artillery shortened its range.

Even then, the cannonading didn't amount to much. Colonel Moore charged the invading force, and the rebels were soon in full retreat. They left Athens in such a hurry that they even forgot their cannons! The threat of invasion had been stopped at the Des Moines River. For the first and only time, Civil War cannonballs fell on Iowa soil, but no Confederate soldiers followed them.

Colonel Grenville M. Dodge was ordered by Governor Kirkwood to organize a regiment of infantry to protect the southern counties of Iowa, but the guerrilla bands in northern Missouri had learned their lesson. There were no more border incidents in that part of the state. Grenville Dodge moved from "Camp Disappointment," where he could find no rebels to fight, to outstanding service with General Sherman in his Georgia campaign. Dodge was retired as a Major-General.

BORDER DEFENSE ON THE NORTH

Northern Iowa was never threatened by Confederate invasion, but it had a serious Indian scare during the Civil War. Soldiers had been withdrawn from some of the forts in Sioux country, because they were needed to suppress the rebellion in the South. Taking advantage of the absence of troops, the Sioux, under the leadership of Little Crow, went on the warpath. The worst Indian massacre in American history occurred in southwestern Minnesota during August of

1862. Four hundred and fifty men, women and children were murdered in New Ulm and other settlements near the Iowa border.

Panic struck the settlers of northwest Iowa, and Governor Kirkwood rushed mounted soldiers to their defense. A chain of forts was quickly built along the northwestern fringe of the state. Of these frontier bastions, Fort Defiance at Estherville was the largest. The stockade was made of planks four inches thick, and it enclosed an area large enough to protect all the people in the settlement in case of danger. The Indians never attacked it.

There was a relentless pursuit of Little Crow and his band of savages, and when they were captured, a mass hanging ended the Indian scare in Minnesota and Iowa. The companies of the Northern Border Brigade were gradually assigned to areas of military activity further south.

THE GRAYBEARD REGIMENT

The war was going badly for the Union in the autumn of 1862. The people of the North had thought they could easily put down the rebellion in a few months, but the South had been winning nearly all the battles. President Lincoln needed more men to strengthen the Union Army. Somebody thought it would be a good idea to form a regiment of men too old for regular enlistment. These men could go on duty behind the lines and release younger men for fighting.

In *The Iowan* magazine for August, 1960, Bob Beasley wrote: "Where could the Union find a whole regiment of old-timers both willing and able to serve? . . . Where were the old men both eager and vigorous enough? The answer was obvious: In Iowa, where many a man beyond the army's 45-year-old age limit had tried to enlist and where there was still enough semi-frontier to keep men rugged and resourceful.

"Secretary of War Stanton gave his approval to the project. And George Kincaid of Muscatine was commissioned a colonel and directed to organize an over-age regiment. . . . By October, the regiment's rolls were filled. . . . On December 15, the 37th Iowa Infantry Regiment was mustered into the Union Army at Camp Strong in Muscatine."

The average age of the men in the so-called "Graybeard Regiment" was 57. More than a hundred of the volunteers were in their sixties. One was 80. The regiment was assigned to guard duties in St. Louis, Memphis, and other points in the western theatre of operations, and it served with distinction for the remaining years of the war.

THE DIET KITCHENS

Help from another unexpected source was provided by the women of Iowa. Early in the war, they had worked tirelessly to make uniforms for the raw Iowa recruits. Throughout the four years of the conflict, they prepared bandages for use in army hospitals, and many of them ran the farms and shops while their husbands were at the front. But the most distinctive contribution of Iowa women to the war effort was the establishment of the Diet Kitchens.

Mrs. Annie Wittenmyer of Keokuk got the inspiration for this boon to sick and wounded soldiers when she visited her brother in an army hospital in Sedalia, Missouri. He was sick with typhoid fever, but he was being given the same food that was served to everybody else in the army—fat bacon swimming in its own grease, black coffee, and stale bread. Since he couldn't eat these rations, he was slowly starving to death. Mrs. Wittenmyer stayed in Sedalia until conditions in the hospital were improved. Then, she went to Washington and persuaded Secretary of War Stanton to give her an order for the establishment of Diet Kitchens in which women volunteers could prepare the proper food for hospital patients.

More than a hundred Diet Kitchens were installed in military hospitals, and, at the close of the war, General Grant declared: "No soldier on the firing line ever gave more heroic service than Annie Wittenmyer rendered." Mrs. Wittenmyer later devoted her time and energy to the Iowa Soldiers' Orphans Homes, which were founded at her suggestion.

ANNIE WITTENMYER was an energetic Keokuk matron who led the battle to establish diet kitchens in army hospitals during the Civil War. Later she championed a home for children orphaned by the war. The state children's home in Davenport is named in her honor.

THE COPPERHEAD WAR

Not all of the people in Iowa were dedicated to the preservation of the Union. There were some who believed that secession was a sovereign right of the individual states, and they gave the South all the help they could. These southern sympathizers were called Copperheads, because they were considered to be as deadly as their "name-snakes." The Copperheads took pride in this label, and even wore badges cut from copper pennies.

After the Union victories at Vicksburg and Gettysburg in July of

1863, the Copperheads in Keokuk County became especially active in gathering arms and ammunition and sending them to the South. The southern sympathizers were led by a young Baptist preacher named Cyfert Talley, who had come to Iowa from Tennessee.

On August 1, 1863, Talley and some of his followers held a meeting in a grove near South English. After the meeting, they drove their wagons through South English on the way back to their homes in the Skunk River valley. Loyal northerners taunted the Copperheads as they rode through town, and, in the heat of the quarrel which followed, somebody fired a shot. Both sides were soon banging away at each other. Most of the shooting was intended to be a bluff, but, either by accident or design, Talley was shot through the head. He was the only man killed in the exchange of gunfire, but this was one too many. The Skunk River party drove off, threatening vengeance.

Word of their leader's death spread through the Copperhead country, and two thousand Talley sympathizers from Keokuk, Wapello, Mahaska, and Poweshiek counties organized the "Skunk River Army." The people of South English appealed to Governor Kirkwood for help, and eleven companies of militia were ordered into Keokuk County. The governor made a personal trip to South English and ordered the Skunk River Army to go home. He left no

doubt that he would use the full military resources at his command if the Copperheads disobeyed him, and the army dispersed. This prompt action by the governor stopped the "Copperhead War."

Today, there is only one reminder of it. In the Rock Creek Cemetery, a gravestone, stained by over a hundred years of weather and neglect, bears a dim epitaph. Although it is almost worn away, these words can still be read: "George Cyfert Talley. Died a martyr to his religious and political beliefs. Shot by highwaymen at South English, August 1, 1863. Aged 29 years, 7 months and 2 days."

VALOR AND VICTORY

The major battles of the Civil War were fought far from Iowa soil, but Iowa was deeply involved in them. The volunteers of the First Iowa regiment fought bravely against a Confederate force five times as large in the battle of Wilson's Creek. Their term of enlistment had expired, but this did not stop them. Many of the wounded were brought back to Keokuk for care and treatment in military hospitals. The only National Cemetery in Iowa was established in Keokuk by the United States government in 1861. Seven hundred and fifty soldiers–eight of whom were Confederate prisoners– were buried in it before the end of the war.

During the four years of conflict

between the states, Iowa furnished a total of 48 regiments of infantry, nine regiments of cavalry, and four batteries of artillery–a total of nearly 80,000 men. At the close of the War, more than 12,000 of this number had been killed in action or had died of wounds or disease. Almost as many more had been disabled by battle injuries.

The victory parades could not bring back the husbands, fathers, and brothers who had given their lives in the service of their country, but every family which mourned the loss of a loved one could feel solemn satisfaction in having helped to save the Union. Governor Kirkwood expressed the sentiment of his people with eloquence and conviction. "When this war began," he said, "ours was a new state without a history, but, today, her name stands on one of the proudest pages of her country's history–graven there by the bayonets of our brave soldiers."

★ ★

THE END of the Civil War gave new encouragement to immigration from northern and western Europe. Rebellion in the United States had been crushed, and the need to repair the waste and destruction of war had created many new jobs. Railroad building had been interrupted by the conflict between the states, and employment was offered to anyone with a strong back and a taste for life in the great outdoors. There was still much land in the west that had not been broken. In the cities, all branches of industry were in need of additional workmen. America was lifting its "lamp beside the golden door."

Hardy settlers from other countries had been among the first to recognize and develop the natural resources of Iowa. Julien Dubuque, a French-Canadian, had been a pioneer in the mining of lead. The Hollanders in Pella had proved the fertility of Iowa soil and the profit in raising dairy cattle. The Germans in Amana had demonstrated what mills could do with native wool and lumber.

Other foreign-born citizens had shown equal ingenuity in combining their native talents with American initiative and independence. Iowa was eager to have more people of this kind within its borders.

The book entitled *A Glimpse of Iowa in 1846, or The Emigrants' Guide,* by J. B. Newhall, had been widely circulated in Europe, but the boosters of Iowa believed that something more was needed. In 1870, the General Assembly created a Board of Immigration with authority to send agents to the eastern states and Europe for the purpose of "blowing Iowa's horn." Nothing much came of this.

The most effective promotion of Iowa was accomplished by a primitive sort of direct-mail advertising. Foreign-born citizens who had found profitable employment in the New World sent glowing reports of their success to relatives and friends in the Old Country. These letters were passed from hand to hand, and all who read them were convinced that they, too, could improve their lot by going to Iowa. As soon as money could be raised for passage, thousands of Europeans joined their compatriots west of the Mississippi.

THE GERMANS

The largest number of immigrants came from Germany. There were two basic reasons why Germans left their homeland. First, they wanted to avoid compulsory military service. Second, and more important,

GUTTENBERG street scene has a tranquil, European air. The solid yet graceful architecture of the large center building was favored by the Germans who settled the picturesque river town.

they believed they could improve their living conditions and open promising careers for their children.

Nearly 36,000 Germans had established themselves in Iowa by the time the Civil War began. In the early years of immigration, many of the people who came to the new state made their homes in counties bordering the Mississippi, where neighbors were not too far away and where access to water power and river transportation was most convenient.

A group of Germans founded a village in Clayton County. They named it in honor of Johann Gutenberg, the inventor of movable type.

Unfortunately, the man who entered the name in the official records made a mistake in spelling. He used two t's instead of one. The town has been Guttenberg ever since.

Contented settlers in the river counties wrote enthusiastic letters to Deutschland inviting their friends to join them. By 1890, the German population of Iowa had risen to 127,000. Farming was the main occupation of the Germans, but they were skilled in a great variety of other professions. Their dedication to agriculture was so remarkable, however, that, by 1920, more than half of the total number of farmers in Iowa were of German descent.

THE SCANDINAVIANS

Among the Scandinavians, the people from Norway were the first to migrate to Iowa in large numbers. Writing in *The Palimpsest* for April, 1962, Homer L. Calkin points out that, in Norway, the farmers could hardly make a living from their barren soil. Many Norwegians in America advanced money to their less prosperous countrymen, with the understanding that these loans would be repaid from the savings of the immigrants after they had worked as farm laborers in Iowa.

The best proof of the thrift and industry of the Norwegians, as well as their art and culture, may be found in the Norwegian-American Historical Museum in Decorah, the largest of its kind in the United States.

Until 1880, more Norwegians than Swedes came to Iowa, but from that time on the situation was reversed. Indeed, by 1890, there were more than 30,000 Swedes in Iowa—enough to rank Iowa third in the nation in the number of immigrants from Sweden.

Many of them settled in Montgomery and Page counties. The Swedish Festival of Lights is still held in Stanton, each year, to mark the opening of the Christmas season. A wreath of greenery embellished with lighted candles is placed on the head of the girl who is crowned Santa Lucia.

The Danes were the last of the Scandinavian groups to arrive in large numbers. The Reverend Claus L. Clausen was one of the early religious leaders. In 1852, he founded St. Ansgar, the westernmost white settlement in Iowa at that time. The Reverend Mr. Clausen visited Denmark in 1869 and spoke fervently for a Danish Lutheran mission among his emigrated countrymen. A. S. Nielsen answered the call and served as a lay preacher to the Danish congregation in Cedar Falls, where the Danish newspaper, *Dannevirke,* was published for many years. The largest settlement of Danes was in Audubon County, with other groups in northern and western parts of the state.

ENGLISH-SPEAKING IMMIGRANTS

The most amazing colony in Iowa was the British settlement in northwest Iowa. Unlike most of the immigrants from the mainland of Europe, the founders of this outpost of the British Empire had plenty of money. Many of them were younger sons of aristocrats who would inherit neither titles nor lands by remaining in England. In the late 1870's, William B. Close and his brothers purchased 30,000 acres of land in Plymouth, Sioux, and O'Brien counties for $2.50 an acre. They formed the Iowa Land Company and promised handsome profits to investors in their rolling farm country.

Training in agriculture was offered to the adventurous young men who had no hope of inheritance in England. These farm pupils (or "pups," as they were called by skeptical Americans) received allowances of $500 to $600 per month, but few of them took their training very seriously. Horses and dogs were imported from England, and there was riding to hounds across the Iowa countryside, or galloping into taverns, fully mounted, for refreshments.

Not all of the English took such a lighthearted view of their farming opportunities. Some of the immigrants made a serious effort to operate their country estates at a profit, but, like the farm pupils, they regarded their part of the world as a colony of the British Crown. LeMars once held the distinction of having the only church in the United States in which prayers were offered for Queen Victoria as the head of the nation. Fourth of July festivities often ended in near-riots when Americans resisted the efforts of the colonists to raise the British flag.

In time, the dry summers and the bitterly cold winters caused most of the British to sell their Iowa land and return to England. Only the names of such towns as Quorn, Sutherland, Granville, and Hawarden are reminders of the English residents of the late nineteenth century.

The Scotch, Irish, and Welsh had the same advantage as the English in coming to America. They didn't have to learn a new language. This fact enabled them to become a part of American life more quickly than the Germans and the Scandinavians, but they never became as numerous. The Scotch were attracted by the farm land in Boone, Keokuk, and Tama counties. "Tama Jim" Wilson, who was Secretary of Agriculture in the cabinets of three Presidents, was born

in Scotland, but he spent most of his life on a farm near Traer.

The Irish came to Iowa to work on the railroads, and many of them settled in the Dubuque diocese. They were willing to do any kind of hard work, as long as it paid well. J. A. Green made a fortune by operating a stone quarry near Anamosa.

Mahaska County had the largest number of immigrants from Wales. Most of them had mined coal in the Old Country. When they came to Iowa, it was natural for them to make their homes in Mahaska, Lucas, and Wapello counties, where they could continue to work as miners. The important difference was that they got higher wages in Iowa than they had earned in Wales.

THE BOHEMIANS

The Bohemians came to Iowa because a revolution in their homeland had failed. The first refugees made a new start in Johnson and Linn counties. In later years, Cedar Rapids became the goal of Bohemian immigrants because the early exiles from their country had found hospitality there. Another Bohemian, or Czech, community was founded in Winneshiek County by Joseph Spielman, who built a sawmill on the Turkey River. The town of Spillville, which grew up around the mill, was so much like a village in Bohemia that the homesick composer, Antonin Dvorak, spent a happy vacation there in the summer of 1893. The house in which Dvorak lived is now a museum in

ANTONIN DVORAK, famed Czech composer, lived with his family on the second floor of this building in Spillville during the summer of 1893. Today it houses the unique Bily Clock Museum.

which the beautifully carved clocks of the Bily Brothers are displayed.

THE AMISH

The "Hook-and-Eye Dutch," who live in farm communities near Kalona and Hazleton, have no historical connection with the Dutch. Their language is German, or Deutsch, but their roots are Swiss. In an article written for the 1964–65 Winter Issue of *The Iowan* magazine, John M. Zielinski traces the ancestry of the Amish to sixteenth-century Switzerland. Here, Menno Simons and his followers took part in the Anabaptist movement and founded the sect known as the Mennonites.

In 1693, Jacob Amman, a Mennonite minister, declared that the rules of the faith were not strict enough. Amman broke away from the church, and he and his converts formed what was to become the Amish. In the nineteenth century, the Amish came to America because of persecution in Europe.

The Old Order Amish still wear plain, buttonless clothing. They use horses and buggies instead of automobiles. No tractors are used on their farms, and their homes have no "worldly" conveniences, such as electricity, plumbing, telephones, or central heating. It is difficult for them to maintain their schools and their "country-minded" way of life in a society which has become increasingly "city-minded."

THE BLESSINGS OF LIBERTY

The advent of the twentieth century in Iowa was marked by a swing of immigration from the British Isles and northern and western Europe to eastern and southern European countries. This change brought Greeks, Italians, Russians, Poles, and other nationalities into the state.

In less than a hundred years, Iowa became the melting pot of many nations and was enriched by the immigrants who made their homes within its borders. Sylvester G. Matson spoke prophetically when he addressed the state constitutional convention of 1846. In urging the fathers of a new state to extend the franchise to foreigners, he said: "They know better how to appreciate the inestimable blessings of liberty than we do."

27. IOWA FIRSTS

It is a well-known fact that Iowa is a leader among the states in the production of corn. Automobile license plates once proudly identified every car owner in Iowa as a native of "The Corn State." Iowa is also a leader in the production of hogs, but automobile license plates have not yet proclaimed Iowa as "The Hog State." (There would be too great a temptation to call Iowa drivers "Road Hogs.")

The black soil which carpets Iowa gives it first place among all states of the Union in Grade "A" land. This greatest of natural resources was Iowa's main attraction when the Black Hawk Purchase opened the prairie to white settlement. It continues to be the principal source of Iowa's wealth. Ninety-four percent of the land area of the state is still devoted to farming. The corn, oats, soybeans, and meat products produced on these 33,000,000 acres have been assessed by the Iowa Development Commission as having a higher value than the output of all the gold mines in the world.

FIRSTS IN TOWNS

But two million acres of the state are *not* being used for farming. Can Iowa claim any "firsts" in its towns and cities? Yes. The first bridge across the Mississippi was completed in Davenport. Herbert Hoover, the son of a blacksmith in West Branch, was the first President born west of the Mississippi River.

The first fresh-water pearl buttons were made in Muscatine. The first rotary pump was built in Cedar Falls. The first gasoline traction engine clanked its way into history from the little town of Froelich. The traction motor was first called a "tractor"

"THE FARMHOUSE" was one of the original buildings on the campus of Iowa State University in Ames. For many years it has been the traditional residence for the dean of the College of Agriculture.

by the advertising manager of the Hart-Parr Works in Charles City. The words "Quaker," "Maytag," and "Sheaffer" all identify products of Iowa which hold first rank in the world of commerce.

FIRST ADVICE TO "GO WEST"

Words have also shaped the destinies of men who became famous in Iowa history. The widely quoted advice, "Go West, Young Man," was first given to Josiah B. Grinnell, the man who founded the city of Grinnell and helped to run the Underground Railroad. Grinnell was a young minister in New York City whose forthright sermons against slavery brought him to the attention of the famous editor, Horace Greeley. The throat of the preacher was not equal to the ardor of his ministry, and, when Grinnell consulted his friend about it,

Greeley said, *"Go West, young man, go West.* There is health in the country and room away from our crowds of idlers and imbeciles."

Others have claimed that they were on the receiving end of this famous advice, but Grinnell told the story about it in his autobiography, and there is no reason to believe that he made it up. He did go west, and his dream of establishing a religious and educational community came true in the city and college which bear his name.

FIRST LAND GRANT COLLEGE

The first Land Grant college in the United States was Iowa State in Ames. This renowned institution of higher learning is now the Iowa State University of Science and Technology, but it began its career under a different name.

In 1858, Governor Ralph P. Lowe signed a bill to establish a State Agricultural College and Model Farm. The Board of Trustees was organized in January of 1859, and it selected Story County as the site of the new school. In 1862, President Abraham Lincoln signed the Morrill Land Grant Bill into law. This new Act of Congress offered large grants of land to States which were willing to offer instruction in agriculture and mechanic arts. Only a few farm buildings had been completed in Ames, so Governor Kirkwood tried to get the land grant for the State University in Iowa City. But it was too late. The legislature had made a start on an agricultural college in Ames, and it accepted the provisions of the Morrill Act in behalf of the new project in Story County. By the terms of the act, the State Agricultural College and Model Farm received an initial endowment of 240,000 acres of land. Since the act also provided for the sale and leasing of this land, the financial help from the United States government enabled the new college to become a reality. It was opened to students on March 17, 1869.

Many Iowa farmers thought a state agricultural college was a waste of the taxpayers' money. Farming, they said, was learned by working in the fields, not in a college classroom. The crafts associated with agriculture were learned by serving an apprenticeship with master craftsmen.

FIRST IN SHOW BUSINESS

Working with a master craftsman was the pathway to skill in many fields. August Ringling had become a skilled harness maker in this way. During the Civil War, business in his harness shop in McGregor was slow, because farmers couldn't afford to buy new harness. They simply patched their old harness and hoped for better times. By 1870, however, traffic on the Mississippi had brought prosperity to McGregor, again. This was fortunate for August Ringling, because he had a family of seven boys to feed.

One day, the boys rushed into the harness shop to describe the wonders of a circus which had unloaded from a steamboat early that morning. A few minutes later, the pole balancer from the circus came into the shop. His leather belt and socket were broken. Learning that the circus man was a former McGregor boy, Mr. Ringling refused payment for mending the belt, and the performer gave the harness maker enough passes to take his whole family to the afternoon show.

The boys were spellbound by the performance. The next day, they began teaching themselves rope-walking, juggling, and other arts of the circus. A tent was made of all the horse blankets and rag carpets they could beg or borrow in the neighborhood. An old billy goat and several dogs were assembled for the menagerie.

When all was in readiness, the first performance of Ringling Brothers Circus was announced, and the children of the town paid ten pins each for admission. The premiere was a resounding success.

It would be a few more years before the Ringling brothers would get real money for their talents as entertainers, but, in time, the Ringling Brothers and Barnum and Bailey Circus would become "The Greatest Show on Earth," an enterprise of first rank in the world of entertainment.

FIRST IN TROTTING

Bareback riding and chariot racing brought fame to the Ringling brothers of McGregor. Charley Williams made Independence the center of the harness racing world with two trotting stallions named Axtell and Allerton.

Williams was a night telegraph operator in Independence. During the day, he bought butter and eggs from neighboring farmers and shipped them to city markets. If there was any spare time, he caught up on his sleep.

As soon as he had saved enough money, he bought two mares from the Iowa Central Stock Farm and shipped them to Kentucky to be bred. His careful attention to the pedigrees of both the dams and the sires of his colts proved that he was a man of rare judgment. Charles W. Williams was the only man who ever developed two horses to hold the world stallion

CHARLEY WILLIAMS, the "scientific horse breeder" of Independence, made his home town the "Lexington of the North." His two stallions, Axtell and Allerton, broke world trotting records.

trotting record. And, as Dr. William J. Petersen observes in *The Palimpsest* for October, 1965, "what is more astonishing, Williams bred them both the same year, and they were the first colts he ever raised."

Axtell and Allerton were foaled in 1886. Charley Williams had his own ideas about training them, and he gave them his personal attention from the time they took their first steps. When they were ready for the sulky, he was the driver who paced them. However, there was more to be done than merely training his colts.

BARN at "Rush Park" west of Independence was built by Charley Williams to house his world-famous racehorses. The now-peaceful fields beyond were once thronged with thousands of spectators.

He bought land west of Independence and called it Rush Park. To make the name appropriate, he built the first kite shaped track in the United States, with only one big turn for a mile race. The speed which this kind of track permitted soon brought Rush Park to world attention.

But the two great stallions trained by Charley Williams didn't need the kite track to break records. Axtell won his first race in Keokuk in 1888. Triumph followed triumph. On October 11, 1889, Axtell flashed around the mile track at Terre Haute, Indiana, in two minutes and twelve seconds, a new trotting record for stallions of any age. That night, Charley Williams reluctantly agreed to sell his champion for $105,000, the highest price ever paid for a horse.

Allerton made a slower start than Axtell, but he, too, won fame and honor for his owner. In 1891, he set a new record for the mile at two minutes and nine and one-fourth seconds.

But Allerton was injured on the track at Davenport in 1892. He never raced again. The stallion champion of the world was retired to stud. In later years, when Charley Williams traded his horses for Canadian land, provision was made for Allerton to be given a comfortable home in Indianola for the remaining years of his life.

FIRST HOBO CONVENTION

Independence became the "Lexington of the North" because of the vision and enterprise of Charley Williams. Britt attracted national interest when the first Hobo Convention was held there in 1900. It began as a practical joke. An editor who identified himself as "Bailey of Britt" announced the event in the belief that it would attract attention to his home town. He had no assurance that any hoboes would attend the convention, but this didn't keep him from writing stories about it. He even predicted that the hoboes would nominate Admiral Dewey as their candidate for President. Among all the wanderers on land or sea, the admiral had demonstrated eminent qualifications by going all the way to the Philippine Islands during the Spanish-American War.

On the scheduled date in August, reporters flocked into Britt from all parts of the country only to discover that the whole thing was a hoax. They entered into the spirit of the occasion, however, and invented stories about hoboes who never existed. The resulting publicity brought hundreds of hoboes to Britt in succeeding summers, and, each year, a "hobo king" is elected and crowned in elaborate public ceremonies.

FIRST IN FLIGHT

Hoboes dropped off the rods of freight trains and clambered out of boxcars for their annual reunion in Britt. Railroads were too slow for Billy Robinson, the "bird man" of Grinnell. He was so impressed by the first flight of the Wright Brothers in 1903 that he soon began experimenting with a motor for an airplane of his own. His preliminary efforts were unsuccessful but by 1911 he had developed a 60-horsepower radial motor which was the first of its kind.

He spent the winter of 1911 learning to fly at an aviation school in Florida. By 1913, he was ready to

BILLY ROBINSON, Grinnell's "bird man" set a new nonstop cross-country record in flying the mail from Des Moines to Chicago.

start his own airplane company in Grinnell. Billy Robinson enjoyed his greatest thrill on October 17, 1914, when he set a new American nonstop record by flying the mail from Des Moines to Chicago in four hours and forty minutes. He was killed on March 11, 1916, when he tried to establish a new altitude record.

"FIRST LADY"

Women were not permitted to fly very high in any kind of activity except housework, but this was before Carrie Chapman Catt went into action. As Carrie Lane, she had been brought to Iowa from her birthplace in Wisconsin at the age of seven. During her years in a country school near Charles City, she made up her mind to become a teacher. She went to Iowa State and graduated at the top of her class. This gave her the first proof that women could successfully compete with men, *if* they were given the chance.

She moved to Mason City, where she was, first, the principal of the high school and, later, the superintendent of the entire school system. It was in Mason City that she married a newspaper man named Leo Chapman. Her husband's poor health caused the couple to move to the warmer climate of California, and Mrs. Chapman became the first woman reporter in San Francisco. Her success in jobs usually reserved for men convinced her that, since women could do the work of men, women should also have the right to vote.

After her husband's death, Carrie Chapman returned to Iowa and made her first big speech for women's rights. She faced a great deal of ridicule by men who believed that women should be content to mend socks and wash dishes, but one man admired Carrie Chapman for her courage and intelligence. His name was George William Catt. Carrie Chapman became Carrie Chapman Catt when she married him in 1890.

For the next ten years, she was closely associated with Amelia Bloomer and Susan B. Anthony in the suffrage movement. When she was elected president of the National Woman Suffrage Association in 1900, the movement went into high gear. Much of the credit for the passage of the Nineteenth Amendment must be given to Carrie Chapman Catt. When the Amendment was ratified in 1920, women were given the same right to vote that men had always enjoyed. Success in the long struggle for equal rights was achieved during the presidential term of Carrie Chapman Catt. She held the distinction of being the only person in American history who was president and "first lady" at the same time.

SETTLERS who had the idea that the black soil of Iowa would make them rich soon discovered that they had to fight for their fortune. First of all, the tough prairie had to be broken. The breaking plow used for this purpose had a beam seven feet long, and it was drawn by as many as six teams of oxen. Even then, it was hard work to keep the big coulter in the ground as it cut the roots of the prairie grass. When the stubborn crust had been broken and the land beneath it had been turned for cultivation, the stirring plow could be used to keep it tillable.

But farming was still no easy life. Weather was unpredictable; summers might be hot and dry, or cold and wet; late frosts could kill a spring planting; hail and wind could destroy an entire crop before harvest. Insects were another menace. Periodically, grasshoppers and chinch bugs devastated whole sections of the state like a plague. Some settlers decided that farming in Iowa was too much of a gamble, and they left the state to seek their fortunes elsewhere. Those who stayed were determined to succeed at any cost. The cost was sometimes very high.

JOSEPH ROSS AND SQUATTERS' RIGHTS

In at least one case, an Iowa farmer killed a man who bid against him in a land sale. Joseph Ross had come to Wapello County and staked a claim shortly after Iowa became a state. In those early days, ownership of a claim was not legally established until the land was put up for public sale.

The time came when the land occupied by Ross was listed for auction. It was generally understood that the settler had the right of purchase. Ross made a bid of a dollar and a quarter an acre, which was the established price in 1849. To his astonishment and anger a doctor in Ottumwa made a bid of a dollar and a half.

Evidently the doctor did not know that Ross had staked out the claim in the first place, but he didn't have time to withdraw his bid. Ross had pulled his gun, and, even though the doctor tried to defend himself, Ross shot first, and the doctor was fatally wounded. Joseph Ross was arrested for murder; a trial was held and the jury quickly acquitted the farmer because he had used his gun to protect his property. Legally, of course, the land was not his property until he had paid for it, but the frontier law of "squatters' rights" had established the title for him.

FIRST STATE FAIR

Five years later, farmers had learned to control their tempers, and it was possible to exhibit farm products and have them judged on their merits without being shot. The first State Fair was held in Fairfield on October 10, 11, and 12, 1854. The daily admission was twenty-five cents per person. Prizes for winning exhibits ranged from one to ten dollars, with three fifteen-dollar prizes. Everybody had a good time, whether he won a prize or not. Ideas on farming were exchanged, the makers of farm implements had a chance to display their new machinery, and entertainment was provided by eighteen young women who demonstrated their skills in horseback riding. After all expenses and premiums had been paid, the fair management showed a profit of fifty dollars. Encouraged by this success, the Iowa Agricultural Society decided to make the State Fair an annual event.

THE BEST-TASTIN' APPLE

Although farmers were willing to accept the judgment of officials at the State Fair, an apple grower near Winterset was considered to be crazy because he insisted that he had grown a better apple than anybody else. His name was Jesse Hiatt. He took special pride in the orchard which he had raised on his farm.

In 1872, he had planted two rows of seedling apple trees which had been sent to him from Vermont. A "sport" or mutation, appeared between the rows, and Hiatt cut it down. The next year it appeared again, and once more it was cut down. When it showed up for the third year, Hiatt, who was a devout Quaker, said: "If thee must grow, thee may." The sport was given careful attention, and in due course it produced its first apple. Jesse Hiatt picked it from the tree, took it to the house with him, peeled it, and ate it with great enjoyment. "Becky," he said to his wife, "this is the best tastin' apple in the whole world!" She had to take his word for it since none was left. The apple was named "The Hawkeye" in honor of the state in which it was born.

As the years passed, the tree produced more fruit, and Jesse Hiatt carried the apples from it wherever he went, trying to get his neighbors to taste them. The farmers merely laughed at Hiatt and refused to admit that his Hawkeye was anything special. An apple was an apple, and they saw no reason to get excited about a freak fruit.

But the Stark brothers of Louisiana, Missouri, caught Jesse Hiatt's enthusiasm and purchased the right to propagate the new apple. The Hawkeye was slightly modified by the Stark brothers, and they renamed it the "Delicious." Only the stump of the original tree remains, today, but there is a monument in the city park in Winterset which honors Jesse Hiatt and his development of "the best tastin' apple in the whole world."

"TAMA JIM" WILSON

Fame dragged its feet in recognizing Jesse Hiatt, but James Wilson of Traer attracted statewide attention as soon as he became a candidate for the legislature in 1867. His platform was: "Fence in the cattle, instead of the crops." Nobody had ever bothered to take the side of the crop farmers against the cattle barons. Herds of cattle were allowed to roam wherever they could find anything to eat. Wilson thought it was high time to put a fence around *them*. He was elected, and he was so persuasive in the legislature that the cattle were soon put in their place.

Wilson was a Republican, but his popularity with the farmers crossed party lines. He was sent to Congress by the voters of the Fifth District in 1872. There was another James Wilson in Washington at that time, and the new congressman from Tama County was called "Tama Jim." The name stuck, and the farm leader from Iowa was known as Tama Jim Wilson for the rest of his life.

While he was a member of Congress, he became a good friend of William McKinley, a congressman from Ohio. Politics, then as now, was a rough business, and in 1884 the Dem-

"TAMA JIM" WILSON was presented with this bust of himself when he ended his long service as U.S. Secretary of Agriculture. Today it is displayed in the Traer Public Library.

ocrats unseated both Wilson and McKinley in election contests. But Tama Jim had bought an interest in the *Traer Star-Clipper,* and he spent all the time he could spare from his farm work in writing a weekly column on agricultural topics. These columns were sold to 75 farm papers, and the wisdom and common sense of James Wilson were widely quoted.

In 1891, Wilson was appointed professor of practical agriculture and director of the Experiment Station at Iowa State College in Ames. Tama Jim had no college degree, but this was no handicap. Janette Stevenson Murray, in her book, *They Came to North Tama,* tells how he handled the job: "Mr. Wilson supplied the ideas, enthusiasm, and practical experience; his young assistants, the science."

In 1897, when William McKinley was inaugurated President of the United States, he appointed Tama Jim as Secretary of Agriculture. Wilson held this position longer than any other Cabinet member before or since. Presidents came and went, but James Wilson remained in office until another Wilson moved into the White House. This Wilson was named Woodrow, and he was not a Republican, so Tama Jim had to go.

He had served his country as Secretary of Agriculture for sixteen years. Before he left Washington, the employees of the department presented him with a bronze bust of their long-time boss. Tama Jim took it with him when he returned to his home in Traer, but he was afraid that it might fall on the heads of his grandchildren if he kept it in the house, so he gave it to the Traer Public Library. It is still there.

THE THREE HENRY WALLACES

Early in his career, James Wilson had discovered that ownership of a newspaper made it possible for him to write and print what he wanted to say. He urged his good friend, Henry Wallace, to follow his example. Wallace took Wilson's advice and bought the *Winterset Chronicle*. In one year, the number of subscribers increased from 400 to 1400.

"Uncle Henry," as he was known, was so successful as a country editor

that he was invited to help James M. Pierce publish *The Iowa Homestead.* Wallace and Pierce made the paper so famous and themselves so rich that Uncle Henry decided he could afford to start his own paper and run it to suit himself. The result was *Wallaces Farmer,* one of the most popular farm magazines ever published. It was the springboard by which the Wallace family jumped into politics.

Henry C. Wallace, the son of Uncle Henry, inherited the editorship of *Wallaces Farmer,* and in 1921 he was called to Washington as Secretary of Agriculture in the Cabinet of President Harding. He was the third man from Iowa to serve in this position. Tama Jim Wilson had been the first; the second was E. T. Meredith, the publisher of *Successful Farming,* who had served under President Wilson.

The grandson of Uncle Henry was Henry A. Wallace. He had grown to manhood with the same interests in agriculture which had made his father and grandfather famous. In 1922, he and Simon Cassady of Des Moines were the first men to successfully develop a hybrid corn involving one or more inbred lines. He became editor of *Wallaces Farmer* in 1924 and held this position until 1933, when he was chosen by President Franklin D. Roosevelt to be Secretary of Agriculture. The grandson had left the Republican family tree and had branched out as a Democrat.

Henry A. Wallace was inaugurated as Vice President of the United

States in 1941. After completing his four-year term, he returned to the Cabinet as Secretary of Commerce from 1945 to 1946.

HENRY FIELD

Another man named Henry became famous in agriculture, but not because of his success as a politician. His name was Henry Field, and he lived in Shenandoah. He got his start at the age of six by raising vegetables in the family garden and selling them from door to door. His customers liked his garden products so well that they asked him to save seed for them. Throughout his boyhood, he harvested and packaged his seeds by hand and sold them at a good profit.

Then as he grew older, he decided to try his luck at selling the seeds by mail. In 1899, he put out his first seed catalog, setting the type by hand and printing it, page by page, on a small hand press. He got so many orders that the Field home be-

came too small to handle the business.

In 1907, the first building of the Henry Field Seed and Nursery Company was completed. More buildings and greenhouses were added as the business prospered. By 1924, Henry Field was talking to his customers over radio station KFNF, one of the first broadcasting installations in the country. Thousands of crystal set owners throughout the United States listened to the daily noontime programs in which Henry talked to them about his family, his ideas about gardening—AND about the seeds he wanted them to try. When the Federal Radio Commission limited the power and frequency of radio stations in 1927, KFNF had to be content with a smaller audience, but, by that time, Henry Field was famous from coast to coast, and his seed business was literally in clover.

NELSON FARM MUSEUM

Machinery has taken over many of the chores that Iowa farmers once performed by hand, and agriculture in Iowa has taken a form which the pioneers would find it difficult to recognize. Fortunately, many of the methods and materials of early farming have been preserved in the Nelson Pioneer Farm and Museum near Oskaloosa. Here, the ghosts of the settlers who broke the prairie can still find comfort among their familiar tools, and visitors of today can appreciate the resourcefulness of the first farmers in the state. ★ ★

HENRY FIELD lived in this house in Shenandoah when he began his seed business.

29. CRIME AND PUNISHMENT

In our last chapter, we noted that a farmer in Wapello County shot and killed a doctor who bid against him in a land sale. The farmer was acquitted by a jury of his peers on the grounds that he had only protected his property. Fifteen years earlier, he might have been hanged.

In 1834, Patrick O'Connor, a miner in the Dubuque area, shot and killed his partner in a drunken quarrel. The settlers around the Dubuque mines thought this was carrying an argument too far. One of their number was picked to prosecute the murderer. The miners wanted to be fair, so they gave O'Connor the right to pick not only his defense attorney, but also the members of the jury. The Irishman was scornful of the whole business. "I'll not deny that I shot him," he boasted, "but ye have no laws in this country, and ye cannot try me."

Try him they did, however, and, after hearing both sides of the case, the jury picked by O'Connor convicted him of murder in the first degree. He was sentenced to death by hanging. O'Connor still wasn't worried. He counted on the fact that there were no laws in Dubuque by which the sentence could be carried out. His confidence was badly misplaced. On June 20, 1834, a crowd assembled at the homemade gallows, and, much to his surprise, Patrick O'Connor was hanged by the neck until dead.

MASSEY VERSUS SMITH

But violence continued despite this exhibition of frontier justice. In 1835, a man named Woodbury Massey bought a mining claim near Dubuque. The title was in dispute. Massey got his rights to the claim established by the land office. Then, he had the land agent go with him to serve notice of possession on the trespassers, a certain Bill Smith and his son. As the agent and Massey approached, the two Smiths fired on them from ambush, and Massey fell dead. The agent made a citizen's arrest of the Smiths and took them to Mineral Point in what is now the state of Wisconsin. Court was in session there, but the judge dismissed the case against the Smiths on the grounds that he had no jurisdiction west of the Mississippi River.

This was too much for the brother of Woodbury Massey. When he met the elder Smith on a street in Galena, Illinois, he shot him dead. Law enforcement being what it was in those days, everybody decided that the score was now even. Everybody, that is, except the younger Smith. He loudly announced that he was going to avenge his father's death by shooting another Massey. The first Massey he met when he returned to Dubuque was Louisa, the daughter of the man he had killed on the mining claim. She had a pistol concealed beneath her cloak in case of need.

Junior didn't know Louisa, so he was considerably surprised when an attractive young woman faced him on the street and said, "If you are Smith, defend yourself!" Without waiting for him to do so, she whipped out her pistol and fired. Smith was saved from death by a package of papers in his breast pocket, but he

was so badly shaken by the experience that he decided to get out of the vengeance business. Iowa later named a county in honor of Louisa.

THE BELLEVUE WAR

Primitive justice had to be mobilized again several years later, when horse thieves took over the town of Bellevue. The outlaws had their headquarters in a hotel on the riverfront, and they felt secure in their thievery because Bellevue had no courts to stop them. Forty law-abiding settlers finally formed a vigilance committee and marched on the hotel to capture the ruffians. In the "Bellevue War" which followed, four men on each side were killed. With their leader dead, the remaining members of the gang surrendered.

A vote was taken to decide whether to hang the captives or to flog them. The voting was done by dropping beans into a box. A white

LAST STAND by river outlaws was made here. All that remains of what was a hotel at the time of the "Bellevue War."

bean counted as a vote for hanging; a red bean for whipping. After the vote had been taken, the box contained three more of the red beans than the white.

The outlaws were given a severe public whipping. Then, they were placed in boats on the Mississippi with the promise of death if they ever returned to Bellevue. Their narrow escape from hanging did not reform the criminals. A short time later, they broke into the house of Colonel George Davenport in Rock Island while his family was attending a Fourth of July celebration in the city bearing his name. The helpless old man was murdered in cold blood, and his house was ransacked. This time, some of the hoodlums were caught and hanged, but most of the gang got away again.

THE REGULATORS

Horse thieves became more numerous in Iowa as settlement increased. The farmers depended on their horses for working the land as well as for transportation. If the horses were stolen, they were in serious trouble. Official law enforcement was weak and slow, so vigilance committees were organized throughout the state to bring the horse thieves to immediate trial. These vigilantes called themselves Regulators, and they held their courts in the woods at night. Few of those accused of horse stealing escaped the verdict of

guilty. There was no more voting with beans for hanging or whipping. Hanging was the fixed penalty, and there was no appeal. During the fourteen years between 1846 and 1860, there were at least 45 illegal hangings in the state.

As so often happens when people take the law into their own hands, the innocent as well as the guilty were punished. Some of the Regulators used their self-anointed power to accuse personal enemies and have them put out of the way. This abuse of authority reached its climax in Cedar County when a man named Alonzo Page was hanged on the false evidence of a Regulator who didn't like him. One of Page's neighbors, Canada McCullough, said that Page had been lynched because of a private grudge. McCullough was told to keep his mouth shut if he didn't want the same treatment, but he refused to be silent. The Regulators decided to stop his talking with a rope.

McCullough was ready for the vigilantes. He loaded all his guns, and when the Regulators rode up to his house, he met them at the door with his best gun in his hands. He calmly promised them that the first man who raised his rifle would be shot through the head. Not one of the Regulators wanted the honor of being a dead hero, and, after a moment of hesitation, the vigilantes backed away. This was the beginning of the end for the Regulators. Their reputation as cowards and bullies

IOWA'S OLDEST COURTHOUSE. The Van Buren County courthouse in Keosauqua is believed to be the oldest building in Iowa which has been in continuous use as a courthouse. The Lee County Courthouse in Fort Madison was started earlier, but the Van Buren County Courthouse was finished first.

gradually caught up with them, and only a few of the night riders remained active as members of the Anti-Horse Thief Association.

THE JONES COUNTY CALF CASE

Courts of law took the place of mob justice as the power of local government increased, but even the courts could not always cope with the devious ways of crime. Robert Johnson of Jones County was accused of stealing four calves from his neighbor, and he spent 26 years of his life, as well as all his savings, before he was able to establish his innocence. The Jones County Calf Case dragged through the courts from 1874 to 1900 before it was settled by the Iowa Supreme Court.

Johnson had promised a friend in Greene County that he would buy four calves for him at the first opportunity. One day, Johnson met a stranger at the general store. The man introduced himself as "John Smith" and said that he was in the cattle business. Johnson noticed that the stranger had four fine calves in his wagon, and he offered Smith $24 for them. The sale was made; Johnson delivered the calves to his friend in Greene County and collected the amount he had paid for them.

When he returned to Jones County, his neighbor accused Johnson of *stealing* the calves from his pasture. But didn't the neighbor remember that Johnson had bought the calves from a stranger at the general store? What stranger? John Smith. Nobody remembered any stranger by that name.

The neighbor made a special trip to Greene County and positively identified the calves as his property. The friend for whom Johnson had done the favor said that he had suspected all along that the calves were stolen, but he hadn't wanted to say anything without proof. The neighbor and the "friend" agreed to bring charges of theft against Robert Johnson.

With his reputation for honesty at stake, Johnson fought the case through eight different trials. Members of the Anti-Horse Thief Association burned his barn, tied a hangman's noose to a tree in his front yard, and left a note saying, "You had better go west!" Johnson stood his ground. The many trials cost him his farm and forced him into bankruptcy, but he finally had the satisfaction of clearing his good name. It was proved that the whole case had been a tissue of lies designed to blacken his character.

Why had his "friend" and neighbor brought charges against him for stealing four calves that cost only $24? And why had the Anti-Horse Thief Association been so determined to get him out of the county? Perhaps it was envy of his success as a farmer. Some people begrudge the prosperity of others and consider a resourceful neighbor to be "high and mighty." This may have been the reason for the plot. Whatever the motive may have been, Johnson was vindicated. In later years, he was elected mayor of Anamosa, where his honor remained firmly established for the rest of his life.

THE ADAIR TRAIN ROBBERY

The old saying that "there is honor among thieves" didn't help Jesse James, who was shot in the back by a member of his own gang. Bob Ford valued the reward for the notorious outlaw more highly than he esteemed loyalty to his leader.

Jesse James left his black mark on Iowa history in 1873, when he and his gang derailed the locomotive of a Rock Island train and robbed the passengers of all their money. They had expected a much richer prize. Word had reached them, earlier, that the train would be carrying a shipment of $75,000 in gold.

Jesse and his brother Frank found a spot west of Adair that had a sharp curve in the track. They noticed that the Rock Island trains always had to slow down at this point. On the night the gold shipment was due, the gang removed the bolts from a fishplate on the track and tied a rope through the bolt holes at one end of the loose rail. Just before the locomotive reached the critical curve, the outlaws pulled the rail out of line, and the engine toppled into the ditch. The engineer was killed instantly, and the train was stopped in its tracks.

The gang climbed into the baggage car, but the gold shipment was not there. It had been delayed for later delivery. The train robbers took what little currency they could find in the safe, then forced the passengers to surrender all their valuables.

The telegraph line had been cut by Jesse James before the robbery, and by the time news of the hold-up reached Adair, the gang had galloped off into the night. Posses trailed the robbers to the Missouri line, but Jesse James had friends in his home state, and the lawmen were not welcome there. He was never caught.

There is a persistent legend that Jesse James robbed the rich to help the poor. R. F. Dibble doesn't have

SECTION OF TRACK at the robbery site shows how the James gang removed the fish-plate in order to derail the Rock Island locomotive.

much faith in this Robin Hood image. In his book, *Strenuous Americans,* he writes: "Who knows? Perhaps from the vantage ground of Abram's bosom, the restless shade of Jesse James is craftily plotting the organization of a celestial James band, which, leading a second revolt of seditious angels, will attempt to succeed where Satan himself once failed."

★ ★

30. POLITICAL GIANTS

WHEN SUCCESS in politics is measured, the championship goes to the man who is elected President of the United States. Iowa has produced only one champion in this class, and he didn't work his way to the top by serving a political apprenticeship as governor or senator.

HERBERT HOOVER

Herbert Hoover was never a candidate for any elective office except President. He won financial success as a mining engineer and as a developer of mining properties. When World War I broke out in Europe, Hoover was in London. Hundreds of Americans were fearful that they would be marooned by the German blockade. Hoover used his organizing skill and his own money to help his fellow citizens get back to the United States.

Belgium was invaded by the German army, and the people of that peaceful nation were suddenly deprived of food. Herbert Hoover headed the Belgian Relief campaign which brought thousands of tons of food to the starving widows and orphans.

Because of his success in mobilizing this mission of mercy, Hoover was appointed Food Administrator of the United States by President Wilson, and he set up the program of food conservation which was in effect during World War I. After the war, he served as Secretary of Commerce under Presidents Harding and Coolidge. He had become so well known by this time that the Republican party decided to make him its candidate for President.

In his book, *As Ding Saw Hoover*, Jay N. Darling observes, "Hoover had everything except a flair

HERBERT HOOVER looked like this when he was inaugurated as President of the United States in 1929.

for politics." During the time that he was a world citizen, nobody knew exactly whether he was a Republican or a Democrat. However, he had served in the Cabinets of two Republican Presidents, so he agreed to accept the Republican nomination for President.

He was elected, and, on March 4, 1929, Herbert Hoover moved into the White House. Even though he was now President of the United States, he still refused to accept a salary. Throughout his career in government, he considered the opportunity to serve the people all the reward he needed.

A worldwide economic collapse called the Depression occurred while Hoover was President, and the Democrats put the full blame for it upon him. As a result, he was defeated by Franklin D. Roosevelt in his campaign for re-election. Throughout

the Roosevelt administration, Hoover was cast in the role of an arch-villain. The name of Hoover Dam was even changed to Boulder Dam, until President Truman restored the original name in 1947.

It was Truman, also, who took the lead in bringing Hoover back to public favor and in offering him new opportunities to serve the American people. The great humanitarian was honored by Democrats and Republicans alike for the remaining years of his life.

Herbert Hoover became a political giant when he was elected President of the United States, even though he had no taste for politics. He entered the political arena only because high office gave him the greatest opportunity to serve the public needs. It was his misfortune to be elected at a time when storm clouds were forming all over the world. His best efforts could not change the international weather.

JAMES W. GRIMES

An earlier Iowan was also the victim of a political tempest. His name was James W. Grimes, and his home was in Burlington. He held the distinction of being the first and only Whig who ever served as governor of Iowa. The first two governors of the state were Democrats. When Grimes was elected as the third governor of Iowa, in 1854, the Whig party was falling apart. Its members were in disagreement on the Free Soil and slavery issues, and the opponents of slavery formed the new Republican party in the same year Grimes was elected governor of Iowa. Since he had been a bitter foe of slavery all his life, he soon became a leader in the new party, and it was as a Republican that he was elected to the U.S. Senate in 1858.

James W. Grimes faced his greatest test of political integrity while he was serving Iowa as a United States Senator. In 1868, the House of Representatives took the first steps to impeach President Andrew Johnson for "high crimes and misdemeanors." (The President had dismissed Secretary of War Stanton.) It became the constitutional responsibility of the Senate to conduct the trial of the President with the Chief Justice of the Supreme Court presiding.

During the two months of the trial, Senator Grimes vigorously defended the separation of powers of the executive and legislative branches of government. He denied the right of Congress to place the President on trial. The attacks upon his character in this debate were so vicious that the Senator was paralyzed by a stroke of apoplexy. However, when the Senate finally assembled to vote on the question of the President's guilt, Grimes insisted on being carried to the Senate chamber. On the critical roll call, Grimes was helped to his feet and, with great difficulty, he spoke the words *"not guilty."* James Harlan, the other Senator from Iowa, voted "guilty."

Two-thirds of the Senators needed to vote "guilty" in order to convict the President. When the votes had all been cast and counted, the Chief Justice announced, "Thirty-five Senators vote 'guilty' and nineteen 'not guilty.' Since *one less* than two-thirds have voted 'guilty,' the President is acquitted."

John F. Kennedy, in his *Profiles in Courage,* credits Senator Edmund G. Ross of Kansas as "the man who saved a President," since no one knew which way he would go. *Any* of the 19 Senators who voted "not guilty" could have claimed credit for deciding the issue, but Senator Grimes alone put his health in jeopardy by appearing in the Senate chamber at the time of the vote. He had been struck down by paralysis only two days before, but he insisted on being present in order that his voice might be heard. If he had permitted his physical infirmity to deter him, the outcome would have been different. Indeed, the ordeal was so great and the damage to his health was so severe that he resigned his seat in the Senate. When he was brought back to his home in Burlington, the local newspaper noted the return of "Judas Iscariot Grimes." But his self-sacrificing integrity was acknowledged before he died. Chief Justice Salmon P. Chase, who had presided at the trial, declared: "I would rather be in your place, Mr. Grimes, than to receive any honor in the gift of our people."

JAMES HARLAN

James Harlan was the Iowa colleague of Senator Grimes at the time of the impeachment proceedings, but he did not share the convictions of his fellow Republican. Harlan had come to Mount Pleasant in 1853 as president of the Mount Pleasant Collegiate Institute. As head of the college, he had obtained substantial support for it from the Methodist Church, and, through his efforts, it was given a new state charter as Iowa Wesleyan University.

In 1855, Harlan became a Republican Senator from Iowa in the United States Congress, and he remained in office throughout the Civil War. He was a close personal friend of Abraham Lincoln. Lincoln's wish

ROBERT TODD LINCOLN and his family knew the comforts of this gracious square house on the Iowa Wesleyan College campus in Mount Pleasant. It was owned by Iowa Senator James Harlan, father-in-law of President Lincoln's son.

to have him appointed to the Cabinet was honored by President Andrew Johnson. Harlan served as Secretary of the Interior for only a year, and, during this time, he won doubtful distinction by firing an employee of the department named Walt Whitman. Then he returned to the Senate, where he remained until 1873.

Harlan's daughter married Robert Todd Lincoln, the eldest son of the martyred President. The house in which they lived in Mount Pleasant has been preserved by Iowa Wesleyan College as the Harlan-Lincoln Home.

James Harlan was chosen by the people of Iowa as one of the two "favorite sons" to be honored in Statuary Hall, the old House chamber of the Capitol in Washington which in 1864 was converted into a gallery for statues of distinguished Americans. Each of the states was allotted space for two statues.

SAMUEL KIRKWOOD

The second Iowa statesman selected for Statuary Hall was Samuel Kirkwood. He had served as Iowa's Civil War governor for two terms. When James Harlan resigned his seat in the United States Senate to accept a Cabinet appointment, the Iowa legislature elected Kirkwood to complete Harlan's unexpired term. Harlan soon found himself in disagreement with the policies of President Johnson, but he wanted to stay in Washington, so he asked the legislature to put him back in the Senate.

United States Senators were not always elected by direct vote of the people as they are now. Until the Seventeenth Amendment was passed in 1913, they were chosen by the various state legislatures. Samuel Kirkwood had hoped that his willingness to fill the vacancy would be acknowledged by re-election to a full term. But Harlan reminded the politicians in Iowa that he had done them a lot of favors, and the legislature restored him to his former seat. There was nothing for Kirkwood to do except clean out his desk in Washington and return to Iowa City as a private citizen.

In 1870, James B. Howell of Keo-

kuk was elected by the Iowa General Assembly to complete the unexpired term of Senator Grimes, and George G. Wright of Keosauqua was elected for the regular term which followed the "short term" of Howell. There would not be an opportunity for Kirkwood again until 1872, when Harlan came up for re-election. By that time, however, his friend, Congressman William Boyd Allison of Dubuque, had entered the race.

In the fight between Harlan and Allison, both of whom were seasoned veterans with long experience in Washington politics, Kirkwood didn't have a chance. In a one-party state, which Iowa was at that time, the candidate chosen by the Republicans was sure to be elected. The contest between the Senator and the Congressman was long and bitter, but Allison won, and, in 1873, he moved from the House of Representatives to the Senate and remained there for the next 35 years.

Kirkwood was persuaded to run for governor again, in 1875, and he became the first man in Iowa who was ever elected to a third term in this office. But he had not given up his ambition to be a Senator. When George Wright announced that he would not run for re-election, both Samuel Kirkwood and James Harlan jumped into the race. This time, Kirkwood won. He resigned as governor, and, in 1877, he had the satisfaction of going back to Washington as a Senator elected to a full term.

But he did not serve the full

term. In 1881, he accepted appointment to the post of Secretary of the Interior in the Cabinet of President James Garfield. Samuel Kirkwood thus became the only man in Iowa history who served as governor, United States Senator, and a member of a President's Cabinet.

WILLIAM BOYD ALLISON

Although Harlan and Kirkwood are the only two representatives of Iowa in Statuary Hall, there was another political giant who achieved greater power than either of his two contemporaries. He served eight years in the House of Representatives and 35 years in the Senate—a total of 43 years, during which he worked with all the Presidents of the United States from Abraham Lincoln to Theodore Roosevelt.

William Boyd Allison first became widely known in his Congressional district during the Civil War, when Governor Kirkwood appointed him a Lieutenant Colonel on his staff of aides. It was Allison's job to organize enlistment in Dubuque and to establish a receiving depot there.

His ability made so favorable an impression that he was elected to Congress in 1862. He began his long period of service in Washington in 1863. In less than ten years, he had won election to the Senate and had become the dominant political leader of Iowa. Dr. Leland L. Sage in his book, *William Boyd Allison,* tells how Allison "although preferring to work

IMPRESSIVE MONUMENT to Iowa's longtime Congressman and Senator, William Boyd Allison, is a feature of the State Capitol grounds in Des Moines.

through others . . . nonetheless directly controlled the selection of all men for the key positions and was consulted on many lesser ones."

In 1888, only two candidates had a serious chance to win the Presidential nomination at the Republican national convention. They were Benjamin Harrison of Indiana and William B. Allison of Iowa. Harrison won both the nomination and the election. Quoting Dr. Sage again: "Iowans in 1888 believed that Allison was cheated out of the Republican presidential nomination . . . by Chauncey Depew, a Senator from New York and the guiding genius of the New York Central Railroad. He unfairly blackballed Allison, they thought, because of his residence in

Iowa, a state that had just passed legislation providing stringent regulation of railroad freight rates." As Dr. Sage points out, this was not the only reason Allison lost his chance to become President, but it proved to be a significant obstacle on his path to the White House.

Did Allison retire from public life because of his disappointment in losing the big prize? Dr. Sage reports that "never a whimper came from him nor a sigh as to what might have been." He returned to his work in the Senate and continued to be a dominant figure in government for the remaining twenty years of his life.

You will look in vain for a statue of William Boyd Allison in Statuary Hall. But there is a monument in his honor on the grounds of the State Capitol in Des Moines. No other giant in Iowa history has been given this distinction—not even Herbert Hoover, who *did* become President.

★ ★

31.

ARTISTS AND AUTHORS

THE INDIANS who were chased out of Iowa had few friends among the white men. The Sauks and Foxes were crowded off their lands by one "purchase" after another until they had been pushed all the way to Kansas.

GEORGE CATLIN

One white man was always welcome in the Indian villages. He was George Catlin, and he was born in Pennsylvania in 1796. George's father wanted to make a lawyer out of him, and, for a while, George obediently studied law. Then, on a fine spring day, some Indians passed the window of his office, and George Catlin closed his law books for good. He made friends among the strange people he had seen, and followed them to their homes across the Mississippi, sketching pictures of them as he went.

He did not stop on the frontier, where the Indians had been corrupted by the whiskey of the white traders. He ventured alone into the wild country where the original Americans were still unspoiled and free. He lived as they lived, and he found them to be cheerfully tolerant of his artistic interest.

Although Catlin made many sketches of Indians in the far west, much of his work portrayed the Indians of Iowa. Today, the drawings and paintings of George Catlin give us a record of Indian life uncolored by the later prejudice of soldiers and settlers.

JOHN JAMES AUDUBON

Another artist who wandered across Iowa before it had been damaged by improvements was John James Audubon. Audubon was born in Louisiana in 1785. He didn't like New Orleans, so, as he grew to manhood, he migrated to Kentucky and became a storekeeper. But what he liked better than anything else was painting pictures of birds. Whenever business was slow, he left his wife and children and looked for new kinds of birds to paint. The southwestern corner of Iowa was a temporary reservation for the Pottawattamie Indians when Audubon crossed it in the course of his travels. The Pottawattamies had been uprooted from their old homes in Illinois and moved to Iowa against their will, but the artist was more interested in the plumage of the birds than in the plight of the Indians. The paintings made in Iowa by this Kentucky artist appeared among the 435 colored pictures which he published in his monumental volume entitled *Birds of America*.

GRANT WOOD

Many years later, a painter in Cedar Rapids continued in the tradition of Catlin and Audubon. Grant Wood was born on a farm near Anamosa in 1892, more than a hundred years after Catlin and Audubon, and he too painted what he knew best. Art for him was a statement of reality—

of people in their working clothes rather than their company manners. He had tried and rejected Impressionism while he was studying in Paris, and he came back to Iowa determined to paint what he saw.

Grant Wood first attracted nationwide attention when his studio was in the carriage house of the Turner Mortuary in Cedar Rapids. Here, he painted "American Gothic" and "Daughters of the Revolution," two pictures which provoked a storm of controversy, but which are now considered to be American classics.

His "Dinner for Threshers," "Fall Plowing," and other paintings of people and places in his home state gave the world a new understanding of Iowa and Iowans. John Steuart Curry of Kansas and Thomas Hart Benton of Missouri joined Grant Wood in emphasizing the regional identity of the Middle West. Many people in this part of the country thought their pictures were not as flattering as they ought to be, but all of the artists lived long enough to be recognized as honest interpreters of rural America.

HAMLIN GARLAND

The Iowa farm was first put into American literature by an author who spent his boyhood near Osage. His name was Hamlin Garland. This was not a flowery penname which he adopted for literary use; he was born with it. In 1860, when he first met his

GRANT WOOD used the top floor of this carriage house behind the Turner Mortuary in Cedar Rapids as a studio. In it he created some of his famous paintings of Iowa life.

parents, his father was so impressed with the new Vice President, Hanniball Hamlin of Maine, that the boy was immediately given the name of Hamlin.

The elder Garland was a farmer. Breaking the prairie, milking the cows before daybreak, and trudging through deep Iowa snows to a cold and drafty country school made a deep impression on young Hamlin. He never forgot the rigors of his youth.

When he left Iowa to seek his fortune in the East, his first poems and stories were cast in a romantic mold which made little impression on the literary world. It was not until he began writing about the hardships of life on the frontier that his work became popular. In time, his reputation was made by the "Middle Border" novels. Four of his highly successful books had these two words in their titles.

George Bernard Shaw asked Garland where the "Middle Border" was located. Garland replied that it was "a line drawn by the plow, and broadly speaking, ran parallel to the upper Mississippi when I was a lad. It lay between the land of the hunter and the harvester." Since the "Middle Border" books were based on the personal experiences of Hamlin Garland, they give a great deal of information about this first famous Iowa author.

HERBERT QUICK

Another Iowan who wrote about farm life was Herbert Quick. His parents, like many other settlers, had come to the Hawkeye State in wagons drawn by ox teams. Herbert was born on a farm in Grundy County in 1861. The country school in which he began his education has been moved to a park in Grundy Center, where it is preserved as a memorial.

Quick was a schoolteacher and a lawyer before he decided to give his main attention to writing. The novels he wrote were inspired by the prairie homes, the tornados and blizzards, the joys and sorrows of pioneer life. Among his best known books were *Vandemark's Folly* and *The Hawkeye*,

both of which told the stories of early Iowa.

ELLIS PARKER BUTLER

But the farm was not the only inspiration for Iowa authors. Ellis Parker Butler, who was born in Muscatine in 1869, made his home town the setting for many of his humorous anecdotes. In these Muscatine stories, the setting is identified as "Riverbank." Over the years, the library of the State Department of History and Archives in Des Moines has made a collection of books written by Iowa authors. When Ellis Parker Butler was asked to donate a copy of his popular *Pigs is Pigs,* he sent the book, but he wrote the following couplets on the flyleaf:

Oh, state of corn, take it from me,
    And ever let thy motto be:
'Three millions yearly for manure,
    But not one cent for literature.'

BESS STREETER ALDRICH

The "state of corn" may not have been willing to spend "one cent for literature," but book publishers paid well for books that had interesting stories to tell, whether they were written by men or women. The first Iowa woman who became famous as a writer was Bess Streeter Aldrich. Bess Streeter was a daughter of Black Hawk County pioneers. She was born in Cedar Falls in 1881. After her schooling had been completed, and before her marriage to Charles Aldrich, she taught for a time at the Iowa State Normal School.

But writing was her main interest. In her childhood, she had heard stories about the adventures of her parents when Cedar Falls was on the frontier of westward expansion. Her novels and short stories were greatly influenced by these family tales. The books by Bess Streeter Aldrich which became best-sellers include *A White Bird Flying, Spring Came on Forever,* and *A Lantern in Her Hand.* Relatives of the writer were the main characters in her best-seller *Song of Years,* and their graves in a cemetery north of Cedar Falls have caused the burial ground to be known as "The Song of Years Cemetery."

RUTH SUCKOW

Another Iowa woman who achieved fame in the world of literature was Ruth Suckow. She was born in Hawarden in 1892, but she lived in many Iowa towns during her father's years in the ministry. Ruth Suckow was a protege of H. L. Mencken, who encouraged her to write honest and detailed word-pictures of prairie life in her home state. In *The Folks,* Miss Suckow described the cornfields, the spare rooms, the parlors, the churches, and the people of her girlhood. The novel clearly defined the strong and stoic quality of farm life and the

younger generation's revolt against it. Other books which made her famous were *The Odyssey of a Nice Girl, New Hope,* and *Iowa Interiors.*

ARTHUR DAVISON FICKE

Ruth Suckow was able to capture the poetry of life in Iowa even though she wrote in prose. Books of poetry have never had a market value as high as novels, but Iowa has produced successful poets as well as successful novelists.

Arthur Davison Ficke, born in Davenport in 1883, had published *Sonnets of a Portrait Painter* and other collections of poems while he was still a young man. He had not grown rich on the sale of his poetry, and the prospects of earning a livelihood as an honest poet looked very dim when the critics began to get excited about "modern verse."

One night, Ficke and his friend, Witter Bynner, attended the theatre to see a performance of *Spectre de la Rose.* During intermission, the talk drifted to the so-called "modern poetry." The two friends had a sudden inspiration. They would create a new school of poetry which would make fools of the critics. And what would they call it? They agreed to name it after the first noun they found on the theatre program. The noun was "Spectre," and the new cult was called "Spectrism." For the next three weeks,

Ficke and Bynner each wrote about six poems a day. One of Ficke's poems went like this:

I have not written, reader, that you may read.
    They sit in bare rows in the school-room reading.
Throwing rocks at windows is better.
    And, oh, the tortoise-shell cat with the can tied on!
I would rather be a can-tier
    Than a writer for readers.

The two plotters made the poems sound as crazy as possible. When enough material had been written to fill a book, the first edition of SPECTRA was published. Ficke had called himself "Anne Knish," and Bynner had taken the name "Emanuel Morgan." When the book appeared, the critics tried to outdo each other in praising "Knish" and "Morgan." The public accepted the endorsement of the critics without question and bought copies of SPECTRA by the thousands.

Even though the money was welcome, Ficke and Bynner were poets who valued their self-respect. They had merely wanted to show the critics and the public how easy it is to be fooled by new fashions. When they were sure they had proved their point, Ficke revealed the truth about the whole thing. The critics quickly changed the subject and wrote about something else.

One man still praised "Spec-trism." He said to Ficke: "I told you before that I liked it, and, by Jiminy, it's still the best you'll ever do!" He was mistaken. Arthur Davison Ficke went back to writing poetry that made sense. His books *Out of Silence, The Secret,* and *Tumultous Shore* were so successful that he later heard himself acclaimed as one of the three greatest living American poets.

★ ★

32.
MILESTONES
IN
MUSIC

EARLY PHOTO of the academy at Bradford. Here Dr. William S. Pitts conducted his singing school.

THE IMMIGRANTS who decided to stay in Iowa brought their interest in music with them, and they were determined to have musical training for their children.

SINGING SCHOOLS

"Singing schools" were popular in pioneer communities. They were held in the fall after cornhusking and, with the help of the "singing professor," young people learned notes and scales, part reading, and group singing. Dr. William S. Pitts, who wrote "The Little Brown Church in the Vale," was employed as a singing professor in Bradford, even though his medical practice was in Fredericksburg.

The Germans, Bohemians, and Welsh immigrants formed instrumental groups, and when the War Between the States broke out, recruiting of young men for the Union Army was quickened by the exciting tempos of local band music.

STATE SONG AND FLAG

It was during the Civil War that Major Samuel H. M. Byers of Oskaloosa wrote the words which were adopted by the Iowa General Assembly as the official state song. Major Byers had heard the soldiers of the Confederacy singing "Maryland, My Maryland," to the melody of "Der Tannenbaum," a popular German tune. Not to be outdone, the Major took the same melody and wrote words to it which honored *his* state. The first stanza went like this:

You ask what land I love the best,
   Iowa, 'tis Iowa,
The fairest state of all the west,
   Iowa, O! Iowa.
From yonder Mississippi's stream
   To where Missouri's waters gleam,
O! fair it is as poet's dream,
   Iowa, in Iowa.

The state flag designed by Mrs. Dixie Cornell Gebhardt of Knoxville was adopted by the General Assembly in 1921. In 1946, E. O. Osborn, also of Knoxville, wrote a poem entitled *Iowa's Flag.* He dedicated it to Mrs. Gebhardt during Iowa's centennial year. The poem was set to music by Esther May Clark of Oskaloosa, and, in 1949, the "Iowa Flag Song" was adopted by the General Assembly.

There is a third Iowa song which is more widely known outside of the state than either of the two songs adopted by the General Assembly. "The Iowa Corn Song" was first used by the Za-Ga-Zig Temple Shriners of Des Moines at a convention in Los Angeles. George E. Hamilton was in the group that was going by train to the west coast, and he put down a chorus to an old song called "Traveling." Later, John T. Beeston, the director of the Shrine Band, took Hamilton's chorus and scored it for a singing band with solo cornet accompaniment. It was copyrighted by Beeston in 1921, and it continues to be sung and played wherever Iowans gather.

The upward thrust of the right arm when singing, "THAT'S where the tall corn grows" is a pledge of allegiance to the Tallcorn State.

ANTONIN DVORAK

The statement is often made that Antonin Dvorak wrote his great symphony, *From the New World,* while he was living in Spillville, Iowa. This is an appealing story, but it isn't true. Dvorak went to Spillville in the summer of 1893 for a vacation.

His temporary job as director of the National Conservatory of Music in New York City had been getting on his nerves, and he needed a place where he could get some rest. He found it in Spillville. The only music he wrote there was the *String Quartet in F Major,* sometimes called "The American Quartet." The symphony, *From the New World,* was a major work which had been completed before the Spillville holiday. In any case, it would be untrue to claim Antonin Dvorak as a native Iowa composer. His roots remained in Europe throughout his life.

FREDERICK KNIGHT LOGAN

Major Samuel Byers, who wrote the words for "The Song of Iowa," and Esther May Clark, who wrote the music for "The Iowa Flag Song," were not the only citizens of Oskaloosa who gave it distinction. Two nationally recognized composers also were born there. Thurlow Lieurance, who was born in 1878, used native Indian themes in his popular composition, "By the Waters of Minnetonka." Frederick Knight Logan, who was born in 1871, also used Indian material in his love song entitled "Pale Moon." The composition on which he collected the most royalties, however, was "The Missouri Waltz," which became the theme song of a piano player named Harry Truman.

Frederick Knight Logan did not use all of his musical energy for composing. He was the pianist for Enrico Caruso on his nationwide concert tours, and he was the musical director of *Peter Pan* when Maude Adams took the famous play from coast to coast. But, as the years passed, he became weary of travel. Logan spent the evening of his life in Oskaloosa, where he gave his full time to composition.

KARL KING

Another musician who tired of being a traveling man was Karl King. From the age of eighteen, he had played in circus bands. In 1913, while playing baritone horn in the Barnum and Bailey Circus, he wrote a march which is still among the most famous of all his compositions. He called it "The Barnum and Bailey Favorite." From 1914 through 1916, King was bandmaster for the famous Buffalo Bill Show. In 1917, he rejoined the "Greatest Show on Earth," but, this time, he was the leader of the band. King married the calliope player, and, when Karl King, Jr. was born, the Kings decided that show business was no business for a family.

The bandmaster put an ad in *The Musician's Journal* for a job as a director of a municipal band. A subscriber in Fort Dodge saw the ad, and Karl King was invited to visit Fort Dodge and look over the town. King wanted a position which would not take all of his time, because he was still interested in composing band music as well as in playing it.

He liked Fort Dodge, and the people of the town liked him. In 1919, Karl King became the director of the Fort Dodge Municipal Band. As soon as he got himself settled, he opened the King Music House to publish his own pieces. In 1921, he also became director of the Iowa State Fair Band, and, for the next 38 years, he spent ten days every summer at the State Fair in Des Moines. He gave up the job in 1959, because his publishing business required most of his time. And well it might! He had written more than 400 marches and compositions for band. Orders for his pieces come to the King Music House from all over the world.

MEREDITH WILLSON

Karl King came to Iowa to complete his band career. Another famous composer *began* it in the Hawkeye State. Meredith Willson was born on May 18, 1902 in Mason City, which later served as the model for "River City" in *The Music Man*. Young Willson first studied piano, but there wasn't much demand for piano players in Mason City. There was a demand for flute players, however, so Meredith learned to play the flute. He immediately became the first flutist (as well as the only flutist) in the school band. After graduating from high school in Mason City, he studied music in New York and got a job playing the flute in the John Philip Sousa Band. In 1924, he became the first flutist with the New York Philharmonic and worked under the direction of Arturo Toscanini and other famous conductors. He learned about music from the best teachers in the world, and he soon became a conductor and composer in his own right.

Meredith Willson first became famous as a conductor on his programs for the NBC radio network, but his compositions were also attracting attention. His popular song, "May the Good Lord Bless and Keep You," sold more than half a million copies in four months. Two symphonies which he wrote were performed by leading orchestras on the west coast. But his greatest hit was *The Music Man,* for which he wrote both the words and the music. It was an immediate success, and it made Mason City famous. As Willson said, "I didn't have to make up anything for *The Music Man*. All I had to do was remember!" The musical recreated Mason City as it was in Willson's boyhood.

C. A. FULLERTON

The band organized by Professor Harold Hill in *The Music Man* could have been suggested by the choirs organized by Professor C. A. Fullerton of Cedar Falls. Few country schools had pianos or teachers who could play them. Professor Fullerton worked out a plan of teaching boys and girls to sing by having them listen to phonograph records and repeating what they heard. The records were made especially for this purpose, and they were used with a book prepared by Professor Fullerton in 1925. He called it *A One-Book Course in Elementary Music and Selected Songs for Schools*. At one time, as many as 50,000 rural school children were learning the songs which were being taught by the Fullerton method. The success of the plan was demonstrated at the State Fair in 1930, when Professor Fullerton directed a massed choir of his pupils from all over the state.

"BIX" BEIDERBECKE

Unquestionably, the songs taught by C. A. Fullerton made vocal music popular among the school children of Iowa. But the term "popular music" commonly identifies the music played by dance bands. One name in Iowa leads all the rest in this field of music.

It appears in the history of Jazz as "Bix" Beiderbecke.

At his birth in Davenport in 1903, the boy was named Leon Bismark Beiderbecke. This was just too much name to handle, and the parents cut it down to Bickie. Boyhood friends made the name even shorter, and it became simply Bix. The family had musical interests, and Bix was given piano lessons. But his main interest was in the cornet. Excursion boats often stopped at Davenport, and young Bix listened in ecstasy to a New Orleans boy who played jazz trumpet. His name was Louis Armstrong.

The elder Beiderbeckes refused to pay for cornet lessons when they learned that Bix was interested in playing jazz instead of Wagner. The boy therefore taught himself. By trial and error, he learned how to blow the cornet and how to finger the valves.

Then, he played along with Victrola records of "The Original Dixieland Jazz Band." His parents decided to send him to Lake Forest Academy, near Chicago, where he might get other ideas for making a living. But Chicago was jumping with jazz, and the style of improvising which Bix had developed brought him to the attention of some of the best dance band musicians in the country.

Bix Beiderbecke reached his peak as a soloist with the big Paul Whiteman dance band. His records and compositions became popular, but the pressures and tensions of his rapid rise to fame were too much for him. He died when he was only 28 years old. In his short life, he strongly influenced the structure of jazz. His melodic ideas and harmonic patterns are milestones which continue to guide the musical traveler.

★　★

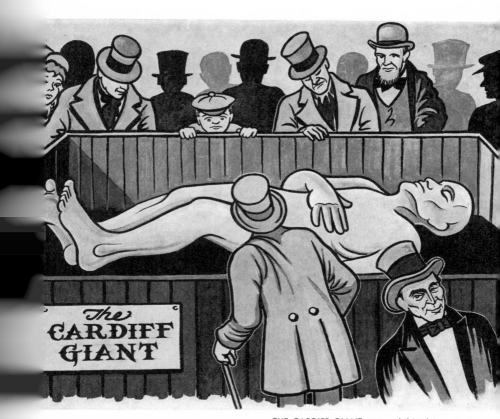

THE CARDIFF GIANT was exhibited in a tent near Cardiff, New York. In the right foreground is George Hull, perpetrator of the gigantic hoax.

33. IOWA IN THE HEADLINES

MANY EVENTS in Iowa history have been of considerable interest to people living within the state, but they have attracted little attention elsewhere. Now and then, however, something has happened in Iowa which has made newspaper headlines in other parts of the country as well.

Often, in the course of its history, Iowa has produced men and women who have risen to national prominence. These giants of politics, industry, literature, art, and music have brought renown to the state in which they were born. Most of them became famous after they left Iowa, but

191

they never disowned their origins. However, one famous giant was thought to be a native of another state, and he did nothing to correct this impression. Despite his silence on the matter, it was finally proved that he was "born" in Iowa.

THE CARDIFF GIANT

In 1868, a man named George Hull was visiting his sister in Ackley, and he heard a preacher talking about "giants in the earth." Hull didn't believe in giants, but the preacher's talk gave him an idea. He hired a farmer to cut a ten-foot slab of gypsum from a ledge east of Fort Dodge. The block was shipped to Chicago, where Hull employed a stonecutter to carve it into the figure of a sleeping giant. Hull then bathed the finished work in sulphuric acid to make it look old.

When the job was done, the stone man was ten feet long, three feet wide across the shoulders, and he weighed three thousand pounds. The giant was packed in a strong wooden box, shipped to Cardiff, New York, and delivered to the farm of "Stub" Newell, a brother-in-law of George Hull. One rainy night, when there were no neighbors around, the giant was taken out of the box and buried behind Newell's barn.

A year later, Newell "decided" that he needed a new well, and he told the well diggers exactly where to dig. About three feet down, one of the workmen uncovered a large foot.

The rest of a huge body appeared as the men dug into the soft, loose dirt. "Jee-rusalem," exclaimed one of the diggers, "it's a big Injun!" That was the belief, also, of thousands of people who swarmed to the pit from neighboring Syracuse and other parts of the country.

They remembered the old Onondaga Indian story about the great warriors whose bodies had turned to stone. Scientists agreed that the giant was a petrified man. Some skeptics thought it looked like a statue of some kind, but visiting ministers insisted that it had once been "a child of God." While all this debate was going on, the people who flocked to see the Cardiff Giant were paying a dollar a head for the privilege, and Stub Newell and his brother-in-law were getting rich.

The day finally came when a man from Fort Dodge took a long, hard look at the giant and said, "You know—that's about the size of a block of gypsum a fellow bought in Fort Dodge, a year ago!"

The reporters asked George Hull if he knew anything about a block of gypsum. "I sure do," he said, "I had that giant carved out of it."

"But," exclaimed the reporters, "you said it was a petrified man!"

"Not me, boys!" replied Hull. "That's what the preachers and scientists said it was."

There were red faces among the scholars, but the public still paid the regular admission price to see the grand old fraud. It remained a popular attraction for a long time, and was even taken on tour. One summer, it was displayed at the Iowa State Fair. Many people still go to see the Cardiff Giant. The most solid citizen ever to leave Iowa now rests in the Farmers Museum in Cooperstown, New York.

THE ESTHERVILLE METEORITE

Another "giant in the earth" was a heavenly body which came hurtling out of space on May 10, 1879, and buried itself in a field near Estherville. This was no fraud. It was a meteorite which came sizzling through the air like an enormous skyrocket. When it exploded, it burst into three large pieces, each piece flying in a different direction, showering the countryside with fragments of molten metal. The largest piece of the meteorite scooped a hole in the ground fifteen feet deep and twelve feet wide.

Most meteorites which enter the earth's atmosphere are totally consumed before they reach the earth. The Estherville meteorite was such an unusual phenomenon that there was immediate bidding for the three big pieces. The largest was sold to the British Museum in London. The second piece was purchased by the museum at the University of Minnesota. The smallest of the three big chunks was acquired by a museum in Vienna. Only the small fragments which had been scattered over the fields were left

in Iowa. They have been preserved as family souvenirs.

KATE SHELLEY

The forces of Nature helped to put Iowa in the headlines again two years later, but this time star billing was given to a fifteen-year-old girl. On the night of July 6, 1881, a raging storm washed out the railroad bridge over Honey Creek, a small stream flowing into the Des Moines River near Moingona. Fifteen-year-old Kate Shelley, standing at the window of her home near Honey Creek, could see the headlight of a track inspection locomotive feeling its way through the torrents of rain. Suddenly, the headlight plunged downward into the creek, and Kate knew that the bridge was gone. She knew also that the Midnight Express would soon come over the same track. Since the track inspection crew had undoubtedly been drowned, someone had to warn the station agent at Moingona to stop the Express.

The Shelley house, in which Kate lived with her widowed mother, was on the east side of the Des Moines River. Moingona was on the west side. Kate lighted an old railroad lantern which had once belonged to her father. Despite the protests of her mother, she left the safety of the Shelley house and struggled against the slashing rain and wind to the long wooden bridge that spanned the Des Moines River.

On hands and knees, she began crawling across the bridge. The glass chimney of her lantern was soon broken, but she felt her way by clinging to one of the rails of the track. The roaring torrent of the river was just beneath her, threatening to sweep the bridge away at any moment. Twisted spikes in the railroad ties tore at her skin and clothing, but she crept painfully onward. After what seemed an eternity, she felt cinders between the ties at the western end of the bridge. Kate staggered to her feet and ran the rest of the way to the Moingona station. She gasped the news about the broken bridge over Honey Creek, and the agent quickly signaled the Midnight Express to a stop. The lives of hundreds of passengers on the train were saved, and Kate Shelley became a national heroine.

The old wooden bridge at Moingona is long gone, but the bravery of a fifteen-year-old girl is still remembered. The lantern carried by Kate Shelley on the night of storm and flood has an honored place in the museum of the State Department of History and Archives in Des Moines.

JUMBO

The fury of uncontrolled water brought nationwide attention to Iowa in a different way in 1886. That was the year in which the people of Belle Plaine decided to tap the artesian springs under their town by drilling a new well. They figured that a two-inch hole would give them enough pressure to serve their needs. The drillers quickly struck water, and a normal flow began to rise.

But this was no ordinary well. In a few hours, a stream of water 18 inches across was spouting out of the ground to a height of five feet. Sand, shells, rocks, wood, and bones boiled out. The mouth of the well widened to three feet, and the townspeople became frantic. Streets were flooded, and ditches were hastily dug to carry the water to the Iowa River. Sandbags by the ton were thrown into the well, but the force of the artesian monster threw them out again.

The "white elephant" soon attacted newspaper reporters from all over the country, and headlines referred to it as "Jumbo." Thousands of visitors came to Belle Plaine to view "The Eighth Wonder of the World." One tourist got too close and fell in, but he came out as though he had been shot from a cannon.

After running wild for over a year and defying all efforts to tame it, "Jumbo" was finally choked off by a complicated system of hydraulic jacks. Today, all is quiet at the corner of Eighth Avenue and Eighth Street, where the monster once roared its defiance. A boulder with a bronze plaque identifies the site of Old Jumbo Well, which is now covered with pavement.

THE BATTLE OF THE HOTELS

The defiance of two bankers created an uproar of another kind in Forest City in 1898. The members of the Commercial Club had decided that the town of 1500 citizens needed a new hotel. Everybody agreed on the project, but there was bitter disagreement on its location. The president of the Forest City National Bank wanted the hotel located on the north side of town, where he had his home. The president of the First National Bank wanted it on the south side of town, where he lived. Since they couldn't agree, each banker decided to build his own hotel where he wanted it. Each tried to outdo the other, and each attracted a loyal following on his side of town. Forest City was divided into two hostile camps.

The hotel on the north side was called The Summit; the one on the south was named The Waldorf. Each had fifty rooms, steam heat, baths, electric lights, billiard parlors, reading rooms, and dance pavilions. The Summit opened its doors in November of 1898. It was decorated in lustrous black throughout. Glistening black Racine coaches drawn by jet black horses were driven down the dirt streets to the railroad station, where the coachmen on the high drivers' seats waited for the guests of the new hotel.

In February of 1899, the great doors of The Waldorf were opened for business. The Waldorf was decorated in gleaming white, and it had white coaches and white horses to meet the trains. Both hotels were popular with traveling men. The dining rooms provided food of such quality and variety that they attracted the people of Forest City as well as the visitors from the outside world who came to see the two luxury hotels.

However, the local backers of one hotel did not enter into the activities of the other. If a salesman came into a store, the businessman would ask, "Where are you staying?" If the salesman was a paying guest in the hotel supported by the businessman, he

LONE SURVIVOR of the Battle of the Hotels in Forest City is now the administration building of Waldorf College. It was once the Waldorf Hotel.

would make a sale. Otherwise, he wouldn't. The traveling men therefore had to stay in one hotel for a night, leave town, come back the next day, and stay in the other hotel in order to do business on that side of town.

Each hotel tried to put the other hotel out of business. A price war brought the rates for rooms and meals down to such a bargain level that neither hotel was able to make a profit. The Waldorf was the first to give up the fight. It sold out to The Summit. Even with The Waldorf closed, The Summit continued to operate at a financial loss, and when it was destroyed by fire in 1915, Forest City had no hotel at all.

The building once occupied by The Waldorf was purchased by the United Lutheran Church, which made a college out of it. The public library of Forest City was built on the site of The Summit. "The Battle of the Hotels" is only a memory now, and the people of the north and south parts of town speak to each other as though nothing had ever happened to divide them.

★ ★

WOODROW WILSON once remarked that "a spot of local history is like an old inn upon a highway where man has passed through." People do not last as long as places, but personalities of the past continue to live in the buildings they have used.

The Old Stone Capitol in Iowa City is such a building. A visitor with imagination can recall the millers, the stagecoach drivers, and the candlestick makers who first assembled in it as members of the Iowa Territorial legislature.

The little white house in West Branch from which Herbert Hoover began his journey to the White House is more than a quaint cottage in a tidy Quaker town. It is a bridge to our personal understanding of a great man. This is the house in which he was born. Its walls continue to radiate his physical presence. Visitors with sensitive antennas can pick up these radiations.

34. HISTORIC SITES

SITES UNSEEN

Unfortunately, the power to tune in the past is not held by everyone. Many of our important landmarks have been destroyed because there was not enough interest in saving them. Old Zion Church in Burlington was rich with historic associations, but it was torn down to make room for a theatre. The theater now is gone, and the site of Iowa's first territorial capitol is today a parking lot.

The house in which Samuel Clemens lived with his mother in Muscatine was ripped apart so that a filling station could be built in its place. The print shop in which the future Mark Twain worked for his brother in Keokuk was bought by a museum and moved to New York State.

The boyhood home of William F. Cody in LeClaire is no longer in Iowa. The owner didn't think the

house amounted to much, so he sold it to the Burlington Railroad, which hauled it to Cody, Wyoming, and made it a part of the Buffalo Bill Museum.

SITES OF NATURE

Some of Iowa's landmarks *couldn't* be moved. We still have the first Pike's Peak. From its top, there is a good view of the junction of the Wisconsin and Mississippi Rivers, where Marquette and Joliet entered Iowa history in 1673. A few miles to the north, the Effigy Mounds tell the story of settlers who came to Iowa long before the white man.

Across the state in Osceola County is Ocheyedan Mound, the highest point in Iowa. It is 1,675 feet above sea level and rises 170 feet above the surrounding countryside. The word Ocheyedan means "spot where they weep." It refers to the

Indian custom of seeking high ground on which to mourn the dead.

Red quartzite, the oldest rock in the state, can be seen in the Gitchie Manitou area in Lyon County. The face of Iowa, as it looked when the ocean had finished washing it, is preserved in the massive lampshell formations of Backbone State Park. These are landmarks of Nature.

SITES OF SETTLERS

Some of our manmade landmarks have been preserved because private groups or individuals thought they should be saved. The Hoover family bought the little cottage in which a president was born and transferred ownership of it to the Hoover Birthplace Foundation. Luther College bought several log cabins which had been built by Norwegian immigrants and moved them to the campus in Decorah. The Gardner Cabin, which survived the Spirit Lake Massacre, was preserved by the Okoboji Protective Association and is now maintained by the State Historical Society of Iowa.

Dr. William J. Petersen, superintendent of the Society, took the first necessary steps in safeguarding "Plum Grove," the home of Governor Robert Lucas in Iowa City. It is now under the care of the State Conservation Commission.

The house built in Pella by Dominie Scholte is still standing. It has been continuously occupied by

HERBERT HOOVER was born in this two-room cottage in West Branch. Restored to its early appearance, it is now visited by thousands.

Scholte descendants since the leader of the Dutch immigrants built it in 1847. The people of Amana take pride in their history, and the Amana Society has preserved many landmarks which hold the past in focus.

SITES OF SANCTUARIES

The Inspirationists of Amana were not the only religious folk who protected monuments of their faith. The Mars Hill Baptist Church, near Floris in Davis County, is one of the largest single-room log buildings ever constructed in Iowa. It is 26 by 28 feet in size. The church was built by volunteer labor in 1857. When the Civil War came along, 35 men in the congregation joined the Union army, and services in the church were discontinued until the war was over.

In the same year that the Baptists were building their log church at Mars Hill, a Wisconsin doctor named William S. Pitts made a stagecoach journey through Bradford. At that time, Bradford was the metropolis of Chickasaw County. Dr. Pitts noticed a beautiful grove at the edge of town, and he thought it would be a perfect setting for a church—a "little brown church in the vale."

When he got home, he wrote a song about it. Five years later, he established his practice in Fredericksburg. Returning by chance to Bradford, he was amazed to discover that a church was being built on the very spot where he had pictured it on his earlier visit. In a conversation with the pastor, he learned that it would be painted brown, because money was scarce and brown paint was cheaper than white. Struck by the coincidence, Dr. Pitts dug into his trunk until he found the manuscript of the song he had written. He showed it to the pastor and was persuaded to sing it in the new church for the first

time. The song not only made the building famous, but also saved it from destruction when the village of Bradford was abandoned. Although most Congregational churches are painted white, there is at least one which is still brown.

The Reorganized Church of Jesus Christ of Latter-Day Saints has preserved Liberty Hall at Lamoni, because it was the home of its president, Joseph Smith III, the son of the Prophet. The only church in Iowa which the Pope has elevated to the eminence of a minor basilica is the Church of St. Francis Xavier in Dyersville. Its 200-foot twin spires have made it a landmark in eastern Iowa since 1880.

SITES OF FULFILLMENT

In contrast, the Chapel of St. Anthony of Padua, near Festina, seats only eight people. It was built in fulfillment of a promise made by a mother whose son fought in Napoleon's army. When Johann Gaertner was sixteen years old, he was drafted for military service. His mother promised in her prayers that, if Johann escaped death in the war, she would build a chapel in proof of her gratitude. She did not live to fulfill her vow, but her son remembered it. After he had migrated to Iowa, Gaertner and his family built what has been called "the smallest church in the world." It is located in farm country beside the Turkey River, two

LITTLE BROWN CHURCH near Nashua was built exactly as depicted in Pitts' song, though the builders knew nothing of the hymn.

200

miles south of Festina. The veteran of the Napoleonic Wars lies buried in the churchyard behind the chapel.

Another unusual landmark built in fulfillment of a vow is the Grotto of the Redemption in West Bend. Paul Matthias Dobberstein was a student for the priesthood in Milwaukee when he became critically ill with pneumonia. As he fought for his life, he prayed to the Virgin Mary to intercede for him. He promised to build a shrine in her honor if he lived. The illness passed, and Matthias Dobberstein was ordained as a priest. He went to West Bend as pastor in 1897.

For fifteen years, he stockpiled beautiful stones. Then, in 1912, he began the actual work of fulfilling his promise. Throughout the next 42 years, until his death in 1954, Father Dobberstein devoted every spare moment to building the largest grotto in the world. The ornamental stones were collected from every state in the Union and from every country on the globe. Statues made of Carrara marble were carved by Italian sculptors, but all of the building was done by the dedicated priest and one loyal assistant. The Grotto of the Redemption is a sermon in stone which attracts thousands of visitors to West Bend every year.

SITES OF STRIFE

The age-old war against Satan is symbolized by the grotto in West

REPLICA of the blockhouse and stockade which gave Fort Dodge its name. The reconstruction does not occupy the original site, but the buildings have been faithfully reproduced.

Bend and by other landmarks of the Christian faith. Wars against Indians and against Secession have left few relics in Iowa.

Fort Madison was burned to the ground by the soldiers who built it. Only the foundations remain. A part of Fort Atkinson is still standing. The State Conservation Commission has converted the officers' barracks into a museum, and the stone blockhouses and powder magazine are sturdy reminders of the only fort ever built by the government to protect Indians from Indians. A replica of Fort Dodge can be seen near that city.

Several stations on the Underground Railroad have been preserved. The parsonage of the Reverend John Todd in Tabor is unchanged. The "Old Slave House" near Lewis brings back memories of John Brown and the Negroes he guided to this place of refuge. The Lewelling House in Salem still has the kitchen trapdoor and the hidden staircase used by fugitives.

There is no Iowa house in which Abraham Lincoln lived, but the Harlan Home in Mount Pleasant was occupied by his son, Robert Todd Lincoln, in the years following the assassination of the Civil War President. Robert Todd Lincoln married the daughter of Senator James Harlan of Iowa, and their children played on the campus of Iowa Wesleyan College.

SITES OF INDUSTRY

Landmarks of pioneer industry in Iowa are not as numerous as they are in some of our neighboring states. The water-powered woolen mill in Amana is still going strong, but few of the old grist mills are left. Pine Creek Mill has been preserved by the Conservation Commission in Wildcat Den State Park. Clayton County has four old mill sites and one restored replica, Winneshiek County has three, and Allamakee County has one. The Bellevue Mill in Jackson County is the last known survivor of the two to three hundred sawmills and grist

mills which once lined the Mississippi River in Iowa and Illinois.

A relic of the lead industry stands on the riverfront in Dubuque, but the Old Shot Tower is only a hollow shell today. Like the tower above Julien Dubuque's grave, a short distance downstream, it is a monument to the lure of lead in the late eighteenth and early nineteenth centuries.

SITES OF TRANSPORTATION

The exciting days of steamboat transportation on Iowa rivers are recalled by the Hotel Manning in Keosauqua and the Mason House in the ghost town of Bentonsport. The plan to make the Des Moines River a navigable stream was implemented by a

RUINS of the old shot tower in Dubuque. Molten lead was poured through a colander at the top of the tower. As the streams of lead fell down the shot tube, they were broken up into round pellets by air resistance and surface tension. The pellets were caught and cooled in a large tank of water at the bottom of the tower.

series of locks and dams, and, for a time, such towns at Bonaparte, Bentonsport, and Keosauqua promised to become busy ports of call for river traffic. But even with locks and dams, the river was too shallow to permit reliable navigation except when rains were spaced just right, and the steamboat hotels now dream of glories that might have been.

The plank roads which gave Iowa its first paved highways are all gone. The lumber was removed and converted into board walks or farm buildings and only the Jimtown Inn, near Danville, remains as a fringe relic of the wooden thoroughfare between Burlington and Mount Pleasant.

The Iowa State Department of History and Archives has preserved some of the vehicles used in early transportation. Among the exhibits in the basement of the Historical Building in Des Moines are a Conestoga wagon, a stagecoach once owned by the Western Stage Company, carriages and sleighs which were custombuilt for prosperous settlers, a high bicycle, the first steam automobile in Iowa, the first Cadillac purchased in the state, and the electric car driven by Governor George W. Clarke.

In his book, *Covered Bridges in Illinois, Iowa and Wisconsin,* Leslie C. Swanson lists twelve covered bridges which are still standing in Iowa. Seven of these bridges are in Madison County, three are in Marion County, and Keokuk and Polk counties have one each. The seven covered bridges in Madison County are all within a 15-mile radius of Winterset, the county seat.

The Age of Steam in railroad transportation has passed, but several Iowa communities have acquired steam locomotives as monuments to the Iron Horse. One of these "high wheelers" is on display at Sioux City.

Most of the steamboats which carried passengers and freight on the Mississippi River have fallen into decay. They have been replaced by diesel-powered towboats. The "Geo. M. Verity," a towboat which inaugurated modern barge service on the Upper Mississippi, is berthed in Victory Park on Keokuk's riverfront, where it has become the Keokuk River Museum.

SITES TO SAVE

Why do we save these relics? What can they contribute to living in the world of today? Blake Clark, writing in *The Diplomat* magazine for December, 1958, declares, "We need authentic, tangible reminders of our national virtues and heroes to make us feel a part of the best of our heritage. . . . If we can save enough of the homes, churches, courthouses, and other places where Americans who went before us lived and worked, we can sense their way of life, their ideals and character. We want our children to sense them, too. . . . A nation with no regard for its past will have little future worth remembering."

★ ★

BIBLIOGRAPHY

AURNER, CLARENCE RAY. *Iowa Stories, Book III.* Iowa City: Clio Press, 1921.

BEASLEY, BOB. "The Graybeards," *The Iowan* (Aug.-Sept., 1960).

BRIGGS, JOHN ELY. *Iowa, Old and New.* Lincoln, Nebraska: The University Publishing Company, 1939.

CALKIN, HOMER L. "The Coming of the Foreigners," *The Palimpsest* (April, 1962).

CARPENTER, ALLAN. *Between Two Rivers: Iowa Year by Year, 1846–1939.* Mason City, Iowa: Klipto Loose Leaf Co., 1940.

CLARK, BLAKE. "Wanton Disregard of Our Heritage," *The Diplomat* (Dec., 1958).

CLARK, DAN ELBERT. *History of Senatorial Elections in Iowa.* Iowa City: State Historical Society of Iowa, 1912.

COLE, CYRENUS. *I Am a Man—The Indian Black Hawk.* Iowa City: State Historical Society of Iowa, 1938.

————. *Iowa Through the Years.* Iowa City: State Historical Society of Iowa, 1940.

DARLING, JAY N. *As Ding Saw Hoover.* Ames: Iowa State University Press, 1954.

DIBBLE, R. F. *Strenuous Americans.* New York: Boni and Liveright, 1923.

GALLAHER, RUTH A. "The Tama Indians," *The Palimpsest* (Feb., 1923).

GRINNELL, JOSIAH B. *Men and Events of Forty Years.* Boston: D. Lothrop Co., 1891.

HARNACK, CURT. "The Iowa Underground Railroad," *The Iowan* (July, 1956).

HART, IRVING H. *Stories of Iowa.* Cedar Falls: University of Northern Iowa, 1953.

HOLLOWAY, JEAN. *Hamlin Garland, A Biography.* Austin, Texas: University of Texas Press, 1960.

Iowa: A Guide to the Hawkeye State. New York: Hastings House, 1949.

JACKSON, DONALD. "Black Hawk—The Last Campaign," *The Palimpsest* (Feb., 1962).

———. "Old Fort Madison—1808–1813," *The Palimpsest* (Jan., 1958).

KENNEDY, JOHN F. *Profiles in Courage.* New York: Harper and Row, 1956.

KEYES, CHARLES R. "Prehistoric Man in Iowa," *The Palimpsest* (June, 1927).

KNISH, ANNE and EMANUEL MORGAN. *SPECTRA—A Book of Poetic Experiments.* New York: Mitchell Kennerley, 1916.

MAHAN, BRUCE E. *Old Fort Crawford and the Frontier.* Iowa City: State Historical Society of Iowa, 1926.

MARTIN, MICHAEL and LEONARD GELBER. *Dictionary of American History.* Paterson, New Jersey: Littlefield, Adams & Company, 1959.

MCKUSICK, MARSHALL. *Men of Ancient Iowa.* Ames: Iowa State University Press, 1964.

MURRAY, JANETTE STEVENSON. *They Came to North Tama.* Hudson, Iowa: Hudson Printing Co., 1953.

NEWHALL, J. B. *A Glimpse of Iowa in 1846, or The Emigrants' Guide,* reprint. Iowa City: State Historical Society of Iowa, 1957.

PELLETT, KENT and J. D. HYLTON. "Jesse Grew a Money Tree," *The Iowan* (June-July, 1957).

PETERSEN, WILLIAM J. *Iowa: The Rivers of Her Valleys.* Iowa City: State Historical Society of Iowa, 1941.

———. "Mormon Trails in Iowa," *The Palimpsest* (Nov., 1956).

———. "The Lexington of the North," *ibid.* (Oct., 1965).

"Picture Magazine" of *The Des Moines Sunday Register.* Dec. 14, 1958.

PRICE, ELIPHALET. "The Execution of Patrick O'Connor," *The Palimpsest* (June, 1959).

RICHMAN, IRVING B. *Ioway to Iowa.* Iowa City: State Historical Society of Iowa, 1931.

RUPPE, REYNOLD. "Man in Early Iowa —Historical Puzzle . . . With Pieces Missing," *The Daily Iowan Magazine* (Dec. 6, 1960).

SABIN, HENRY. *The Making of Iowa.* Chicago: A. Flanagan Co., 1900.

SAGE, LELAND L. *William Boyd Allison.* Iowa City: State Historical Society of Iowa, 1956.

SALTER, WILLIAM. *Iowa, the First Free State in the Louisiana Purchase.* Chicago: A. C. McClurg & Company, 1905.

SHAMBAUGH, BENJAMIN F. *The Old Stone Capitol Remembers.* Iowa City: State Historical Society of Iowa, 1939.

SHAMBAUGH, BERTHA M. H. *Amana That Was and Amana That Is.* Iowa City: State Historical Society of Iowa, 1932.

SHANE, GEORGE. "Iowa's Plank Road a Boon to Pioneers," *The Des Moines Sunday Register* (Dec. 15, 1957).

SHARP, ABIGAIL GARDNER. *History of the Spirit Lake Massacre and Captivity of Miss Abbie Gardner,* 5th ed. Des Moines: Iowa Printing Co., 1902.

SWANSON, LESLIE C. *Covered Bridges in Illinois, Iowa and Wisconsin.* Moline, Illinois: Leslie C. Swanson, 1960.

SWISHER, JACOB A. *Iowa—Land of Many Mills.* Iowa City: State Historical Society of Iowa, 1940.

TEAKLE, THOMAS. *The Spirit Lake Massacre.* Iowa City: State Historical Society of Iowa, 1918.

The Book That Gave Iowa Its Name. A reprint of ALBERT M. LEA's *Notes on the Wisconsin Territory.* Iowa City: State Historical Society of Iowa, 1935.

THWAITES, REUBEN GOLD (ed.). "Marquette's First Voyage," *The Jesuit*

Relations and Allied Documents, Vol. LIX, 1673–1677. Cleveland: The Burrows Brothers Co., 1930.

VAN DER ZEE, JACOB. *The British in Iowa.* Iowa City: State Historical Society of Iowa, 1922.

WALSH, JAMES E. *Black Loam of Iowa.* Lake Mills, Iowa: Graphic Publishing Company, Inc., 1964.

YAMBURA, BARBARA S. and EUNICE WILLIS BODINE. *A Change and a Parting: My Story of Amana.* Ames, Iowa: Iowa State University Press, 1960.

ZIELINSKI, JOHN M. "Vision From the Past," *The Iowan* (Winter, 1964–65).

INDEX